"A gifted teacher, communicator, and evangelist, Ajith Fernando has produced a most timely resource to equip today's generation. In recent decades the church in the West has struggled to develop mature disciples. We have retreated into our dwindling communities with the occasional foray outside in the attempt to make converts. Fernando calls us to the task of developing mature disciples, and through the deepening of our faith we are better equipped to engage in the wider world."

Stephen Skuce, Director of Global Relationships, The Methodist Church in Britain

"Grounded in Scripture, rooted in decades of ministry, and colorfully illustrated from Sri Lanka and around the world, Ajith Fernando's *Discipling in a Multicultural World* will enrich God's people as we seek to make disciples among all nations. Much more than a classroom guide, it will motivate us to follow Fernando's example, pouring our lives into others' just as others poured their lives into his."

David Greenlee, Director of Missiological Research and Evaluation, Operation Mobilization

"How do we make disciples of Jesus in contexts of increasing ethnic, cultural, and religious diversity? Few people are as qualified to answer this question as the global Christian statesman Ajith Fernando. Drawing upon four decades of ministry worldwide and a seasoned scholar's understanding of Scripture, Fernando provides us with a rich and wise guide to forming disciples among those from various cultural backgrounds. Essential insights for effective ministry today!"

Harold Netland, Professor of Philosophy of Religion and Intercultural Studies, Trinity Evangelical Divinity School

"In *Discipling in a Multicultural World*, Ajith Fernando moves beyond techniques and programs to the life-on-life realities of discipleship in the emerging context of multiculturalism. This book is a gem for those who are prepared to come face-to-face with the real cost of discipleship. Filled with practical examples, the book is a real-life tutorial from one of the great giants of discipleship in our day. A truly formational book!"

Timothy C. Tennent, President and Professor of World Christianity, Asbury Theological Seminary

"Ajith Fernando has been living the message of this book for more than four decades, and now he shares his insights in this comprehensive work. Integrating thorough biblical study, extensive experience, deep understanding of cultural dynamics, and vulnerable storytelling, *Discipling in a Multicultural World* is essential reading for any leader who—like Paul the apostle—aspires to 'present everyone mature in Christ' (Col. 1:28)."

Paul Borthwick, Senior Consultant, Development Associates International; coauthor, *The Fellowship of the Suffering*

Discipling
in a
Multicultural
World

Other Crossway Books by Ajith Fernando

The Call to Joy and Pain: Embracing Suffering in Your Ministry

Deuteronomy: Living Obedience to a Loving God

The Family Life of a Christian Leader

Jesus Driven Ministry

Discipling
in a
Multicultural
World

Ajith Fernando

Foreword by Robert E. Coleman

CROSSWAY®
WHEATON, ILLINOIS

Royalties from the sale of this book have been assigned to education and literature projects of Youth for Christ, Sri Lanka.

Library of Congress Cataloging-in-Publication Data

Names: Fernando, Ajith, author.
Title: Discipling in a multicultural world / Ajith Fernando; foreword by Robert E. Coleman.
Description: Wheaton, Illinois: Crossway, 2019. | Includes bibliographical references and index.
Identifiers: LCCN 2018026105 (print) | LCCN 2018044340 (ebook) | ISBN 9781433562860 (pdf) | ISBN 9781433562877 (mobi) | ISBN 9781433562884 (epub) | ISBN 9781433562853 (trade paperback)
Subjects: LCSH: Discipling (Christianity) | Christianity and culture.
Classification: LCC BV4520 (ebook) | LCC BV4520 .F47 2019 (print) | DDC 269/.2—dc23
LC record available at https://lccn.loc.gov/2018026105

To the community at
Trinity Evangelical Divinity School
with gratitude for
a generous sabbatical to write this book
and delightful friendships

Contents

Foreword

Jesus taught that everything commanded in the Law and the Prophets comes down to loving God and neighbor as yourself (Matt. 22:37–40). From this Great Commandment flows the Great Commission given by Christ to his disciples before he ascended back to heaven to take his place of authority at the right hand of God: "Go . . . and make disciples of all nations . . ." (Matt. 28:18–20).

The word "disciple" could be translated as "learner," in the sense of an apprentice, and in the Christian context means a follower of Jesus. So Jesus's invitation to persons wanting to become disciples was simply "Follow me." Here was the essence of his plan to change the world. By following him, disciples would learn both his way of life and his vision for the nations.

With this objective in view, love finds its most relevant expression in reproducing the ministry of "the Son of Man [who] came not to be served but to serve, and to give his life as a ransom for many" (Matt. 20:28). This is not to say that one can replicate his atoning sacrifice. That work was finished once and for all at Calvary. But the way Jesus prepared disciples to bring the good news of his completed mission to the ends of the earth can be repeated. It is called discipleship.

The disciples could understand what Jesus expected for they had seen Christ's last command lived out before their eyes. In principle, by following the patterns of Christ's servant ministry, we can make disciples today. The Great Commission is not a special call for privileged saints to become clergy or overseas missionaries; it is a command to the whole church to adopt a servant lifestyle by which all Christians can experience their priesthood.

To be sure, developing this commitment to kingdom living requires all the resources of grace that one can summon by faith. Love is costly. Learning to shoulder the cross and follow Jesus is not easy. Obedience is learned though suffering and self-denial. Mentoring disciples is like raising children, and there is no exemption from duty.

Helping baby believers find their footing in salvation is a necessary first step, of course. But there is much more to learn in the deeper dimensions of holiness and Christlikeness as teacher and follower grow in grace and knowledge together. The more difficult task may come in igniting satisfied church members to become active disciple makers. Your joy comes when persons in whom you invest begin to bear fruit, with much more to come.

That is why this book is so welcome. It offers practical help where needed most—in bringing disciples into daily life. Ajith Fernando's concern is not with programs or fast tracks to success. Rather, building on the biblical principles of growing a spiritual family, he weaves the Great Commission into the way we live out our ministry in our homes and work places, helping people we love "become mature, attaining to the whole measure of the fullness of Christ" (Eph. 4:13 NIV).

Giving the study a ring of authenticity is Ajith's personal pilgrimage of disciple making. He tells it like it is, both the good and the not so pleasant. Whether that is leading in a small church of multicultural converts, mentoring young people hooked on drugs, or raising leaders to take over the work he leaves, it's all for real.

What he doesn't talk about are the many books he has written or the great conferences he has spoken at around the world. Even with all his recognition, he has not lost identity with the poor people of Sri Lanka, where he lives and continues to minister. I think most noteworthy is that his children follow in his steps.

We can learn from this man. Experienced disciples especially will appreciate some of the delicate issues he comes to grips with in telling his story. Thankfully, God is not finished with any of us yet.

I would be challenged and blessed to sit at Dr. Fernando's feet. This book affords us all that opportunity.

Robert E. Coleman
Distinguished Senior Professor of Evangelism and Discipleship
Gordon-Conwell Theological Seminary

Preface

This book on discipling seeks to help nurture Christians to maturity and fruitfulness while taking into account an exciting challenge we face today. Many who come to Christ, even in the West, may have different cultural backgrounds from those who disciple them. They may be from other faiths or no faith. In the non-Western world the church is reaching people from other faiths. At the same time, there is a growing phenomenon in the West of religiously unaffiliated people who are called the "nones."[1] Recently the periodical *Christian Century* reported that 29 percent of Americans between the ages of 30 and 39 would classify themselves as religiously unaffiliated. The figure rises to 38 percent when it comes to the ages 18–29. Starting with 8 percent of those above 80 years old, the figure climbs steadily for each age group.[2] This trend is more marked in Britain,[3] and even more so in other Western countries.[4] So disciplers in the Western or the non-Western worlds may be called upon to disciple people whose approach to life and religion has been quite distant from the Christian approach. I try to be alert to this challenge in this book.

1. James Emery White, *The Rise of the Nones: Understanding and Reaching the Religiously Unaffiliated* (Grand Rapids, MI: Baker, 2014). White wrote later, "A recent survey of thirty-five thousand Americans by the Pew Research Centre found that the rise of the nones has grown to encompass 23 percent of American Adults." White, *Meet Generation Z: Understanding and Reaching the New Post-Christian World* (Grand Rapids, MI: Baker, 2017), 11.

2. Daniel Cox and Robert P. Jones, "America's Changing Religious Identity," PRRI (website), September 6, 2017, https://www.prri.org/research/american-religious-landscape-christian-religiously-unaffiliated/. The figures for other age groups are 40–49, 23 percent; 50–59, 18 percent; 60–69, 16 percent; 70–79, 12 percent. I am grateful to my friend James Moore of Trinity Evangelical Divinity School for instructing me about the religiously unaffiliated.

3. "A Majority of Britons Now Follow No Religion," *The Economist*, September 9, 2017, https://www.economist.com/britain/2017/09/09/a-majority-of-britons-now-follow-no-religion.

4. See Gabe Bullard, "The World's Newest Major Religion: No Religion," *National Geographic*, April 22, 2016, https://news.nationalgeographic.com/2016/04/160422-atheism-agnostic-secular-nones-rising-religion/.

My intention was not to write a "how to" manual on discipling. I hope to give biblical principles about discipling and to present examples about how they apply in daily life and ministry. The exact way in which a person disciples varies according to the personality of the discipler, the personality and maturity of the disciplee, and the context in which the discipling takes place.[5] The diverse histories and cultures of churches or organizations can result in different ways in which they do interpersonal work. My hope is that people reading this book will become convinced of the biblical principles for discipling and find ways of putting those principles into practice in their situations.

Over the years I have been asked to write handbooks on how to do various aspects of ministry. Such books can be very helpful. But I believed that my calling was first to teach biblical principles of life and ministry with vibrant practical application and then to present that material in written form. I have left it to hearers and readers to apply the principles they have learned in their situations. Hopefully this has helped nurture many people who are continuing to serve God wherever they are.

There are many excellent, biblically based, practical books about discipling.[6] The fact that so many of them have been written within the past ten years reflects a welcome trend to emphasize the importance of discipling in today's church. Some of the books deal with some aspects of discipling more comprehensively than my book does. Two books

---

5. See below, p. 20, for how I use the terms *discipler* and *disciplee*.

6. E.g., Christine Dillon, *1-2-1 Discipleship* (Sevenoaks, Kent: OMF; Ross-shire, UK: Christian Focus, 2009); Edmund Chan, *A Certain Kind: Intentional Disciplemaking That Redefines Success in Ministry* (Singapore: Covenant Evangelical Free Church, 2015); Robert E. Coleman, *The Master Plan of Evangelism* (Grand Rapids, MI: Revell, 1963, 1964, 1993); Mark Dever, *Discipling: How to Help Others Follow Jesus* (Wheaton, IL: Crossway, 2016); Leroy Eims, *The Lost Art of Disciple Making* (Grand Rapids, MI: Zondervan, 1978); Bobby Harrington and Alex Absalom, *Discipleship That Fits: Five Kinds of Relationships That God Uses to Help Us Grow* (Grand Rapids, MI: Zondervan, 2016); Walter A. Henrichsen, *Disciples Are Made Not Born: Helping Others Grow to Maturity in Christ* (Wheaton, IL: Victor, 1974); Bill Hull, *The Disciple-Making Pastor: Leading Others on the Journey of Faith* (Grand Rapids, MI: Baker, 1988, 2007); Lam Kuo Yung, *Total Discipleship: Experiencing Jesus and His Abundant Life* (Singapore: Katong Presbyterian Church, 2017); Dennis McCallum and Jessica Lowery, *Organic Discipleship: Mentoring Others into Spiritual Maturity and Leadership* (Columbus, OH: New Paradigm, 2012); Rainer Mittelstaedt, *Ministering Forward: Mentoring Tomorrow's Christian Leaders* (Winnipeg, MB: Word Alive, 2017); Greg Ogden, *Transforming Discipleship: Making Disciples a Few at a Time*, rev. ed. (Downers Grove, IL: InterVarsity Press, 2016); K. Thomas Resane, *Mentoring: A Journey to the Best One Can Be* (Kempton Park, South Africa: AcadSA, 2010); Dann Spader, *Discipling as Jesus Discipled: Seven Disciplines of a Disciplemaker* (Chicago, IL: Moody Publishers, 2016); Paul D. Stanley and J. Robert Clinton, *Connecting: The Mentoring Relationships You Need to Succeed in Life* (Colorado Springs: NavPress, 1992); and David L. Watson and Paul D. Watson, *Contagious Disciple Making* (Nashville: Thomas Nelson, 2015).

written recently are from the missionary/missiological community: *Making Disciples across Cultures*, by Charles A. Davis[7] and the more academic *Intercultural Discipleship*, by W. Jay Moon.[8] Using different approaches, they contribute significantly to the literature on biblical and culturally sensitive discipling. I decided to focus on a few key areas that need special attention today and to reflect on them biblically and practically. My main concern has been on nurturing godly and fruitful disciples of Christ, and I have tried to address some challenges faced when doing this.

As an ardent advocate of discipling in my preaching and teaching for many years, I have come to realize that discipleship is not something that people take to naturally. Many Christian leaders in Sri Lanka and abroad have told me that, despite the wide-ranging discussions on discipling in books and seminars, few people are really doing it. There seems to be something about our culture that resists this activity. All of this has made me think a lot about the cultural, spiritual, ministerial, and personality issues that render Christian leaders all over the world so reluctant to give themselves to this ministry. I hope to address these issues in this book.

I must pay tribute to those who have discipled me. First and foremost is my mother, who taught her children the Bible from the time we were little. It was she who led me to experience personal salvation when I was in my early teens and who taught me the basics of the Christian life. Around that time, we were blessed with a wonderful pastor, Irish missionary George Good, whose influence helped me decide on vocational Christian work and convinced me of the glory of the Christian life, of preaching, and of worship. My father was a model of hard work and commitment to excellence in all he did. In my later teens, I became a volunteer in Youth for Christ and had the privilege of being discipled by our leader Dr. Sam Sherrard. He taught me many of the practical principles that undergird my ministry today.

As a student at Asbury Theological Seminary I had the amazing privilege of coming under the influence of Dr. Robert E. Coleman, who

---

7. Charles A. Davis, *Making Disciples across Cultures: Missional Principles for a Diverse World* (Downers Grove, IL: InterVarsity Press, 2015).

8. W. Jay Moon, *Intercultural Discipleship: Learning from Global Approaches to Spiritual Formation* (Grand Rapids, MI: Baker Academic, 2017).

had written the classic book on discipling *The Master Plan of Evangelism*. I fear that, though much of what I have written in this book has been influenced by Dr. Coleman's book, I am not able to give sufficient documentation of that fact. His teaching has become part of my life and thinking. He was firmly committed both to theology and evangelism, and he helped me develop the theological convictions that have undergirded my ministry. I did graduate studies in New Testament at Fuller Theological Seminary and had Dr. Daniel Fuller as my mentor. He mentored me in the fullest sense of the term, spending unhurried time alone with me, giving me godly counsel, and teaching me how to study and argue for truth. Dr. Fuller's influence is seen in all the study and writing I do today.

Shortly after returning to Sri Lanka following my studies in the United States, I married Nelun and had the privilege of living close to one who practiced what I preached better than I did.

To these personal influences I would add my three brothers—Kumar, Duleep, and Priyan—and my sister, Anusha; my seminary teachers; my colleagues in Youth for Christ; my friends and accountability partners; the many pastors and other Christian workers I have befriended; and the biographies I have read. All of these have deeply influenced me in my walk with God. I have tried to footnote the sources of my ideas, but I am painfully aware that the influence of many people has not been acknowledged.

Since I have been so blessed by the discipling of others, it should be no surprise that discipling is very much a part of my ministry too. It has been one of the primary tasks I've engaged in while serving in Youth for Christ, first as a volunteer beginning in 1966 and then as a staff worker beginning in 1976. For the past thirty-five years, this ministry has primarily (not exclusively) been with first-generation Christians from other faiths. My grassroots ministry is in a church we have been involved in for over thirty-five years. Most of the members there are converts from other faiths. Since stepping down from the national directorship of Youth for Christ in 2011, I am giving more time to discipling and mentoring than ever before. Because I see this as an urgent need in Sri Lanka, I have had to reduce my preaching to devote more time to personal work. From disciplees and my own children, Nirmali and Asiri, I have learned a lot about Christian nurture and living. A day's meeting with those I disciple and mentor shortly before I left on sabbatical gave me many helpful ideas about discipling.

Many lessons that I have learned have come through failure. Some of those I have discipled have not turned out as I wished they would, and with everyone I have discipled I have made many mistakes. They have also suffered from the disadvantages that come from my own weaknesses. I will generally not mention the failures, as I would like to protect the privacy of individuals involved. Sometimes I use an example having changed the details of the story to guard the identity of the persons concerned. My failures and weaknesses have convinced me that those I disciple should be exposed to the influence of others who will compensate for my limitations.

This book was written on the campus of Trinity Evangelical Divinity School in Deerfield, Illinois, in the United States, which offered me an unbelievably generous six-month sabbatical package. The kindness that my wife and I experienced from the Trinity community is a wonderful example of God's unmerited favor on us. We were blessed not only by the material facilities they gave us but also through interaction with some of God's choice scholars who teach there. We were also warmly welcomed and enriched by the Arlington Heights Orchard Evangelical Free Church family of which we were a part during our time in the United States. My friends Brian and Ellen Relph kindly gave me a book grant to purchase books for this sabbatical. I also wish to thank my friends who supported us financially during the sabbatical and prayed for the writing of this book.

I am grateful to be working with Crossway once again, and with Thom Notaro, whose meticulous editorial work greatly improved this book.

———

Investing personally in people's lives can be done in different ways with differing intensity. Paul Stanley and Robert Clinton have a helpful classification of different types of discipling, mentoring, and coaching in their book *Connecting: The Mentoring Relationships You Need* to *Succeed in Life*. In this book I am using the word *discipling* to refer to most kinds of personal investing in others. When I distinguish between discipling and mentoring, *discipling* will refer to intensive caring for relatively new believers and *mentoring* will be used for less intensive caring for more mature believers.

In this book, I use the terms *discipler* and *disciplee* rather than *master* and *disciple*. The discipler's aim is to help his or her disciplees to become disciples of the Master, Jesus Christ. Our aim is not to nurture "our disciples" but to help people to become faithful disciples of Christ. I believe this approach helps overcome some of the dangers of discipling that I will describe. *Disciple makers* is another good term used in several books for those I refer to as disciplers.

However, I must say that in the Bible people are called disciples of groups or individuals other than Jesus. The Pharisees and John the Baptist had their disciples (Mark 2:18). The Jews considered themselves disciples of Moses (John 9:28). But the Gospel of John records that John the Baptist oriented his disciples toward Jesus (John 3:25–30). John's disciple Andrew, impressed by John's comment about Jesus, followed him as he walked, and the ensuing conversation resulted in Andrew becoming a disciple of Jesus (John 1:35–41).[9] Most of the other instances of the word *disciple* (*mathētēs*) are for followers of Christ, and it often is a synonym for Christians in general.[10] So I trust I have adequate reason for using the terms *discipler* and *disciplee*. The ambition of the discipler could be described in the words of John the Baptist: in the life of the disciplee, Christ "must increase, but I must decrease" (John 3:30).

---

9. I am indebted to Edward L. Smither, *Augustine as Mentor: A Model for Preparing Spiritual Leaders* (Nashville: B&H Academic, 2008), 5, for these insights.

10. Smither, *Augustine as Mentor*, 5.

Bible Versions Used

All emphases in Scripture quotations have been added by the author.

Part 1

INTRODUCING SPIRITUAL PARENTHOOD

1

Spiritual Parenthood

So Needed, but Why So Neglected?

I find that every church I go to is talking discipleship and disciple-making as a core value—but I somehow don't see it. It is what I call a preferred value rather than an actual value, much like evangelism is in many church situations. It's what we are supposed to do—rather than what we do, and I guess it is because our culture of individualism sees it as a program rather than a lifestyle of sacrifice and inconvenience.

Richard Brohier[1]

The above words from my Australian pastor-friend Richard Brohier aptly describe a crisis facing the church. And they get to the heart of the problem: "Our culture of individualism sees [discipleship] as a program rather than a lifestyle of sacrifice and inconvenience."

At the start of this book, I want to present discipling as a kind of parenting. Parenting is messy and inconvenient. Many couples today opt out of parenting because of the inconvenience, stress, and

1. Richard Brohier, Geelong, Australia, email message to author, July 2, 2017.

disruption to life that children bring. If people are opting out of literal parenthood, it would not be surprising to find Christians opting out of being spiritual parents of people with whom they have no biological or other "essential" tie.

In this chapter and the next, I will explore the biblical model of spiritual parenthood and the challenges it brings. This may give us a clue to why so many Christians are reluctant to launch a ministry of discipling.

Introducing a Metaphor

The Bible says that people are "born again" when they are saved (John 1:12–13; 3:3–8; 1 Pet. 1:3, 23). A newborn child needs to be cared for by parents. Most basically, God is our Father (John 1:12), but God often uses people to mediate the blessings of his fatherhood in our lives. So we shouldn't be surprised to find that the Bible often refers to the nurturing of believers using the metaphor of parenthood. It fittingly describes the relationship between disciplers and disciplees.

Even though there wasn't much of an age gap between Jesus and his disciples, he sometimes referred to them as his children (Mark 10:24; John 13:33; 21:5). Paul sometimes spoke of whole congregations as his children (1 Cor. 4:14; Gal. 4:28; 1 Thess. 2:7, 11). But Paul especially named people he had personally discipled as his children. He mentioned Timothy in this way—six times (1 Cor. 4:17; Phil. 2:22; 1 Tim. 1:2, 18; 2 Tim. 1:2; 2:1)—as he did Titus (Titus 1:4) and Onesimus (Philem. 10). And Peter referred to Mark as his son (1 Pet. 5:13).

Peter used the common Greek word for son (*huios*) when referring to Mark. This word appears 380 times in the New Testament. But Paul, when referring to his spiritual children, used a less common word, *teknon*, which appears ninety-nine times in the New Testament.[2] *Teknon* can be used for "a person of any age for whom there is a special relationship of endearment and association,"[3] and this seems to be the way Paul used it when alluding to those he discipled. The term conveys the affection that exists between discipler and disciplee.

---

2. In John 13:33, John uses a related word, *teknion*, when presenting the words of Jesus. This word appears seven times in 1 John also, each translated "little children" in the ESV. In John 21:5 we find the unrelated word *paidion*, which, like *teknon and teknion*, also carries the sense of an affectionate relationship.

3. Johannes P. Louw and Eugene A. Nida, *Greek-English Lexicon of the New Testament: Based on Semantic Domains*, 2nd ed., vol. 1 (New York: United Bible Societies, 1996), 109.

As William Barclay says, "Over and over again, there is affection in Paul's voice when he speaks of Timothy."[4]

Paul's affection for Timothy is more strikingly presented in 2 Timothy, where he refers to Timothy as "my beloved child" (*agapēto teknō*), after which he says, "Recalling your tears, I long to see you, so that I may be filled with joy" (2 Tim. 1:2, 4 NIV). Here we see both the joy and the pain of parenthood. Of the runaway slave Onesimus, Paul says, "I appeal to you for my child, Onesimus, whose father I became in my imprisonment. . . . I am sending him back to you, sending my very heart" (Philem. 10, 12). The word translated "very heart" literally means "bowels," which were considered the seat of feelings in those days. This "word is repeatedly used by Paul to convey the sense of affection."[5] The brilliant upper-class scholar had become "a very dear friend and intimate companion"[6] of a slave who had run away from his Christian master; and he looked at his leaving as similar to losing his very heart!

Paul's affectionate, parent-like love is vividly described in 1 Thessalonians 2:7–8, where he uses the mother metaphor: "But we were gentle among you, like a nursing mother taking care of her own children. So, being affectionately desirous of you, we were ready to share with you not only the gospel of God but also our own selves, because you had become very dear to us." "Affectionately desirous" is the translation of a single Greek word (*homeiromenoi*) that appears only here in the New Testament and was "rare even in the literature of the era." It was "found in such contexts as a funerary inscription that tells how the parents long for their deceased son."[7] Paul yearned for the Thessalonians and, he says, that is why he opened up his own self to them.

In this book we are looking at discipling as an affectionate relationship of caring between people who see themselves as having a parent-child relationship. The way I generally describe a discipling

4. William Barclay, *The Letters to Timothy, Titus, and Philemon*, 3rd ed. (Louisville: Westminster John Knox, 2003), 25.

5. F. F. Bruce, *The Epistles to the Colossians, to Philemon, and to the Ephesians*, New International Commentary on the New Testament (Grand Rapids, MI: Eerdmans, 1984), 214.

6. Douglas J. Moo, *The Letters to the Colossians and to Philemon*, The Pillar New Testament Commentary (Grand Rapids, MI: Eerdmans; Leicester, UK: Apollos, 2008), 412.

7. Gene L. Green, *The Letters to the Thessalonians*, The Pillar New Testament Commentary (Grand Rapids, MI: Eerdmans; Leicester, UK: Apollos, 2002), 128.

relationship is to say that the discipler "looks after" the disciplee. As Paul said to the elders of the church in Ephesus, "Pay careful attention to yourselves and to all the flock, in which the Holy Spirit has made you overseers, to care for the church of God, which he obtained with his own blood" (Act 20:28). The metaphor used for leadership here is that of a shepherd. This is another very good way to describe discipling, and the idea of shepherding will appear occasionally in this book, as well. Drawing upon an intimate knowledge of the life and work of a shepherd, biblical scholar Timothy S. Laniak has brilliantly described this aspect of leadership in his book *While Shepherds Watch Their Flocks*.[8] The truths in Laniak's book have influenced me more than the footnotes can indicate.

Multiplication

The fruit of a ministry of spiritual parenting must not be underestimated. Spiritual parenting is the key to multiplying disciples. As the famous discipling text says, "What you have heard from me in the presence of many witnesses entrust to faithful men who will be able to teach others also" (2 Tim. 2:2). Four generations of Christians are mentioned here. (1) Paul teaches (2) Timothy, who in turn teaches (3) faithful men, who will be able to teach (4) others also. It is a process of multiplication rather than addition of disciples.

In the mid-1960s, when the ministry of Youth for Christ in Sri Lanka was a few months old, its founder, Sam Sherrard, was looking at a list of all those who had committed their lives to Christ at the various evangelistic events we had conducted. He was suddenly struck by the fact that he had almost no contact with most of the scores of people who had made "decisions" for Christ. Around this time, he read two books that had a marked impact on him: Robert Coleman's *The Master Plan of Evangelism*[9] and Waylon B. Moore's *New Testament Follow-Up*.[10] Sherrard decided to start discipling a few people.

---

8. Timothy S. Laniak, *While Shepherds Watch Their Flocks: Forty Daily Reflections on Biblical Leadership* (n.p.: ShepherdLeader, 2007). Laniak has written a more scholarly book, *Shepherds after My Own Heart: Pastoral Traditions and Leadership in the Bible*, New Studies in Biblical Theology (Downers Grove, IL: InterVarsity Press, 2006).

9. Grand Rapids, MI: Revell, 1963, 1964. References to this book hereafter will be from a newer, 1993 edition.

10. Grand Rapids, MI: Eerdmans, 1963. A newer edition is dated 1984.

Plans to move into new cities were shelved until he was able to nurture a group of leaders in Colombo. The international leaders of Youth for Christ were initially puzzled by this approach, but they wisely did not insist that he change it.

I was a member of the first group that Sherrard discipled. Gradually more and more leaders emerged, and the ministry started working increasingly with people who had no contact with churches. These were discipled and channeled to churches. Some stayed on as volunteers in the work. Because there is a shortage of leaders in the churches, we decided generally not to look for volunteers and staff from outside the movement. Today we have about eighty staff and about 450 volunteers in ministries all over the country. New ministries start when a center has leaders they can release to go to a new area. In addition to nurturing our own staff and volunteers, hundreds of people discipled in this ministry are active in leadership roles in churches. About eighty-eight are serving in pastoral roles, and a large number serve in other Christian organizations. This is significant, considering that the total Protestant population of the country is less than three hundred thousand.

I was leader of this work for thirty-five years, and since stepping down seven years ago, I have served as a kind of mentor and Bible teacher in the movement. It has not been easy to keep up this emphasis on discipling. Sometimes a local ministry would lose its discipling momentum. And if remedial steps were not taken, that would be the death of that work. We are a youth evangelistic movement. When one generation of youth graduates from that work and gets settled in churches, we have to find a new generation from outside the church— that is, through reaching the unreached. And those who are found need to be discipled till they are settled in churches. If we don't do that, the ministry will have to close up. Each division of the ministry is always one generation from closing down!

I have felt the need to preach to and teach our staff and volunteers about discipling all through my forty-two years in this work. It is so easy to let a program orientation eclipse discipling as everyone gets busy seeking to reach the lost. While programs are vital for our survival, if the discipling drops off, those who are reached through the programs will fall away. And the ministry will be left without youth to carry it through to the next generation. So each year we need to keep stressing the importance of discipling.

Commitment: The Key to Parenthood

If spiritual parenthood is so needed, why is it so neglected? In the rest of this chapter we will look at the main reason why people are reluctant to launch into a ministry of discipling, and the next chapter will take up additional reasons.

Commitment to Discipling, Deemed Too Costly

If affection is the characteristic ingredient in spiritual parenthood, the fuel that keeps it going is commitment. When I am teaching on discipling, I often ask the audience how one can nurture affection, like that of a parent toward a child, among those who are not physically related. The most popular response I hear is that the discipler needs to spend a lot of time with the disciplee. In this busy world, that takes a lot of commitment. Let's look at how can we foster such commitment.

We must first clarify that we cannot actively care for everyone in the world. Only God can do that. Even when Jesus was on earth, he needed to concentrate on a few. Similarly, we can pay the price of commitment to a few people. Parenthood is inconvenient, but most parents unhesitatingly take on the inconvenience because of their commitment to their children. We like to have our lives nicely ordered and planned. But when a child gets sick and needs to be taken to a hospital, her parent does not say, "That wasn't on my schedule." Though we cannot keep breaking our plans for everyone, we will for our children—both biological and spiritual. That calls for commitment.

Yet every culture has some features of Christianity that believers find difficult to follow. One of the key countercultural features of Christianity today is commitment. Christianity is a religion of commitment. We are committed to Christ and his cause and to the people God leads us to. But many view Christianity from the viewpoint of consumers. They choose a church based on what the church has to offer. If the church loses its attractiveness and what they consider its usefulness, they simply change churches. That is how many choose their Christian friends also. With such an attitude toward Christian community, it is difficult to muster the kind of commitment that nurturing spiritual children requires. We may do so for physical children because we must. But many Christians view discipling as an option. And many opt out.

Consequently, many people in the church today live with disappointment over leaders who abandoned or ignored them when they most needed help. Jesus talks about this in John 10:12, where he says that the hired hand abandons the sheep and runs away when he sees the wolf coming. Many sheep in the church have suffered because those they trusted abandoned them at tough times in their lives. How can one be healed of consequences of such abandonment? In the next verse, Jesus says: "I am the good shepherd. The good shepherd lays down his life for the sheep" (John 10:11). Wounded sheep can be healed through the costly commitment of a shepherd. Disciplers follow Christ and adopt this kind of commitment.

Those who have grown up with rejection by family and society will tell you how hard it is for them to believe that even God is truly committed to them. But some, seeing the costly commitment of their disciplers, become open to the fact that they are worthy of somebody's commitment. That, in turn, opens the door to accepting that God is truly concerned for their welfare.

There is a crisis in many churches today because many members are not committed to the church and its program. People are unwilling to pay the price of costly involvement. Often churches organize mobilizing campaigns and seminars to resolve this problem. While these can be helpful, they do not strike at the root of the problem. We need a culture of commitment, and leaders must model that. The key then is leaders who will lay down their lives for the sheep. If the leaders die for the people, the people will die for the church! Paul said, "Even if I am to be poured out as a drink offering upon the sacrificial offering of *your faith*, I am glad and rejoice with you all" (Phil. 2:17). He was willing to die for the faith of the Philippian Christians and even happy to do so. Jesus said, "For [the disciples'] sake I consecrate myself, that they also may be sanctified in truth" (John 17:19). The context shows that the consecration Jesus was taking about was his death.[11]

---

11. See D. A. Carson, *The Gospel according to John*, The Pillar New Testament Commentary (Grand Rapids, MI: Eerdmans; Leicester, UK: Inter-Varsity Press, 1991), 567.

The Strain of Caring for Both Family and Disciplees

There is another problem that causes people today to shun costly commitment to people in the church. Many children of Christian leaders say that their parents cared for so many other people that they didn't have time for them. Often these children have abandoned the church because of this. Such neglect of family is clearly wrong. Caring for our family members is a primary responsibility of church leaders. One older translation of 1 Corinthians 14:1 says, "Make love your aim" (RSV). My great ambition in life should be to serve my wife and children and do all I can to see that they are satisfied and happy. But I also have a call to serve others. We must attempt to do both.

But we are not messiahs. We have physical and emotional limitations. Therefore, as I will show below, we must keep our responsibilities at a manageable level. We must make sure we do not take on too many people to disciple. We must make sure we do not take on too many public assignments and committee responsibilities. If we have too much on our plates, our disciplees, our families, and we ourselves suffer.

Even if we have been wise in taking on responsibilities, the balance may be difficult to maintain. A principle I have found helpful is that the balanced life is our cross. When I speak of the balanced life, I don't mean doing everything in moderation. Rather, the balanced life is found in obedience in all areas of life. We are to care for our families and our disciplees and do a lot of other things. That is not easy. It could be quite tiring. It is our cross. But if we know that the cross is an essential part of the Christian life, we will pay the price of our commitments without being upset about it.

When my children were youths, they would sometimes ask me whether I could pick them up late at night from a party. Sometimes I was very tired and was looking forward to going to bed early. But, to my knowledge, I never refused such a request. Why? Because I know that it is God's will for me to cheerfully serve my children. It was a cross for me in that I was tired. But the Bible says that the cross is an essential aspect of a Christian's life; it is God's will for us. Because the will of God is perfect, we will not only do it; we will also be happy doing it.

That kind of approach should help to avert the impression that children are neglected because their parents are committed to ministry. And because we have a place for such difficulty in our theology, we won't be disillusioned by the inconvenience it brings on us.

The Vulnerability and Strain of Being Parents
Openhearted Ministry Can Be Painful

Discipling also makes one vulnerable to hurt and stress. Caring for people can be emotionally strenuous. Today we find much good advice on how to avoid stress. Given the competitiveness of our society and the drivenness it has produced in people, we should heed this advice. The driven, competitive kind of stress harms us and often leads to burnout. But discipling produces a different kind of stress—the stress of love. Speaking of his ministry in general, Paul says, "And, apart from other things, there is the daily pressure on me of my anxiety for all the churches. Who is weak, and I am not weak? Who is made to fall, and I am not indignant?" (2 Cor. 11:28–29). He addressed the Galatians as "my little children, for whom I am again in the anguish of childbirth until Christ is formed in you!" (Gal. 4:19). When you love people, you yearn for their welfare, and you hurt when they are hurt or have failed.

This kind of affection is the fruit of an openhearted approach to ministry. It is also expressed in these words from Paul:

> Make room in your hearts for us. We have wronged no one, we have corrupted no one, we have taken advantage of no one. I do not say this to condemn you, for I said before that you are in our hearts, to die together and to live together. I am acting with great boldness toward you; I have great pride in you; I am filled with comfort. In all our affliction, I am overflowing with joy. (2 Cor. 7:2–4)

His feelings run deep, and he is not ashamed to express them.

I have heard people say that we must exercise some reserve to avoid making ourselves vulnerable to hurt from the people we serve. There is some truth in this. Pain must be kept at a manageable level. But, as we shall show below, while those who minister deeply with people cannot avoid vulnerability to hurt, God equips them with the strength to face the pain.

The Goal of Discipling

Paul tackles these issues well in Colossians 1:28–29, where he describes the goal of discipling: "Him we proclaim, warning everyone and teaching everyone with all wisdom, that we may present everyone mature in Christ" (Col. 1:28).[12] The goal is to "present people mature in Christ." Paul uses the same verb, "present" (*paristēmi*), and the same tense (aorist) in verse 22: "You . . . he has now reconciled in his body of flesh by his death, in order to present you holy and blameless and above reproach before him." Scholars like F. F. Bruce have shown that in both these verses Paul seems to be talking about presenting people to Christ at the second coming.[13] Just as parents do all they can to help their children succeed in exams, disciplers do all they can to present their disciplees mature in Christ at the ultimate final exam: the second coming and its accompanying events. It will be our great joy to present the fruit of our labors to God at the judgment. On that day, the people we have invested in will be to us what the Philippians were to Paul: "my joy and crown" (Phil. 4:1).

When my daughter was little, I used to take her to her preschool each morning on my motorcycle (the standard means of economical transport for middle-class people in Sri Lanka). I would often see a lady who brought four or so little children to school in a passenger van. They would get off the van with her and then hold on to her, each one holding a finger, as she led them to school. I often think that this is the way I would like to go to heaven—taking along with me several people in whose lives I have invested.

Toiling

But preparing people for the second coming involves hard work. Paul goes on to say to the Colossians, "For this [goal of presenting them mature] I toil, struggling with all his energy that he powerfully works

---

12. There is a more comprehensive discussion of these two verses in Ajith Fernando, *The Call to Joy and Pain: Embracing Suffering in Your Ministry* (Wheaton, IL: Crossway, 2007), chaps. 27–29.

13. Bruce, *Colossians, Ephesians*, 87.

within me" (Col. 1:29). Two key verbs express the challenge of discipling here. The word translated "toil" (*kopiaō*) takes the meanings "work, work hard, labor . . . ; become tired, grow weary."[14] Discipling is hard and tiring work. Any discipler would agree that often we feel we are too tired, too weighed down with other responsibilities, to respond to the needs of disciplees. But the work must be done, though it is tiring.

We may need to visit our disciplees when it is not convenient to do so. Sometimes we must work hard to equip them for a challenge they face. A disciplee may be struggling with an issue unfamiliar to us, like homosexual temptation or harmonizing Christianity and science. A disciplee may have a problem understanding a biblical passage. We may have to do some homework to find out about these issues so that we can help him or her adequately. We may need to ask someone else for advice on an issue. We may need to read up on the issue. This looks like a big price to pay, with everything else we have to do in this busy world.

Struggling

The next verb is "struggling" (*agōnizomai*). It can mean wrestling, fighting, battling, and struggling. This reminds us that we are battling for the souls of people. I have experienced many failures in my discipling, when people I have worked with have begun to behave badly or backslide. All disciplers face such struggles. A disciplee falls in love with a nonbeliever. Another seeks revenge against someone who has hurt her. Another fails to have a regular time alone with the Lord or is too lazy to do the study needed for an upcoming exam.

Sometimes when they behave badly, people blame us because of our connection with them. When we refuse to give up on them, they think we are naïve and blind to their faults. Being called a naïve simpleton is hard to take. But just as Jesus bore our shame, we are called to bear the shame of our disciplees and work with them to help them grow to maturity. We must not condone the bad actions of our disciplees, but we can defend their sincerity and continue to hope in the possibilities of grace in their lives. One will need to pay a price to do so.

---

14. Barclay M. Newman Jr., *Greek-English Dictionary of the New Testament* (n.p.: United Bible Societies, 1993), electronic version in Logos Bible Software.

This is particularly true of youth work. Young people often make mistakes and are rejected or severely criticized by the church. Then they often become alienated from the church and leave. At such times, they need older Christians who will stand by them and support them and help them grow into mature servants of God. I often tell the Youth for Christ community that taking on the shame of our youth is part of the call of youth workers. The one thing we must strive to ensure is that those we disciple are truthful. We can work toward solving the problems of those who are honest with us. They deserve our taking on shame on their behalf. (We will look at the issue of truthfulness in chap. 11.)

Sometimes you have to carve out a time in your already busy schedule to make an unplanned visit as a disciplee is facing some special crisis. Perhaps he has angrily left a meeting, not wanting to talk to anyone. You may need to go to him even though it is late and you are feeling weary. When you catch up to him, he may tell you he has decided to leave the church. You may have to grapple with him for a long time until he gives up his intention to leave.

Then, there are some who backslide. And often when that happens, guess whom they blame? Their discipler! It dismays us when people come and tell us what our spiritual child is saying about us. Yet the loving shepherd, like our heavenly Father, leaves the ninety-nine in the fold and goes in search of the lost sheep (Matt. 18:10–14). We sometimes romanticize the idea of going after lost sheep, forgetting what a difficult job searching the rugged terrain is without knowing where the sheep have gone. But that is what we must do. Even though they may be speaking ill of us, we don't hit back. Instead, we will use every legitimate method to persuade the backslidden to return to the Lord. (I will talk about battling for people in prayer in chap. 9.)

Strength from God

Will having to spend so much energy on discipling, with all the other work we have to do, harm us? Will we end up burned out through overwork? It should not harm us permanently, because God always compensates for the price we pay doing it. Paul ends Colossians 1:29

saying the toil and struggling is done "with all his energy that he powerfully works within me." Discipling is primarily a spiritual exercise, and for that we need spiritual energy. God "powerfully works [that energy] within" us. But we must be in vital touch with God. There is no better preventative to burnout than time spent with God in the Bible and prayer.

I believe the major cause for burnout among leaders is insecurity, which can make us drive ourselves to achieve results that prove our worth. Time spent with God addresses this insecurity. We sense the reality that

> the eternal God is [our] dwelling place,
>   and underneath are the everlasting arms. (Deut. 33:27)

That truth attacks our sense of inadequacy. As David put it,

> Those who look to him are radiant,
>   and their faces shall never be ashamed. (Ps. 34:5)

As the radiance of God heartens us during our time with him, our shame is taken away, and our insecurity defused.

Unhurried time set apart to be alone with God also has a way of slowing us down and restoring our equilibrium after the battles of life have caused imbalance. If the time with God is a nonnegotiable aspect of our daily schedule, then we will set this time aside, however busy we may be. And we do not have to rush, because the same amount of time has been reserved whether we are busy or not. That fixedness of the time with God has a way of ministering to our tired and rushed souls and letting the peace of Christ restore our equilibrium.

I have said that the stress caused by discipling is the stress of love. We can always be equipped with the love needed for this work because God's love is an inexhaustible resource. As Paul says, "God's love has been poured into our hearts through the Holy Spirit who has been given to us" (Rom. 5:5). Kent Hughes explains that the word translated "poured" carries "the idea in the Greek . . . that God's love has been and continues to be poured out within our hearts. This is a picture of unstinting lavishness. The old commentator Bengel uses the

Latin word '*abundantissime.*' Our hearts have been filled to overflowing with divine affection."[15] There is no shortage here.

My biggest battle relating to mixing interpersonal work with a preaching and teaching ministry has been the battle for time to prepare my talks. I strongly believe that if we are to reflect the glory of God in what we do, our talks must be well prepared. Now and then an emergency has resulted in my having to preach while completely unprepared. Once on Pentecost Sunday in our church the preacher didn't turn up. I was leading the service and hoping that he would come in time for the sermon. He didn't. So I took my Bible and went through the second chapter of Acts, expounding it. I had preached on this text many years before. With the outline already in the back of my mind as I was going verse by verse, I somehow delivered a sermon, and I believe the Lord used it. This is one way in which the Lord gives us strength for preaching. But that is an exception to the rule.

Usually we preachers and teachers need to be well prepared. For me, finding time to prepare is often a struggle. I know I need God's grace for this. I have a group of friends who pray for me, and I often send them urgent text messages explaining my need to be prepared. Sometimes, partly because of my bad planning and partly because of unexpected personal ministry or family needs, I'm forced to be up almost the whole night in order to be ready to preach the next morning. Of course, I come home and have a good sleep in the afternoon. (The ability to sleep anytime is a gift God has given me.) We must not ruin our health by having insufficient sleep.

I have been preaching for over fifty years, over forty of them as a full-time worker. Somehow God has seen me through. I have experienced the reality of Paul's statement that God's grace is sufficient and that our strength is made perfect in weakness (2 Cor. 12:9). My sense of desperation and weakness makes me depend more on God, which in turn becomes an occasion for God's grace to be unleashed. I have found that preparing talks is an exhilarating task. Indeed, it is tiring and involves the demanding work of careful Bible study and relevant application. But handling the truth has a way of bringing freshness to our lives. After all, as David said,

---

15. R. Kent Hughes, *Romans: Righteousness from Heaven*, Preaching the Word (Wheaton, IL: Crossway, 1991), 109.

The law of the Lord is perfect,
    reviving the soul. (Ps. 19:7)

If you struggle with having to combine person-to-person work with study, preparation, and proclamation, I want to encourage you not to give up. It is demanding work, and you must be careful to arrange your schedule so that you will not hurt yourself by unplanned living. But God will see you through. The energy he supplies is sufficient for you.

The Necessity of Suffering

The preceding discussion has responded to the main reason why discipling is not as popular as it should be in the church. Many are unwilling to pay the physical and emotional price that it entails. Sadly, with all the emphasis on "the blessings of God" in the church today, we are woefully lacking in a biblical understanding of the necessity of suffering in the Christian life. Many Christians think that if someone is suffering from emotional pain, tiredness, stress, or inconvenience, something has gone wrong. Such problems have not been factored into their understanding of a fulfilling life.

Paul would disagree. He followed his Master's teaching and example, and included suffering as an essential aspect of his life. In light of that, when suffering came, he was not disillusioned, nor did he try to avoid it. Instead, he had learned that deeper than the pain of suffering was the joy of the Lord. The joy of the Lord gave him the strength to face the pain of suffering. It was from prison that he wrote, "Rejoice in the Lord always; again I will say, rejoice" (Phil. 4:4). How could he say that from a bleak Roman prison? The answer comes a few verses later: "Not that I am speaking of being in need, for I have learned in whatever situation I am to be content" (Phil. 4:11). He was in prison; but he was not in need, because there was something deeper than every situation he faced: the Lord and his sufficiency.[16]

------

16. I have dealt in some detail with the issue of experiencing joy and pain at the same time in my book *Call to Joy and Pain*, chaps. 1–8.

I have seen some people start the work of discipling and then give up before long. If they had remained close to the Lord and his ways, and if they had applied to their commitment to their disciplees the biblical teaching about suffering, they may not have needed to give up.

2

Objections and Pitfalls

... the deceptive mathematics of worldly thinking that considers pouring out one's life on a hidden few as a scandalous waste of one's potential.

Kent and Barbara Hughes[1]

In our opening chapter I described the need for discipling, as well as the main reason why people avoid it. Because there are more reasons, and the crisis of neglect of discipling in the church is so serious, we need to explore these other objections before going further.

A Countercultural Activity

Numerous cultural factors today make discipling a countercultural activity for leaders.

Discipling Looks Like an Inefficient Use of Time

Efficiency and productivity are key values today. People are told that they must push for measurable results, and usually those results are measured in terms of numbers. In a Christian setting, such an emphasis could result in concentrating on increasing attendance, events,

---

1. Kent Hughes and Barbara Hughes, *The Disciplines of a Godly Family* (Wheaton, IL: Crossway, 2004), 16.

programs, and buildings. These visible goals can take so much time that there is no time left to give concentrated attention to personal discipling. Granted, the fruit of person-to-person discipleship is not immediately visible. And a biblical leader should be concerned with numbers because the numbers represent people who have come within the sound of the gospel, and programs and physical structures are helpful in developing mature Christians. But the focus on numerical growth must not be at the cost of nurturing saints.

I will show below how Jesus combined public and personal ministry. Here let me say that despite the welcome emphasis today on discipling, mentoring, and coaching, leaders generally find it difficult to prioritize unhurried times with those they supervise. Today people present similar objections to the calling of parenthood. Referring to the reluctance to rear children today, Kent and Barbara Hughes talk of "the deceptive mathematics of worldly thinking that considers pouring out one's life on a hidden few as a scandalous waste of one's potential."[2]

We should battle these false values. As we grow in leadership, we often need to pass up what look like wonderful opportunities of service so that we can have sufficient time for personal ministry. These days I meet many young pastors and Christian workers for mentoring or counseling. I have been surprised and saddened to hear that many of them have never had an unhurried conversation about their personal lives with their leaders in ministry. Most of these pastors serve in churches that are growing numerically. A friend of mine in a South Asian country did a survey for a research paper on the relationship between senior pastors and junior pastors. He concluded that often when a young worker joins the staff of a church, he considers the senior pastor his hero. But after a few years, some begin to consider him a demon! They see themselves as pawns used to fulfill the agendas of senior pastors who do not seem to have time for them or interest in their welfare.

If the top leaders in a church or organization do not give time for personal work, it is unlikely that there will be a culture of discipling in the groups they lead. The leaders must demonstrate by example that investing in others is a key aspect of Christian ministry. When

---

2. Hughes and Hughes, *Disciplines of a Godly Family*, 16.

I was leader of Youth for Christ in Sri Lanka, I always tried to disciple a few young staff. This gave rise to an awkward situation, as some people felt I was giving preferential treatment to these staff. But I felt that this problem was worthwhile because of the high place personal work deserves in the culture of our movement. If the leader finds time to disciple, others are also encouraged to give time for it, despite all the other things calling for their attention.

As the possibility of an imbalance in our priorities is very real, we need to keep revising our list of priorities constantly while growing in leadership. Unhealthy baggage can accumulate in our lives without our realizing it. I need to be careful about accepting too many speaking engagements, serving on too many committees, and, more recently, taking on too many people to mentor; mentoring or discipling too many can result in too little time to comprehensively disciple or mentor a few. I've developed a value statement for myself, which I do not universally recommend as a biblical rule but will present for your consideration: "Prominence is a burden that goes with the call of some people. Personal work is our badge of honor." Principles like this help us develop priorities that, in turn, enable us to evaluate the opportunities for service that come our way.

As leaders grow, they should constantly divest themselves of some responsibilities so that they can concentrate on the most important ones. Timothy Laniak tells of a senior elder in a church who "handed in his resignation after many years because, in his words, 'all this business keeps me from shepherding the flock.'"[3]

Discipling Runs Counter to Today's Activity Orientation

People are very busy today. Besides physical work, they are often "busy" in the cyber world with social media or are watching TV. In Sri Lanka if you visit a family in the evening and they happen to be watching a favorite TV program, they may just invite you to join in the watching, without shutting off the TV to talk to you. In this environment people find it a strain to interrupt their activities for a long one-on-one conversation. Such rootless busyness has produced an

---

3. Timothy S. Laniak, *While Shepherds Watch Their Flocks: Forty Daily Reflections on Biblical Leadership* (n.p.: ShepherdLeader, 2007), 118.

insecure generation. They are missing the completion and security that come from committed relationships with trusted friends and relatives. Suicide rates among teenagers have increased markedly, and analysts say a major contributor is a preoccupation with their smart phones and the cyber world.[4]

Based on today's attitude toward time, Christianity could be considered a religion of wasting time. We "waste" a lot of time each day in prayer and Bible reading. Klaus Issler has written a book on Christian spirituality entitled *Wasting Time with God*.[5] We could say the same about discipling appointments. Close relationships do not develop through highly structured and restricted conversations. As we linger with each other, chatting about our lives during the discipling appointment, ties develop that engender trust. Once trust is won and the environment created through long conversations, people have the freedom to talk about the deep secrets of their lives. A side benefit of this is that it dispels damaging insecurities of constantly being rushed. Discipling appointments slow us down.

About ten years ago, I discipled a Youth for Christ volunteer in his early twenties. He was from a westernized background. When he heard I was writing a book on discipling, he sent me a letter describing his appointments with me. I will quote a few extracts from it:

- We met once every 6–8 weeks. Each meeting lasted for about 2–2 ½ hours. [With newer believers we would need to meet more often than once every six to eight weeks, and perhaps for a shorter time]. There was hardly any other thing you did during that time—it was undivided attention at its best. . . . I always wondered how is such a busy man spending long hours with a brat like me.
- We always met in your office room. That was such an amazing room. The whole world slows down in there. It was exceptionally quiet. The books, your papers on the table and portraits of your Christian heroes—all of them just added to the tranquility.

---

4. See, for example, Jericka Duncan, "Smartphones, Cyberbullying Seen as Possible Causes of Rising Teen Suicide Rate," *CBS Evening News*, August 4, 2017, http://www.cbsnews.com/news/smartphones-cyberbullying-targeted-as-causes-of-skyrocketing-teen-suicide-rate/.

5. Klaus Issler, *Wasting Time with God: A Christian Spirituality of Friendship with God* (Downers Grove, IL: InterVarsity Press, 2001).

- You spoke slow. You spoke very little. You would ask me questions in a nonthreatening manner. You gave the opportunity for me to ask questions. [Most meetings I walked in with lists of questions.] You shared your experiences. Everything done in slow motion . . .
- You slowed me down and I am so grateful for this. . . .
- To date that investment is paying off. . . . As Christians, we need to slow down. The world out there is spinning real fast. We won't be able to pick things that God wants us to hear on the run.[6]

Discipling Runs Counter to the Superficiality of Today's Relationships

People today have hundreds, perhaps thousands, of friends on Facebook. They openly share about themselves, but often in superficial relationships with people unwilling to pay the price of costly commitment to them. They don't need to be honest; they can even tell lies about themselves. (I am told that people often enter wrong ages in dating website profiles!) And if the friendship gets inconvenient, you can simply "unfriend" another person. How sad that "unfriend" has become a popular word today.

When you get used to multiple superficial relationships, you may find it difficult to nurture deeper, more trusting bonds. You may not make time for such relationships and may find it awkward to share deeply with others. But how important it is for us to nurture deeper friendships. Proverbs has sage advice to our generation with its addiction to social media:

> A man of many companions may come to ruin,
>> but there is a friend who sticks closer than a brother.
>> (Prov. 18:24)

How much we need such friendship! Discipling offers that to us.

People Are Afraid to Trust Others with Their Personal Details

There is so much abuse of personal information nowadays that people are afraid to trust others with details about their lives. They are afraid

---

6. Sam Arasaratnam, Bahrain, email message to author, June 27, 2017.

of betrayal. They don't confide in people enough to entrust themselves to their care. Sometimes they may not personally like the leader who has been assigned to disciple them. So everyone keeps a "safe distance" from others. This is a major trap in large congregations, where it is very easy to remain anonymous and be lost in the crowd. Today you find people who have been hurt in small, more personal churches moving to large churches where they can remain anonymous.

This problem must be confronted with persevering commitment by the discipler. I am convinced that everyone needs the kind of accountability and trust that a discipling relationship affords. Some may not accept this fact, but if they launch into healthy relationships of accountability, they will appreciate them. In an environment that is unfriendly to such close ties, the discipler has the challenge of winning the trust of the disciplee. I do not think we should force people to "submit" to a discipler of our choice. Disciplees should have a say in who disciples them. But sometimes we may have to disciple people who are not fond of us.

Over twenty years ago, I was asked to supervise the drug rehab ministry of Youth for Christ. This meant I would be discipling three young staff workers in that ministry. The previous leader was extremely effective and had done an excellent job of nurturing these three staff. I soon realized that they were not happy that their former leader had left and that I had been assigned as their supervisor and discipler. It took me about two years to win their trust. I prayed earnestly to God to open their hearts to me. I visited their homes often. I spent a lot of time with them, just chatting with them. I studied books on drug rehab ministry and taught them about the topic. (The books were in English, and they were not fluent in English.) The Lord engineered a situation that forced us to spend a lot of time together. We had acquired funds for the purchase of land for our rehab center, but we couldn't find a suitable site. For an entire year we drove hundreds of miles, all over the country, looking at different locations. That gave us good opportunities to chat.

Even though I was their leader, my attitude toward these three staff was that of a beggar, pleading with them to accept me. After about two years, the tone of our relationship changed. We became and continue to be very close friends. God gave me a burden for drug rehab ministry that is still very strong. Now I am discipling or mentoring six former or recovering drug dependents, four of them in vocational Christian ministry. The sovereign Lord can change situations to bring fruit out of our efforts at winning people's confidence.

Discipling may be culturally distant and practically inconvenient to many people today. But it can be done, and there is an urgent need for all Christian leaders to commit themselves to it.

The Danger of Insecure Disciplers

All of us suffer from insecurities. But if those insecurities cause us to seek ego gratification from those we disciple, there can be dangerous results. This happened with the popular discipleship (or Shepherding) movement in the United States in the 1970s and 1980s. Leaders started having an unhealthy influence over their people, and the groups became like cults.[7] We will look at four examples of how insecurity can harm discipling relationships and then briefly consider three security-building activities.

Too Much Control over People's Lives

Christians belong to communities where members are supposed to be accountable to each other, of one accord, and of one heart, soul, and mind (Acts 4:32; Phil. 2:2). Yet God made each of us as an individual with a will of his or her own with which to decide on preferences. In the Christian life there are often different legitimate ways to do the same thing, and the method used can depend on the personality of the individual. Disciplers need to be careful about insisting on things that are not taught in Scripture.

In Sri Lanka, many marriages are still arranged by parents. But when people become Christians from other faiths, their parents are not able to do this for their children. So in our ministry we often have to assume the role of matchmakers, gently suggesting a possible spouse, or mediating on behalf of someone who has an interest in another.

---

7. B. Barron, "Shepherding Movement," in *Dictionary of Christianity in America.* ed. D. G. Reid, R. D. Linder, B. L. Shelley, and H. S. Stout (Downers Grove, IL: InterVarsity Press, 1990), Logos Bible Software version.

Often people choose their marriage partners and take steps toward relationships without our mediation. If a prospect is not a believer, we can object and seek to persuade the believer against entering that relationship. If the believer refuses to give up this relationship, he or she will be disciplined in some way, as the Bible is clear that marrying unbelievers is wrong. Sometimes in our situation, a person may choose a believer who a leader might think is not suitable. Then the leader has a right to counsel the person and warn of potential problems. But we have no right to prohibit the relationship. We have had situations in our country where parents and leaders have tried to stop a marriage because they didn't personally like the potential mate. But if no biblical principles are broken, we have no right to insist, even though we can share our opinion that this may not be a wise decision.

When leaders insist on their own personal preferences in the lives of others rather than on what the Bible says, they act in a cultic manner. They may be exercising too much control over those under their care. Some followers will repress their individuality, be absorbed in the will of the group, and stay on, finding security in this cultic cocoon. Others will rebel after a time and leave. But they usually leave with deep hurts. I have had to counsel people who have left such cultic groups. Because their identity was so wrapped up in the group, leaving it was a traumatic and wounding experience. They usually took a lot of time to recover and develop sufficient trust to commit to active involvement in another Christian group.

Parenthood as a Matter of Status Rather Than Responsibility

The lifestyle of a biblical leader is that of a servant. So spiritual parents are servants of their spiritual children. Paul claimed to be the father of the Corinthian Christians (1 Cor. 4:14–15). But he also said he was their servant: "For what we proclaim is not ourselves, but Jesus Christ as Lord, with ourselves as your servants for Jesus' sake" (2 Cor. 4:5). Moreover, Paul said that Jesus took upon himself "the form of a servant" (Phil. 2:7). If spiritual parenthood is an aspect of servanthood, then the parenthood cannot be a means to gaining status. It is the responsibility of caring for people. Regarding the authority and power that the Pharisees and Sadducees exercised (Matt. 23:2–8), Jesus said,

"And call no man your father on earth, for you have one Father, who is in heaven" (23:9). He was talking about the kind of fatherhood that insists on status.

A person may serve as a spiritual parent and later hand off that role. Barnabas would probably have considered himself a spiritual father to Mark. But later Peter called him "my son" (1 Pet. 5:13). Something like this happens in a parent-child relationship when the child is released to get married. There continues to be love, prayer, and respect, but the level of parental involvement and the extent of authority is much less.

Sometimes a spiritual parent ends up having a spiritual child as his or her leader. I suppose we could say that something like this happened when Paul became more prominent than Barnabas, the person who nurtured him in ministry. I had the wonderful privilege of ministering in India together with James Hudson Taylor III, the great-grandson of the legendary missionary to China by the same name. We became good friends. Dr. Taylor led the movement his great-grandfather founded (now known as OMF International) for several years. On a visit to Hong Kong, I met Dr. Taylor after his retirement from leadership and asked him how his son Jamie was. He happily told me, "He's my boss." After his retirement from executive responsibilities, Dr. Taylor still worked with a division of the ministry focusing on China, though now under the son's leadership.

Even when they are under our care, we need to expose our disciplees to the ministry of other Christians. Some disciplers don't like that. In fact, some leaders get upset when their members go to meetings led by others. There are some "evangelical grasshoppers" who hop from meeting to meeting and don't settle down and take responsibility in one place. That needs to be discouraged. But we leaders have so many weaknesses, and there is so much we don't know. Others can fill what is lacking in our input to our spiritual children. Besides, our aim is to communicate the Word to them, not ourselves. So we gradually work toward our disciplees becoming independent of us and dependent on Christ and the Word.

At the end of his life, Jesus told his disciples, "No longer do I call you servants, for the servant does not know what his master is doing;

but I have called you friends, for all that I have heard from my Father I have made known to you" (John 15:15). This is a key discipling verse, and I will refer to it again in this book. One of our aims in discipling is to be friends of those we disciple. Once they have been exposed to our lives and teaching, they feel one with us, and we can enjoy beautiful friendship in the truth, in mission, and in communion with Christ. Discipling, then, has to do with responsibility, not status.

Exclusive Relationships

A third problem is also related to insecurity. Disciplers can develop unhealthy emotional attachments to their disciplees. They look to their disciplees for the affirmation they should be getting primarily from the Lord, their family members, and their peers. Disciplees become a boost to their flagging egos! Sometimes these disciplers face rejection from their families and peers. A wife is always, with some justification, scolding her pastor-husband for working too hard and not giving enough time to the family. He feels rejected by her. Those feelings are temporarily eclipsed by the admiration of the disciplees.

In such relationships, leaders can become jealous if their disciplees admire other leaders. They get uneasy if their disciplees develop close friendships with outsiders, even though those outsiders are good Christians. So the group of disciplees huddles together, becoming a clique and excluding outsiders. Others are turned off by the group because it gives the impression that its members are superior to the rest. Jealous leaders will not be willing to release their disciplees when it is time for them to leave the group. The primary concern of good disciplers is the welfare of their disciplees. Sometimes it is best for disciplees to move on to another location, position, or organization. Insecure disciplers don't like to release them in this way. And if disciplees leave, they leave with a lot of hurt.

Some jealous disciplers are not sufficiently concerned about the relationships disciplees have with their families. A key aspect of Christian discipleship is relating in a biblical way to one's family. Even if parents are not Christian and are reacting with hostility to their child's commitment, the child must honor them, must love them, and must contribute to the welfare of the home—even at great cost to self in terms of energy, time, and resources. (I will discuss this issue in chap. 4.) A disciplee must not be so busy doing the "Lord's work" that he or she has no time for family responsibilities. I believe that one of the primary callings of a youth worker is to reconcile young people to their families. So in Youth for Christ, we encourage our workers to make friends with the families of our youth, even with those who persecute the disciplees for becoming Christians.

If a discipleship group with insecure leadership belongs to a church or an organization, it is easy for group members to do things so independently of the larger body that the group detracts from the body. To avoid such an unhealthy situation the leaders of the larger body must ensure that they have a warm and open relationship with all the small group leaders working within that larger body. Sometimes the leaders of the larger body are insecure and suspicious of the small group, which may yearn for revival within the larger body. The leaders of the small group must humbly labor to nurture friendly ties with the leaders of the large group and seek to submit to their authority. Laboring to build relationships in this kind of unfriendly environment may seem like a waste of time. But our commitment to the body of Christ requires that we pay the price of investing time for its good.

Unhealthy Emotional Ties with the Opposite Sex

Discipling or mentoring relationships involving an insecure leader become a huge problem when the disciplee is of the opposite sex. Emotionally laden relationships with a person of the opposite sex can soon turn sexual. Sometimes there may be no serious physical contact, but the two have crossed a line. The result is an "emotional affair."[8] Sadly, emotional affairs sometimes descend to full-blown sexual affairs.

The problem is compounded if either the discipler or the disciplee has an unsatisfactory homelife. A husband works very hard at his job and then in the voluntary ministry at church. His wife is unhappy about his involvements. When he comes home, she complains about him not giving sufficient time for the home. And her complaint may be

---

8. See Debbie Cherry, "Emotional Affairs," *Focus on the Family*, accessed August 12, 2017, http://www.focusonthefamily.com/marriage/divorce-and-infidelity/affairs-and-adultery/emotional-affairs.

justified, but he feels rejected. What a contrast that is to the admiration he gets from the young girl in the committee of the youth ministry of which he is advisor. Why, she has even started calling him Daddy! That's how much she values him. He feels affirmed and takes too much satisfaction from the relationship. So he begins to long for more time with her. An emotional affair has begun.

It is preferable that discipling takes place within one's sex; that is, men discipling men and women discipling women. But sometimes one may need to disciple, or more often mentor (less intense), someone from the opposite sex. It is better to do such discipling/mentoring in groups rather than individually. Even then, one must be careful not to cross boundaries. Cultural differences may determine what is acceptable and what is not in these situations. But we must be constantly aware of the pitfalls. It is normal for a man to feel like the father of a woman he is doing ministry with (or vice versa), but he must be careful in the way he allows the relationship to develop.

I often request that my wife do things with a woman on my behalf, like giving very personal advice. I also show my wife all the personal correspondence I have with women. If I send greetings for a birthday, I send it from both my wife and me, often asking her to send it. Where a man and a woman meet is important. It should not be in a room hidden from outside view. I generally keep the door open when I meet a woman. Glass doors are another solution. The key is not to keep any activity too private. All told, I believe it is best to disciple people of one's own sex. But that should never be an excuse for failing to do everything necessary for the welfare of those of the opposite sex whom we lead.

I need to add that there is enrichment that comes to a group when people of both sexes work together. Men and women can contribute in different ways to a team, and healthy teams having men and women can be encouraged, with a display of mutual respect and admiration toward each member. Respect for each other helps us not to cross boundaries that could end up hurting each other.

Toward a Solution to Insecurity

All of us suffer from numerous insecurities. Only when we get to heaven will we be fully secure in our identity in Christ. But while we are on earth, we need to take time for the security-building activities that God provides for us. Most important is our time with God. In the last chapter, I cited Psalm 34:5:

> Those who look to him are radiant,
>   and their faces shall never be ashamed.

Exposing ourselves to the love and almightiness of God buttresses our security.

Second, we need to nurture the most important human relationships in our lives: our relationships with our families. I am not saying that the person who lacks a happy family life cannot disciple others. But that person needs to be aware of the dangers and be conscientious in feeding on those things that help him or her develop security in God. Whether you have a happy family life or not, your family should be given priority so that you leave no stone unturned in giving them a chance to be healthy.

Third, we need to have friends and peers in whose presence we can relax and be affirmed. The affirmation of friends is very important for our emotional health and security. Just to be able to relax in the company of people we can trust helps reduce the pain of ministry. Sharing our problems and disappointments with sympathetic friends helps combat the tendency for us to be bitter and angry people. For many years, I have been advocating that pastors and Christian leaders have good friends. I have even written a book on the topic.[9] It distresses me how so many leaders say that they can't take the risk of nurturing close friendships because they fear it will result in hurt and betrayal.

Early in his Christian walk John Wesley went to see someone he described as "a serious man" who told him: "Sir, you wish to serve God and go to heaven? Remember you cannot serve him alone. You must therefore find companions or make them; the Bible knows nothing of solitary religion."[10] This is what I would urge all Christian leaders to do today. *Find* companions, or if you can't find them, *make* them. Friends help us avoid many of the dangers associated with discipling ministry.

---

9. Ajith Fernando, *Reclaiming Friendship: Relating to Each Other in a Frenzied World* (Scottsdale, PA: Herald, 1993).

10. Quoted in Augustine Birrell, "An Appreciation of John Wesley's Journal," in *The Heart of John Wesley's Journal* (Peabody, MA: Hendrickson, 2008), 11.

Can We Care for Both the Many and the Few?

One more objection needs to be discussed before we move on to the discipling process. I have often heard people say about a discipler that he cares for a few in the group and neglects the others. If that objection was raised against the greatest discipler of all, Jesus Christ, it is not recorded in the Gospels. Jesus spent time with a few, but most of his prominent acts of kindness were with others. As a human, he could not give everyone the level of care he showed to the disciples. (Thank God that in his exalted state he is able to do that.) We too are limited in our ability, and it would be impossible for us to provide specialized care for all.

It is significant that, in addition to the many times Paul used the parent metaphor with reference to his disciplees, he also used it with reference to whole congregations (1 Cor. 4:14–15; Gal. 4:19; 1 Thess. 2:7, 11–12). Leaders have parenting responsibility for the whole flock under their care. They teach them from the Word. They visit their flock and care for them pastorally. Speaking to the Ephesian elders, Paul said that he communicated God's truth to the church comprehensively: "I did not shrink from declaring to you anything that was profitable" (Acts 20:20a); that is "the whole counsel of God" (Acts 20:27). He taught them "in public and from house to house" (Acts 20:20). Then he warned them of the dangers they faced (Acts 20:28–31). Leaders who disciple today also have a wider ministry. They serve as parents to a wider group than to just their disciplees.

However, note that Paul told the Ephesian elders, "Pay careful attention . . . to all the flock, in which the Holy Spirit has made you overseers" (Acts 20:28). He had trained these elders to care for the flock. Acts 20 records a special meeting he had with them. Later he sent two detailed letters to Timothy, whom he had put in charge of the church in Ephesus. Timothy was someone Paul had comprehensively discipled, as his comment about him to the Corinthians bears out: "That is why I sent you Timothy, my beloved and faithful child in the Lord, to remind you of my ways in Christ, as I teach them everywhere in every church" (1 Cor. 4:17). Timothy knew how Paul acted and what he taught. So Paul had a ministry with the whole congregation in Ephesus. But he also concentrated on discipling a few to leadership, especially Timothy.

Leaders cannot intimately care for everyone in a group as large as a congregation. But they must ensure that everyone is cared for. And the best way to do that is by training people to share in the load of caring. As a lay leader in my church, I lead a small group of six men whom I am trying to disciple. One of them is a leader in the church; the others are not. After the Sunday service, I find myself almost automatically going toward the members of my small group to talk to them. They are my friends, and I like being with them. But I consciously have to make it a point not to do that and instead to speak to others, especially visitors. I have told the group members also to avoid talking to each other after church and, especially, to speak to people who need someone to speak to them. A discipler should not announce by his public behavior that his disciplees are his favorites.

This concern for both the many and the few was the pattern of Jesus's life too. He ministered to large crowds, but he also took time to be alone with his disciples. It would be instructive to see the sequence of some of his ministry actions before and after his death. He spent an extended time with his disciples during what we call the Last Supper. He washed their feet, had an extended teaching session with them, and discussed with individuals and the whole group some of the things that would happen. He climaxed the evening by praying for them (John 13–17). Then he went with them to the garden of Gethsemane, where he prayed alone, but with his disciples near him. In the heat of his subsequent trial, he took time to look at Peter, resulting in Peter's remorse over denying him (Luke 22:61). On his way to be crucified, he looked at the mourning and lamenting women and spoke words of comfort to them (Luke 23:27–31).

Jesus's first recorded words from the cross were words of forgiveness to those who put him to death (Luke 23:34). He was dying for the sins of the whole world. That is the widest extent of ministry possible. But amidst the agony of bearing the sin of the world, he led an individual robber to salvation (Luke 23:40–43)! Then, seeing his mother, he handed over the care of her to John (John 19:26–27). He also saw to his own needs and responsibilities as he said, "I thirst" (John 19:28), committed his spirit to God (Luke 23:46), and finally proclaimed that he had completed the work he came to do (John

19:30). After his resurrection, he spent most of his time with his inner circle of men and women. But he also "appeared to more than five hundred brothers at one time" (1 Cor. 15:6). He had a ministry with the many and with the few.

Jesus gave special time to his disciples. But he also did both kinds of personal ministry: pastoral care, when he ministered to the women who were lamenting, and personal witness, when he led a robber to the Lord. Then he cared for his family and himself. This is a fully rounded ministry.

Some Examples from History

The leaders who had the greatest impact on the history of the church were people who integrated interpersonal work with their preaching and theologizing. Paul was arguably the most influential theologian of the church. But he was also an evangelist, a pastor, and a discipler. British historical theologian Tony Lane calls Augustine, "The greatest Christian theologian since the apostle Paul."[11] Augustine was forced, reluctantly, to leave his monastery in Tagaste and the life devoted to theologizing, teaching, and contemplation that he treasured. He moved to Hippo as a pastor and stayed there for almost forty years. Yet his resulting interaction with people and the issues of their lives surely contributed to the massive impact of his writing. In a book about Augustine's work as a mentor,[12] Edward L. Smither examines several examples of mentoring in the third and fourth centuries, detailing Augustine's approach in particular. It exemplifies the principle of multiplication we saw in the first chapter (see above, "Multiplication," p. 28).[13]

Martin Luther's priceless book *Table Talk* is made up of his sayings taken down by his mentees mainly around the dinner table at his house and in other places. He was a discipler in the fullest sense of the term. Many who read the brilliant writings of John Calvin do not realize that he was a busy pastor, and that his writings grew out of that busy life of ministering to people. Calvin once said, "It is not

---

11. Tony Lane, *The Lion Concise Book of Christian Thought* (Herts, UK: Lion, 1984), 40.
12. Edward L. Smither, *Augustine as Mentor: A Model for Preparing Spiritual Leaders* (Nashville: B&H Academic, 2008).
13. Smither, *Augustine as Mentor*, 145–48.

enough that a pastor in the pulpit should teach all people together, if he does not add particular [personal] instruction as necessity requires or occasion offers."[14] He also wrote, "Since my arrival here I can only remember having been granted two hours in which no one had come and disturbed me."[15]

John Wesley mastered the art of caring for new believers as he developed his class meetings (like our house groups) and bands (like our accountability groups). Charles Spurgeon had his pastors' college, "which focused on developing students at their own pace." Dayton Hartman comments, "Such an approach required intimate and specific knowledge of each student's intellectual capabilities based on personal interaction."[16] These students were discipled. The brilliant English scholar of biblical and early Christian literature Joseph Barber Lightfoot was for a time professor at Cambridge University and then bishop of Durham. When in Durham "he used to have living with him at Auckland Castle six or eight young graduates who were training for the ministry."[17]

————

Discipling is not something for famous preachers only. Many famous preachers would point to unknown lay persons—Sunday school teachers, brothers and sisters in Christ, youth advisors—who discipled them. This is something all Christians can do. But it is necessary for the leaders to model it so that the others in the church can follow their example.

---

14. Quoted in Scott M. Manetsch, *Calvin's Company of Pastors: Pastoral Care and the Emerging Reformed Church, 1536–1609*, Oxford Studies in Historical Theology (New York: Oxford University Press, 2013), 281. This book shows that Calvin and his fellow ministers had a vibrant personal ministry in addition to their theologically oriented preaching, teaching, and writing.

15. J. van Zyl, "John Calvin the Pastor," in *The Way Ahead* (Haywards Heath, UK: Carey, 1975), 73; quoted in Derek J. Tidball, *Skillful Shepherds: An Introduction to Pastoral Theology* (Grand Rapids, MI: Zondervan, 1986), 190.

16. See Dayton Hartman, *Church History for Modern Ministry: Why Our Past Matters for Everything We Do* (Bellingham WA: Lexham, 2016), 27.

17. R. E. Nixon, "Lightfoot, J(oseph) B(arber) (1828–1889)," in *The New International Dictionary of the Christian Church*, 2nd ed., ed. J. D. Douglas (Grand Rapids, MI: Zondervan, 1978).

3

Born into a Family, Incorporated into a Body

So those who received his word were baptized, and there were added that day about three thousand souls. And they devoted themselves to the apostles' teaching and the fellowship, to the breaking of bread and the prayers. . . . And all who believed were together and had all things in common.

Acts 2:41–42, 44

God is relational in his essential being. That is expressed in the community of the Trinity. As humans are made in the image of God, they should also be essentially communal beings. When humans fell into sin, God's ideal of community was spoiled, and the first child of the first humans even murdered his brother. Ever since then there has been strife among people in the world. But God has created a new humanity—the church—which is called to carry through his ideal of community. Christianity cannot be seen apart from this new humanity. When people are converted to Christ they are born again into a family. They become children of God, who is the Father of this family (John 1:12). Using another metaphor, the Bible says that the convert becomes part of the body of Christ. Family and body, of course are the two favorite metaphors for the community of believers in the Epistles. Now Christians cannot think of life without reference to this family and this body.

Discipling and Body Life

The first thing said about the first church in Acts is that after the first believers were baptized, they devoted themselves to activities as a group (Acts 2:41–42). Many see discipling primarily as one individual taking care of another individual. But that is not the biblical model. In the Bible Christians grow in community. This was true not only of the first church in Acts but also of the first disciples of Jesus. We will see in chapter 8 that most of the teaching and training Jesus did with them was when they were together as a group. Jesus took them with him on his travels. They quarreled and debated together. They were sent for ministry in groups, and they reported back to him as a group. When the lost sheep, the lost coin, and the lost son were found, their return in each case was celebrated with the community.

We are involved in church not primarily because it helps us to be good Christians but because Christianity is essentially a corporate life. You cannot have Christianity without corporate life, because you cannot have an individual part of a body, like a finger or a toe, without its connection to the body. Community living is an aspect of who we are. Take worship, for example—that key segment of the Christian life. Worship is most often described in the Bible as something corporate.

When many of us were young, we used to sing songs about battling alone to live the Christian life: it was just Jesus and I. But the emphasis was wrong. Some people think of the Christian life as a lonely pilgrimage with Christ as our companion. Jesus is a wonderful friend, and a helper greater than anyone else we could think of. But he intends us to live for him and battle for Christlikeness in community.

One of the great riches of the Reformation and of the evangelical movement that has carried on its message has been its emphasis on personal salvation. It liberated the church from the idea that salvation is through the church and its sacraments. The Roman Catholic Church emphasized the idea of a ritualistic corporate salvation. While correctly affirming the glorious message of individual salvation through faith, we evangelicals may have gone beyond that to view salvation as something individualistic. Critics of Christianity in Sri Lanka blame the Protestant Reformation for ruining the solidarity that characterizes our cultures. They say the Reformation caused the West to become individualistic by making salvation a personal thing. And, they say, that individualism has infected our non-Western cultures too.[1]

I believe it is unfair to blame the Reformers, like Luther and Calvin, for the individualism of Western culture. Western culture did move in an individualistic direction during the time after the Reformation, but that was a move away from the kind of religion advocated by the Reformers. They themselves were very committed to community life. In chapter 2 I described how Luther kept young workers in his home (see p. 56).[2] Calvin has even been criticized for insisting too much on solidarity in doctrine in the church he led.

Western culture took a good thing—individual initiative and responsibility—that thrived among Protestants after the Reformation and divorced it from its biblical context—community life—and let it develop into individualism, thus losing corporate accountability. Sadly, that cultural shift also affected the expressions of Christianity in the West. Many church communities have diluted the biblical idea of the solidarity of the community and its importance in the life of a Christian. When Western "Protestant" nations like England, the Netherlands, and Germany ruled many nations in the non-Western world, the individualism of those Western cultures influenced these other nations too.

The adjective *individual*, from which the word *individualistic* comes, had its origin in the early fifteenth century. It can be traced back to the Latin *individuus*, meaning "one and indivisible, inseparable," and it was used "with reference to the Trinity."[3] How far the concept has changed from its origins![4] One of the great challenges of

---

1. I am grateful to my friend Suren Raghavan for alerting me to this.

2. Luther's sermon "Two Kinds of Righteousness" presents a rounded understanding of how he viewed the Christian life and highlights the importance of community; accessed in February 2017, http://www.mcm.edu/~eppleyd/luther.html. I am grateful to Canadian Luther scholar Dennis Ngien for directing me to this sermon.

3. From the *Online Etymological Dictionary* © Douglas Harper 2001–2017; accessed October 3, 2017, http://etymonline.com/index.php?term=individual&allowed_in_frame=0.

4. I am grateful to S. Steve Kang of Trinity Evangelical Divinity School for alerting me to this piece on the history of the term *individual*.

disciplers today is to inculcate the sense among their disciplees that they belong inseparably to the body of Christ. I have given a lot of space to the issue of individualism, which I see as a major obstacle to living the complete Christian life. Christians must return to a biblical understanding of what it means to be in solidarity with other Christians belonging to the family of God.

One of Paul's descriptions of Christian maturity is the metaphor of a body that has grown so that each part works in harmony with the whole. He says, "We are to grow up in every way into him who is the head, into Christ, from whom the whole body, joined and held together by every joint with which it is equipped, when each part is working properly, makes the body grow so that it builds itself up in love" (Eph. 4:15–16). In a mature church the parts that make up the body get closer to Christ, which means that they get closer to each other, working in harmony and mutually building up the church. It is well known that much of the material about Christian growth in the epistles of Paul is addressed to readers in the plural—though that is not immediately noticeable in the English translations. We grow together.

The model of Jesus's circle of twelve disciples shows us that small discipleship groups could be an ideal unit for growth within the Christian community. Ideally the disciplers will have individual appointments with the disciplees. Discipling is individual; but it is not individualistic. The context of the discipling relationship is the group. That's where the bulk of the teaching and training takes place. Through the discipler's efforts this small group involvement will lead to commitment to the wider body of Christ, until that commitment becomes the context in which the small group operates.

As noted earlier, when people think of church today, they often think like consumers. What does it have to offer? "If the program is good, I'll go there." "If today's preacher is not good, I won't go to my church this Sunday." But that's the way you choose how to spend a free evening devoted to entertainment. And the reason for going to church is not entertainment. We go to church because that is an essential part of our life, like eating or drinking. The church is part of who we are, part of what it means to be a Christian. Disciplees need a sense of this from the moment they become Christians. Right from the start of their lives in Christ, they must realize that their new normal is life in a body. The disciplers' attitudes go a long way in fostering this conviction in new Christians.

You might think that I am advocating a dreary commitment to duty that is a burden rather than a joy. What if you don't like the church or the group you are with? I do not deny that there are times a person may need to leave a local church. But the consumer mentality results in people changing churches far too often. When I was doing my postgraduate studies in theology, I joined the young-adult group in the church I became part of. The leader of the group was a first-year theology student, and I felt his teaching was not up to the mark. But this was my group, and I faithfully went every week. I cannot adequately describe the blessing that group was to me. Over forty years later, I still have contact with some of its members, even though I live halfway around the world. We miss the blessings of community when we try to avoid the inconveniences that come with community. Sadly, inconvenience has become a very bad thing today. If Jesus and Paul thought that way, the history of the world would be very different!

Our community life could become one of the great attractions of Christianity in this present age. People in the postmodern West (and also the rapidly changing East) are looking for authentic community. In fact, a reaction against consumerism and its adverse affect on society is largely what produced postmodernism. As people seek authentic community today, will they see in the church an expression of the consumerism they revolted against? Will they see that our main attraction is a brilliant program that people come to devour as consumers? If so, they will likely look elsewhere for authentic community.

If people come to a church for the wrong reason, driven by a love for entertainment, that could keep them from the challenge of becoming a community where members live and work in solidarity with each other. The programs that draw consumers to the church may, ironically, make the church unattractive to a lost world. The lost are seeking the kind of flock that only the Good Shepherd can supply. If they look at us, will they find what they were looking for?

Extending Solidarity to the Wider Body

Smaller Groups within the Body of Christ

Today, the discipleship group is often where people are introduced to the idea of being part of the body of Christ. It is very important that this ethos, and its benefits, be experienced as soon as they become Christians, because it is so countercultural in our highly individualistic world. The love people experience in the discipleship group should open them to the blessings and joy of loving community life. After the "body of Christ" idea becomes ingrained in the minds of new believers through their fellowship in the discipleship group, they will gradually learn to extend it to the wider community, which is the local church. Then they will extend it even wider to the universal church. This will happen only if the discipler has this "body of Christ" attitude, which helps new believers to expand their thinking beyond the small discipleship group to understand their connectedness to the whole body of Christ.

Youth for Christ works primarily with those who have no contact with the church. One of the biggest challenges we face is discipling people so that they become fully incorporated in local congregations. If we're not careful, our staff and volunteers could neglect this as they concentrate on the growth of new converts and the Youth for Christ program. So we need to remind them constantly that unless our youth are firmly incorporated in churches, we have failed in our mission.

The programs in most churches will usually not match the appeal of the program in a specialist youth organization. So one of the key concepts we try to communicate is that we go to church not for the program but because we are Christians, because that is our family. We recommend to our staff that their primary volunteer involvement be in a local church and try to ensure that all those who lead discipleship groups are involved in local congregations. Their example of involvement in the church will encourage the youth also to get involved.

This same challenge confronts youth ministries within the local church. One of the most important callings of youth workers is to reconcile the youth with adults, especially parents. Many young people may end up leaving the church in later years because they were not integrated into the life of the wider church when they were young.

Insecure youth workers risk being so gratified by the response of the youth to their brilliant programs that they don't make an effort to integrate the youth into the whole church. They might even criticize other groups within the body of Christ to show how much better their small group or youth group is. This will encourage young people to think that life revolves around them, but the leader must discourage such thinking. Godly leaders teach their disciplees to heed Paul's advice: "Be humble, thinking of others as better than yourselves" (Phil. 2:3 NLT). A key in all this is working hard to get youth to experience the unity of the body of Christ so that this connectedness is what keeps them in church, not the brilliant program of the youth group.

Usually any small group that is somewhat separate from the whole church is treated with suspicion by the larger group. It may be a discipleship group committed to radical discipleship. It may be a youth group filled with enthusiasm but sometimes lacking wisdom. They make one mistake, and many pounce on them with accusations. The members of the group react with hostility to what they see as unfair criticism by the dead traditionalists in the larger group. And the rift begins to grow.

Mediators are needed in such situations. They could be senior members who are respected by the church and understand that those in the small group or the youth group have the genuine desire to please God. A mediator can act as an advocate for the small group, as Barnabas did for the young, fiery Saul of Tarsus. Because the larger group trusts him, their criticisms may be less harsh or completely silenced. And the small group can avoid being disillusioned with the larger group and losing hope of working well in this environment. I think the best person to act as such a mediator is the pastor himself. It is so important for the senior-most leader of the church to have a good relationship at least with the leaders of all the different groups connected to the church.

Baptism as Incorporation into the Body

Another act that helps give people a sense of belonging to the community is baptism. Sometimes today people are baptized by a small group or at some exotic place like the River Jordan. I do not want to be harsh about this practice, but it misses one of the key blessings associated with baptism. Baptism is a sign of a person's incorporation into the body of Christ. It is best done within the community to which the person will belong. This increases the sense of body identity that is an important aspect of Christian identity.

When Problems Arise in a Small Group

The sense of connectedness to the whole body of Christ is particularly helpful when a local situation turns sour. The leader of a discipleship group can fall into serious sin and give up all his ministry. A group can experience conflict that destroys unity. Or a church can go through a painful split. Christians who derive their primary identity from the group can feel completely let down and helpless at such times. Their belief in Christian groups now shattered, they may not reach out to another group of believers. But if they have been well trained to see themselves as part of the whole body of Christ, they will likely seek to nurture fellowship somewhere, despite the initial hurt.

So it is extremely important to train people in such a way that they don't get an unhealthy sense of security from the small group to which they belong. Secure leaders will delight to introduce their disciples to the beautiful bride of Christ with its variety and richness.

Life in a Covenant Community

We can learn many lessons from the community life of Old Testament Israel. These were a people bound together by a covenant. Their community life, of course, harmonizes well with the community values in honor-and-shame-oriented cultures, which are collectivist rather than individualistic in approach (see chap. 11). The identity of people in Old Testament communities was wrapped up in their being part of the covenant community, and that had a marked influence on their attitudes and behavior. This is a value needed in Christian communities, whether in individualistic or collectivist societies.

Body-Life Events That Bind the Group Together

Many of the significant events in the corporate life of the people of Israel had to do with the values that bound the people into this covenant community. The covenant was frequently renewed, and the people participated together in the renewal. There was frequent public repetition of the law—for example, of the Ten Commandments. The Methodist church has a covenant service, usually on the first Sunday of the year, where people together renew their commitment to live faithful lives. That is the most meaningful service of the year to me.

Can we have meaningful rituals of renewing our commitment, periodic reminders that we are a community bound together with an ethos that identifies us? Church anniversaries are often boring encumbrances for members, especially young members who are often made to perform in front of an audience. Can anniversaries be transformed into joyous times of celebration and of renewal of commitment to the historic values of the church or movement?

The Israelites made pilgrimages to Jerusalem every year, which again buttressed their identity as a nation. They sang important and joyful songs, like the Songs of Ascents found in Psalms 120–34, as they climbed up Mount Zion. Several festivals were holy and joyful times. But always these events reminded the people of the ethos that bound them together. A key to the growth of any believer is his or her identity as a member of the people of God, bound together by an exciting history and ethos.[5]

Muslims, who have an amazing sense of community solidarity, have used the idea of festivals and pilgrimages to good effect. I have been at the airport in Colombo, Sri Lanka, when charter flights have arrived carrying Muslim pilgrims back from the Hajj pilgrimage to Mecca. The pilgrims are welcomed with loud shouts of elation and tears. In some ways the solidarity of Muslims is closer to biblical form than the radical individualism of many Christians. In fact, among the things Muslims fear as Western culture permeates the world is that their children will give up this solidarity and become culturally individualistic. This is sad, because Christians have an amazing theology that says we all are members of the one body of Christ. This should bind us together in a closer-knit solidarity than Muslim communities express.

---

5. For a fuller discussion about pilgrimage festivals, see Ajith Fernando, *Deuteronomy: Loving Obedience to a Loving God* (Wheaton, IL: Crossway, 2012), chap. 39.

Leaders must do all they can to foster an atmosphere where people see themselves as bound both to Christ and to his body. A very important aspect of this is the way we make our festivals meaningful and affirming of Christian values. The Old Testament gives many detailed instructions on how festivals should be conducted. Feasting and joy played a major role in them. Deuteronomy 16 describes three festivals. It has high regard for the feasts involving special food. Twice it asks the people to "rejoice" (16:11, 14). Once it says that, as a result of the feast, the people would be "altogether joyful" (16:15). Exuberant praise also was an important part of Old Testament community life, especially during festivals. The psalmist urges the people:

> Clap your hands, all peoples!
> Shout to God with loud songs of joy! (Ps. 47:1)

The psalm goes on to proclaim their God as the Lord of all nations, who is committed to the welfare of the nation of Israel.[6]

Moments of eating together, of joy, and of fear play an important part in a person's formation. The fearful proclamation of curses was balanced by great and emotional expressions of joy. Let's look at some of those fearful proclamations.

Curses for Breaking the Covenant

The covenant had a lot to do with morality, and when the covenant was made or renewed, the people pledged to be holy. They agreed that those who kept the covenant would be blessed and that those who didn't would be cursed. "Cursed" is a strong term. In many Christian churches we are accustomed to hearing the worship leader say, "And all the people said . . . ," and the people respond, "Amen." That sequence, or something like it, appears a few times in the Bible. Three times it is associated with giving praise and blessing to God (1 Chron. 16:36; Neh. 8:6; Ps. 106:48). Once it comes in connection with God's blessings to his people (Jer. 11:5). Once it represents Jeremiah's cynical response to a false prophet's prophecy of blessing to the people

---

6. Some scholars think this psalm is connected to a festival, while others dispute that.

(Jer. 28:6). Three other times it relates to pronounced curses on the disobedient (Num. 5:22; Deut. 27:15–26; Neh. 5:13).

In Deuteronomy 27:15–26 the Levites are to pronounce curses twelve times for various kinds of sin. And the people respond with "Amen" after each curse. The list of sins is instructive. Five of the curses are for sins relating to what I am calling personal morality: dishonoring parents (27:16), lying with one's father's wife (27:20), lying with an animal (27:21), lying with one's sister (27:22), and lying with one's mother-in-law (27:23). One curse is for a religious sin: idolatry (27:15). Four are for communal, interpersonal sins: moving a neighbor's landmark (27:17), misleading a blind man (27:18), striking down a neighbor (27:24), and taking a bribe to shed innocent blood (27:25). Once the sin pertains to justice: perverting justice toward the sojourner, the fatherless, and the widow (27:19). The last one is a general statement: a curse for those who do not do the law (27:26). The whole gamut of behavior is included here. And the people, as part of their identity, commit themselves to it together, and to the tragic consequences of disobeying it. You can see how community solidarity can be an incentive to holy living.

Sin Is Individual and Corporate

There is another factor of a covenant community that helps in placing holiness as a high value in the group. This is the biblical teaching that sin is both a personal and a corporate matter. Sometimes the sin of one person is regarded as the sin of the whole community. When Achan sinned, the whole community suffered (Joshua 7). When the tribes east of Jordan tried to act independently of the rest of the people, they were challenged over their independence. In the message sent to them were these words: "Did not Achan the son of Zerah break faith in the matter of the devoted things, and wrath fell upon *all the congregation* of Israel? And he did not perish alone for his iniquity" (Josh. 22:20). All the people shared in the responsibility for Achan's sin. Two righteous leaders, Daniel and Nehemiah, confessed the sins of the people as if they were their own (Neh. 1:6–7; Dan. 9:5–6). Twice, in his prayer, Daniel said, "To us . . . belongs open shame" (Dan. 9:8; see also 9:7).

Usually, especially in honor-and-shame-oriented cultures, when one implicates the community of sin, the messenger is considered to have done something very wrong. Nationally the person is dubbed an unpatriotic traitor. That was what prophets like Jeremiah had to face. His condemnation of the people came out of deep pain. He said, regarding the judgment he proclaimed,

> Oh that my head were waters,
>   and my eyes a fountain of tears,
> that I might weep day and night
>   for the slain of the daughter of my people! (Jer. 9:1)

Christians must highlight wrongdoing to help free the church from its effects. But we must do so with a sense of humble, penitent identification with the wrong that is done.

Today when a Christian does something shameful, some believers gloat over his fall from grace, especially if he is a prominent leader in another church. Though they may put on a sad face, they enjoy gossiping about the scandal and feed the attitude that they are not like that. But biblical Christians hurt when anyone in the body has done wrong, as if they themselves have done the wrong. As one who is often tempted not to identify with the downfallen, I am rebuked by the thought that I have not yet developed a biblical attitude of solidarity with the whole people of God.

Security through Solidarity

This idea of corporate solidarity must be inculcated early in the discipling process. Disciplees must see themselves not as lone individuals trying valiantly to live the Christian life but as connected first to their discipleship group, then to the church to which they belong, and then to the whole body of Christ. This does a lot to bring security and stability to their lives, especially as they face temptations to compromise their faith under pressure from outside the faith community. Realizing that they are a part of a complex and intricate body that spans the whole of human history gives them immense strength.

I often use stories from church history when I am teaching and preaching to new believers. This method is used throughout the Old

Testament, as the people are reminded of the ways God has blessed them or punished them. I want new believers to get the sense that they are part of the grand movement of the Lord of the universe that encompasses the whole of human history. The work that God is doing will surely and steadily go from victory to victory until its final triumph, when "the kingdom of the world has become the kingdom of our Lord and of his Christ, and he shall reign forever and ever" (Rev. 11:15).

The past eighty years or so have witnessed a turning of Muslims to Christ as never before in history. Yet analysts say that during this period there has also been a fairly large-scale return to Islam among the same converts. This testifies to the power of the community in which they have grown up and had their identity and security. These days this power often takes the form of militant force. And for some, this force is too great to resist. We have seen this in our ministry with converts to Christ from Buddhism and Hinduism, as well as the few Muslims we have worked with. If it were firmly planted in their minds that they belong to a community that will finally triumph, the push to return to their former faith would lose some of its appeal. True security comes from belonging to the body of Christ, which is the eternal kingdom of the Lord of lords.

———

The second half of this chapter, on life in a covenant community, may seem out of place in a book on discipling. But I have a strong reason for including it here. I believe one of the hardest aspects of Christianity for believers to accept today is the importance of the body of Christ. This is particularly so in the Western world. The individualism that we see has many features that are contrary to Christian belief and practice. We need to rethink how we can bring community solidarity back into the church. I have given biblical and practical means for doing so in this chapter. May Christians young and old recapture the glorious doctrine of the body of Christ.

4

Belonging to Two Families

Honor your father and your mother, that your days may be long in the land that the LORD your God is giving you.
Exodus 20:12

I have come to set a man against his father, and a daughter against her mother, and a daughter-in-law against her mother-in-law. And a person's enemies will be those of his own household.
Matthew 10:35–36

The first four of the Ten Commandments have to do with our relationship with God (Ex. 20:3–11), and the next six, our relationship with other humans (Ex. 20:12–17). The first of the commands relating to other people is the command to honor parents (Ex. 20:12), which Paul described as "the first commandment with a promise" (Eph. 6:2). Jesus spoke of situations in which following him may result in going against one's parents (Matt. 10:34–36). Yet he did not abrogate the fifth commandment. He not only upheld it; he also strongly rebuked people who made religious excuses for not caring for parents (Matt. 15:3–9).

This paradox regarding parents illustrates that Christians are citizens of two worlds—on earth and in heaven—and are members of two families—their earthly family and the family of God. Paul addressed the Philippians as "saints *in Christ Jesus* who are *in Philippi*" (Phil. 1:1, literal trans.). We live concurrently in both worlds and have responsibilities in both. Romans 12 presents principles governing how we relate to other members of the family of God, and Romans 13 gives principles governing how we relate to authorities in the earthly society to which we belong. Here I want to deal with the ramifications of belonging to and being committed to two families and two communities.

Honoring Family Commitments

Family Obligations

When the ministry of Youth for Christ first began to see young people coming to Christ from non-Christian backgrounds, we were naturally very concerned about the persecution they would face, especially from their family members. We warned them and tried to ensure that the rejection they experienced at home would be offset by warm acceptance in the Christian community. Soon, however, we realized that our emphasis may have been unwise. Often disciplers don't realize how important it is to disciplees to maintain good relationships with their physical families. Disciplees themselves may not think of this in the initial glow of excitement about their new-found faith. While the importance of family ties may not be initially evident in a time of persecution, it will surface sooner or later.

We needed to do all we could to encourage our disciplees to have healthy relationships with their families. While we continued to warn the youth about the possibility of persecution, we began to emphasize how they could be good members of their families. In fact, the moment a young person got involved with us, our staff and volunteers tried to meet the parents and develop a friendly relationship with them. We soon found that, even though the parents were unhappy that their children had become followers of Christ, some came to our staff and volunteers for advice and help when they had problems with their children.

We encouraged the youth in their studies, which was something most parents liked.[1] We encouraged our leaders to talk to the youth

---

1. Some parents from very poor families wanted their children to leave school and start earning income for the family, and were not very happy with our emphasis on education.

about relationships at home and to try to help the children resolve conflicts with family members. The practice of visiting family members of those we disciple presented an important aspect of discipling, especially if the disciplees were having problematic relationships at home. In our evangelistic camps we always had a session on parents. And it was invariably the most popular talk at the camp. Clearly, we were dealing with a felt need: the need to relate well to moms and dads. Not only did the talks share about how Christianity is committed to family life; they also gave hints on how to be good children and how to be healed of the wounds inflicted by unreasonable parents.

One of the biggest reasons why people reject the gospel, even after being convinced it is true and desirable, is the hurt it would cause their families. Jesus had this problem in mind when he said: "I have come to set a man against his father, and a daughter against her mother, and a daughter-in-law against her mother-in-law. And a person's enemies will be those of his own household" (Matt. 10:35–36). If Jesus warned of this possibility, we too must warn people of it. Yet that is not the whole story. I said at the start of this chapter that the Bible teaches that Christians should be committed to the earthly structures to which they belong. The family is the most important of those structures. Therefore, most of the principles of family life given in the Bible apply also to families that are not Christian. The only exception to obeying parents would be when doing so involves clearly going against God's Word (such as worshiping idols).

It is wise to share these ideas about family responsibilities when people are considering whether to accept the gospel, as well as after they have become Christians. They should know that honoring parents is one of the vitally important Ten Commandments of Christianity (Ex. 20:12). The Bible has harsh words for those who treat their parents in a bad way. Severe punishment is meted out to "a stubborn and rebellious son who will not obey the voice of his father or the voice of his mother, and, though they discipline him, will not listen to them" (Deut. 21:18–21). Harsh words are also directed at one "who does violence to his father and chases away his mother" (Prov. 19:26), one who "curses his father or his mother" (Prov. 20:20), and one who "robs his father or his mother" (Prov. 28:24). We need to show how

Jesus harshly criticized as "hypocrites" those who made religious excuses for avoiding family responsibilities (Matt. 15:3–9). Another such statement comes from Paul: "But if anyone does not provide for his relatives, and especially for members of his household, he has denied the faith and is worse than an unbeliever" (1 Tim. 5:8).

Christians can demonstrate their commitment to the family by showing genuine concern for their parents. Sometimes parents will notice the marked change in the behavior of children who have become Christians. This has resulted in some parents themselves becoming open to the gospel. The mother of a young convert to Christ in our ministry died after a time of illness. At the funeral some of the convert's siblings accused him, saying that their mother died of a broken heart because he had changed his religion. A sister had been working abroad and had come back to Sri Lanka for the funeral. She told everybody that this was not true, but that their mother had told her often of how this son was a great comfort to her because he was so loving and kind to her.

Some parents of children in our ministry were very unhappy about the change in the values of their children after they became Christians. They didn't like their child marrying someone from a socioeconomic position they considered inferior to theirs. They were unhappy about the God-honoring vocational choices of their children, which resulted in lower earnings than they could have had. Yet these children especially cared for their aging parents. Though they were not economically wealthy, they took more responsibility for their parents' care than their more affluent siblings. This resulted in the parents ultimately being very proud of and grateful for their children.

I know of Christians who kept their obligations to their non-Christian parents even though the parents completely cut off ties with them. The children sent monthly financial gifts to the parents' bank accounts even though the parents refused to have any contact with them. The parents took the money, but they did not acknowledge having received it. After many years (ten years in one case) these parents reestablished ties with their children. Christians should fulfill all the responsibilities they have toward their parents, whether doing so is appreciated or not. It is a source of healing to believing sons and daughters to know that, even though their parents did not acknowledge it, these believers did what they needed to do. And sometimes it results in the healing of the relationship.

Informing Family Members about Conversion

Disciplers need to discuss with disciplees when and how they should inform family members of their conversion to Christ. Jesus told the man who was delivered from demons in the country of the Gerasenes, "Go home to your friends and tell them how much the Lord has done for you, and how he has had mercy on you" (Mark 5:19). Such news will be a huge blow to a non-Christian family. In this chapter I say a lot about how to allay the fears of family members relating to conversion. Despite those precautions, if a member leaves the family religion, the family will generally react very negatively.

Sometimes informing them immediately may not be wise. Usually some members of the family are more tolerant of conversion than others. It may be best to tell the less-volatile members first. Sometimes prospective disciples informed their family members around the time they are deciding to become Christians. Then, with their parents' permission, they follow Christ. Even if family members don't give permission, they feel included if they are informed prior to the decision. But this strategy does not work when there is strong opposition to conversion.

Sometimes family members are prepared for the news by seeing changes in those who have become Christians. They see new converts reading the Bible or praying. In some homes, however, doing that may be prohibited, and the new believers must find another place to do it. I know of children who prayed with the room lights off after the other members had gone to bed, or read the Bible behind a closed door. Others went to a church building that was open during the day to have their own time with God. When family members know that the convert is going regularly to a Christian meeting, they become prepared for news of conversion. They can also be prepared by seeing how much more conscientious their family member is in doing household chores, and how much more loving and kind.

Sadly, some parents remain very angry even after a child, who may have been ruining his life with drunkenness and immorality, has given up all that to become a Christian. The betrayal and shame they feel by the child's leaving the family religion is greater than what they felt from his ruinous lifestyle. One of the worst scenarios is when young converts spend so much time with their Christian activities that they curtail time at home and in their studies. That should be discouraged.

I do not think we can make universally binding rules about when and how one should inform the family. But the topic must be brought up soon after conversion. Generally family members will know sooner or later about what has happened. In extreme cases, as in some strong Muslim families, a person may secretly remain a believer while finding a way to fellowship with other Christians. In the next chapter I will briefly discuss the so-called "insider movements," in which followers of Christ remain within the non-Christian religious community to which they belonged (e.g., Muslim or Hindu) without discarding their identity as members of that community.

Obeying Parents

Most Christians face challenges when it comes to obeying their parents. Those whose parents are not Christians generally have the more serious problems. The values held by parents, whether Christian or non-Christian, often differ from those of their Christian children. Some parents ask their children to do things that clearly contradict Christian principles. Disciplers need to discuss often with disciplees how they should respond to the requests and commands of their parents.

Greg Jao's chapter "Honor and Obey" in *Following Jesus without Dishonoring Your Parents*[2] is so good that I will unashamedly borrow from it here. Jao describes how, when there is a clash of principles with parents' wishes and commands, counselors from westernized cultures tend to focus on passages like Matthew 10:35–37:

> For I have come to set a man against his father, and a daughter against her mother, and a daughter-in-law against her mother-in-law. And a person's enemies will be those of his own household.

---

2. In Jeanette Yep et al., *Following Jesus without Dishonoring Your Parents* (Downers Grove, IL: InterVarsity Press, 1998), 43–56. Chen Pei Fen, a convert to Christianity, has written a heart-warming testimony of her struggle to relate to her family in the booklet *Keeping the Faith: The Cost of Following Christ* (Grand Rapids, MI: Our Daily Bread Ministries, 2017).

Whoever loves father or mother more than me is not worthy of me, and whoever loves son or daughter more than me is not worthy of me.

Counselors from Asian cultures, on the other hand, use texts like Ephesians 6:1–2: "Children, obey your parents in the Lord, for this is right. 'Honor your father and mother' (this is the first commandment with a promise)."[3] The community solidarity of non-Western cultures places a very high value on obedience to parents even after children grow to adulthood.

These two texts bring us to the heart of the problem. Paul's statement from Ephesians is very strong. His words are even stronger in Colossians 3:20: "Children, obey your parents *in everything*, for this pleases the Lord." That looks like an absolute command without exceptions. In Ephesians Paul gives a reason from natural law (or general revelation),[4] saying about obeying parents, "for this is right." That means common sense would tell us that this is the best thing to do. Then Paul appeals to God's special revelation in the Ten Commandments: "this is the first commandment with a promise." All this presents a compelling case for obeying parents fully.

But Jao also discusses exceptions.[5] On the one hand, he observes that Paul's "commands provide no clear exception to the reach of a parent's authority," and he cautions us about being quick to talk of exceptions. On the other hand, he notes Dick Lucas's exposition of Colossians in which Lucas says that Paul characteristically gives "a basic rule for the churches without qualification," and leaves "it to experience and spiritual wisdom to discover the inevitable limitations of such rules."[6] As an example of a rule without qualification, Lucas cites Paul's statement "Let every person be subject to the governing authorities. For there is no authority except from God, and those that exist have been instituted by God" (Rom. 13:1). As an example of inevitable limitations to such rules, Lucas cites the response of Peter and John following the prohibition of evangelism by the authorities:

---

3. Jao, "Honor and Obey," 46. I have used the ESV here. Jao uses the NRSV.
4. Jao, "Honor and Obey," 46.
5. Jao, "Honor and Obey," 47.
6. Dick Lucas, *Fullness and Freedom: The Message of Colossians and Philemon* (Downers Grove, IL: InterVarsity Press, 1980), 162.

"Whether it is right in the sight of God to listen to you rather than to God, you must judge, for we cannot but speak of what we have seen and heard" (Acts 4:19–20).

Jao points to Paul's "directive [to fathers] to avoiding exasperating (Ephesians 6:4), embittering or discouraging (Colossians 3:21) their children."[7] This brings another factor into the discussion: parents can be at fault too. We know that parental error can go to an extreme; parents might be physically or emotionally or sexually abusive. In such cases children need to be protected from their parents. There are also times when parents can try to force their children into doing things that the children know to directly contradict God's laws. Parents sometimes try to force their children to marry unbelievers. They sometimes try to get their children to join them in doing what is clearly wrong, like fraud or taking violent revenge against an enemy. In such cases, the children need to respectfully refuse.

Taking the various strands of Scripture together, I have concluded that we should advise children to generally obey their parents. Sometimes the children will not like what is commanded. It may be unreasonable, and obedience could be inconvenient and tiring. But out of respect for parents, they should obey. Sometimes, however, doing so would mean clear disobedience to God's Word or calling. Then the child must disobey. Darrell Bock describes the strong emphasis on obeying parents in the Old Testament and Jewish literature, and says: "The only exception, according to Deut. 33:9, is when one is enticed to be unfaithful to God by someone in the family."[8] The passage from Deuteronomy refers to the incident of the golden calf when the Levites, by placing God above family ties, did not spare their own families (Ex. 32:27–29).

Even though family responsibilities are important, they cannot be fulfilled at the expense of obedience to Christ. When a would-be follower of Christ came to him and said, "Lord, let me first go and bury my father," Jesus showed that he would not tolerate any hindrance, even a family responsibility, to following him. He said, "Follow me,

---

7. Jao, "Honor and Obey," 48.
8. Darrell Bock, *Jesus according to Scripture* (Grand Rapids, MI: Baker; Leicester, UK: Inter-Varsity Press, 2002), 176.

and leave the dead to bury their own dead" (Matt. 8:21–22). This applies to choices that set the direction of one's life, like marriage and the call to ministry.

Sometimes children postpone acting on matters of conscience in the hope that their parents will change their minds, as in decisions about marriage or the call to the ministry. Disciplers may need to intervene. I have visited parents who opposed what seemed like a very good decision by a child to marry another believer. I have gone and given my fullest commendation of the person in question. Sometimes this outside opinion has helped the parents to approve the marriage.

Disciplers, then, must be seriously involved with disciplees on difficult issues with parents. It can be a lonely, emotionally wrenching, and heartbreaking time for young believers. They need all the support they can get. This is particularly true when vocational and marriage decisions must be made. Parents are particularly insistent in these areas as the decisions have long-term implications for all parties. And sometimes Christian children end up deciding to go against their parents' wishes. This is a time not for rash decisions but for prayerful, patient, and humble grappling to know God's will.

While children may have to go against the wishes of their parents, they must always be respectful. The call to honor parents stands, whatever the circumstances. This is not easy. Even very patient people tend to become impatient during conflicts with immediate family members. Here they must exercise utmost restraint and, with God's help, refuse to let their behavior toward their parents be disrespectful. Disciplers must always be alert to such issues relating to the earthly families of their disciplees.

Family Traditions

The relationship that converts to Christ have with their families also gets complex when it comes to family traditions. Like vacations, family parties, and other such gatherings, traditions such as weddings and funerals are among the most important and memorable events in the life of a family. Often religion is incorporated into these events. It is important that we prepare new Christians to face these challenges. We should talk with them about what they can and cannot do. Often new converts have very negative attitudes toward the past way of life that held them in bondage. Therefore, they may not want to have anything to do with anything remotely connected to their former religion. But some traditions can be upheld without compromising biblical principles. We must discuss these things with disciplees and let them arrive at ways to handle specific situations. The following list augments what I have dealt with in some detail in my book *Sharing the Truth in Love*.[9]

- Family vacations might involve going to a famous temple or a shrine of the parents' faith. Believing children could be advised to go with the family on the vacation but not participate in the worship. We could discuss where the believer should stay when the other family members are worshiping. The biblical example of Naaman may not lead to a binding principle, but it could give some hints on how to act in difficult situations, especially as Elisha did not contradict Naaman's decision. In 2 Kings 5:17, Naaman says, "[I] will not offer burnt offering or sacrifice to any god but the LORD." However, because of Naaman's position, the king will lean on him when the king is in the house of his god Rimmon. Naaman asks God's pardon for this (2 Kings 5:18). Elisha does not prohibit this role but says, "Go in peace" (2 Kings 5:19). Naaman's job took him into a temple worship ritual even though he did not believe in the god Rimmon. He said he would worship Yahweh only. Here is an example of submission to authority that requires being in a place not otherwise appropriate for a Christian, yet without actively participating in prohibited rituals.
- Special meals, like those held in honor of a dead family member, are very important to a family. But they are loaded with religiously objectionable practices. Food may be given to monks to accrue merit to the dead person, thereby improving his future lives. Clearly Christians cannot subscribe to this. They should avoid worshiping and serving the monks. But they can help with cooking and washing dishes and cleaning the house.

---

9. Ajith Fernando, *Sharing the Truth in Love: How to Relate to People of Other Faiths* (Grand Rapids, MI: Discovery House, 2001).

Food may be offered to idols before being served to the people. That makes partaking of it problematic.

- Chinese converts to Christianity will buy gifts for their family members and celebrate the New Year with them. They will help in the special family responsibilities in connection with the New Year. But they will not participate in the religious ritual associated with the New Year activities that contradict their Christian beliefs.

- Respect for parents and ancestors is an important part of the Chinese culture. But Christians cannot participate in rituals involving ancestor worship, which is part of Chinese popular religion. This has resulted in the charge that Christians do not honor their ancestors. Chua Wee Hian lists ways in which they can counter this charge with positive acts that are compatible with Christianity. "They will always respect and honor their relatives while they are alive," he says. After they have lost loved ones, "many are prepared to be the first in cleaning family tombs, and some Christians have even set up halls of remembrance for their forebears. Non-Christian relatives and friends may be invited to special memorial services where Christ is proclaimed as victor over the grave."[10]

- In some cultures, New Year rituals are aimed at persuading the gods and other forces to send blessings. Similar rituals are performed at the start of a farming or building project. Often small items made out of precious substances, like gold, are blessed and included in the foundation of a building during a foundation-laying ceremony. Instead of participating in these, Christians can pray—in public if possible, or otherwise in private—for God's blessings upon the farming, building, or other venture the family is involved in. Even if the family does not permit them to pray publicly, the believers can assure their family members that they have prayed privately. These activities have biblical precedents.

- I know several converts from Buddhism and Hinduism who do not eat beef because that is something their non-Christian

---

10. Chua Wee Hian, "The Worship of Ancestors," in *Eerdmans' Handbook to the World Religions*, ed. Pat Alexander (Grand Rapids, MI: Eerdmans, 1994), 247.

family members find repulsive. Similarly, converts from Islam can refrain from eating pork. At Youth for Christ evangelistic camps, we usually have a few special meals, and often pork is a delicacy at such meals. But we will not serve pork if we have Muslim youths at the camp, for that would be unnecessarily insensitive to Muslim scruples. If some of them come to Christ, we may need to tell them that out of sensitivity to the misgivings of their family members, they would be wise to abstain from eating pork for the rest of their lives.[11]

Marriage and Weddings

The most important events in the lives of families in many cultures are weddings and funerals. One of the biggest fears of non-Christian families is that a member who converts to Christianity will dishonor the family in matters relating to conducting weddings and funerals. It is very important for disciplers to be sensitive to family and community customs at such times so that unnecessary conflict and hurt are avoided.

- A major concern of parents is who their son or daughter will marry. In many cultures marriages are arranged, and, sadly, we have seen that some new Christian youth succumb to pressure from their parents and marry the non-Christians their parents have chosen. Disciplers need to be proactive in talking about the choice of a marriage partner, and even be willing to do what parents would do in helping the believer to find a spouse. We have seen that sometimes, when the children keep refusing the people their parents have chosen for them, the parents look to us to do what they could not do—find a partner for their child. This is a responsibility that many pastors and Christian leaders all over the world take very seriously.
- A young convert from Buddhism may delay his marriage by a few years so that he can save money to provide for his sister's marriage. This is a family obligation in many cultures where there are close family ties, and where it is normal for family members to help each other at considerable cost to themselves.

---

11. The last four bullet points are from Fernando, *Sharing the Truth in Love*, 194–96.

This may seem very strange to Christian leaders in individual-istic cultures. They would be wise to consult Christians from within the unfamiliar culture before advising new believers faced with the prospect of delaying their marriage.

- Parents usually play a very important role in Buddhist and Hindu wedding rituals, but not in Christian marriage services. This is so even in Asia, where the church has been influenced by individualistic Western culture. I know of Christians in Sri Lanka who include as part of the wedding service a beautiful chant extolling the sacrificial contribution of the parents in the lives of their children. While this is sung, the children give gifts to their parents.[12]

- Couples generally do not like parents interfering much in their wedding preparations. Often discussions on that topic devolve into unpleasant arguments. It would be good for Christian couples to show utmost patience here and accede to the parents' wishes whenever possible without breaking Christian principles. This accords with the biblical culture of commu-nity solidarity, which may sound strange in our individualistic world. It can be an opportunity for Christian children to show love and respect for their non-Christians parents.

Funerals and Acts of Remembrance

In many cultures funerals are major community events involving elaborate rituals. This is another area where new believers need to talk with other Christians to clarify what they may and may not do. Sometimes they unnecessarily avoid practices that are essentially more cultural than religious and therefore would not contradict Christian principles.

We have had situations in our church where believers who were the only Christians in their families died. The non-Christian relatives insisted on having funerals according to Buddhist rites, and we had no legal right to insist on a Christian funeral. Instead, we had a Chris-tian service before the final burial rites were performed. Now we tell believers to leave in writing that they would like their funerals to be

---

12. The last two bullet points are from Fernando, *Sharing the Truth in Love*, 194.

done according to Christian rites. A few months ago, after a believer died, we went to her home and found in the main hall a framed letter stating her wish for her funeral arrangements to be done by our church.

In many cultures, Christian funerals seem to be plain affairs in comparison with the funerals of non-Christians. Non-Christians sometimes think we do not honor our dead in the way we conduct our funerals. In Sri Lanka, Protestant funerals, unlike Roman Catholic funerals, are generally sanitized events, as influenced by the Dutch and British cultures of those who introduced Protestant Christianity to the country. Catholicism was introduced by the Portuguese, whose southern European culture was very different from the western European culture. In the Bible there is a tradition of funerals being public, community events, which seems to be out of sync with Protestant Christian practices today.

Public weeping and days of mourning were part of the biblical culture. The Bible says that when Moses died, "the people of Israel wept for Moses in the plains of Moab thirty days. Then the days of weeping and mourning for Moses were ended" (Deut. 34:7–8). There were thirty days of mourning for Aaron too (Num. 20:29), and seven days for Jacob and Saul (Gen. 50:10; 1 Sam. 31:13). Jeremiah asked skillful people to come to wail over the dead (Jer. 9:17–20). Was he speaking of a class of professional mourners? A dynamic equivalent for this today would be a choir, for music is very much a part of Christianity. When Lazarus died, many Jews had come to console Mary and Martha, and they were there even four days after the burial (John 11:19). This is very much in keeping with Asian culture, where people spend extended time in the home of the bereaved as an expression of their solidarity with them. We know that Jesus wept at the funeral of Lazarus (John 11:35).

This kind of mourning did not stop after the resurrection of Christ. Public expressions of lamentation continued into the life of the New Testament church. After the first martyrdom, "Devout men buried Stephen and made great lamentation over him" (Acts 8:2). After Dorcas died, "All the widows stood beside [Peter] weeping and showing tunics and other garments that Dorcas made while she was with them" (Acts

9:39). Here we have public expressions of sorrow and praise. These practices are quite normal in many non-Christian cultures. Giving expression to our sorrow is also a way of healing that we may miss with our heavily sanitized funerals.

These funeral practices were community events with opportunity for the people to participate. We too can make our funerals events where the whole community is involved. Neighbors can contribute meals or drinks for visitors and help decorate the road and house for the funeral. This helps the people to realize that the Christians are true members of the community.[13]

It is common in many cultures to have special events of remembrance a week, a month, three months, or a year after the death of a loved one. Usually these include religious rituals and a good meal. Christians could combine a good meal and a Christian service of thanksgiving in honor of the dead person. Having a meal in honor of or in thanksgiving for a person does not break Christian principles. And, culturally, it is a good thing. It can be done with distinctly Christian elements, like prayer and singing. This could actually be a prime opportunity for us to present the hope-filled way in which Christians look at death.

The greatest thing about a Christian funeral is that it proclaims the hope of the resurrection. Christians funerals should show how we can experience the joy of the Lord while having a broken heart, which is one of the most amazing ironies of biblical Christianity. Sadly, with the overemphasis on blessings and the neglect of suffering and the cross, this glorious paradox is missing in a lot of Christian preaching and living. We must demonstrate the reality of this biblical paradox.[14] We publicly express deep sorrow over the loss of beloved and treasured believers, and we praise God for the admirable things in their lives. But we also rejoice in our unassailable hope of the resurrection. By embracing this paradox, Christian funerals throughout history have had a great witness to the glory of the gospel.

---

13. For some helpful tips relating to funerals in Buddhist villages in Asia, see Jane Barlow, "Suffering, Death, and Funerals in Thailand," in *Suffering: Christian Reflections on Buddhist Dukkha*, ed. Paul H. De Neui (Pasadena, CA: William Carey Library, 2011), 104–21.

14. On this, see Ajith Fernando, *The Call to Joy and Pain: Embracing Suffering in Your Ministry* (Wheaton, IL: Crossway, 2007).

Baptism: When? Where?

Every new disciple needs to be baptized at some stage along the path to maturity. Peter includes the call to be baptized along with the evangelistic call to repent, showing how basic that is to Christianity: "Repent and be baptized every one of you in the name of Jesus Christ for the forgiveness of your sins, and you will receive the gift of the Holy Spirit" (Acts 2:38). Baptism is the definitive act of witnessing to conversion and of incorporation into the body of Christ. In the first church it seems to have been done immediately after repentance and conversion to Christ, as is implied in Peter's words quoted above and with the baptism of the Ethiopian and Cornelius's household (Acts 8:26–38; 10:46–48). "Later," as Philip Schaff says, "when great caution became necessary in receiving proselytes, the period of catechetical instruction and probation was considerably lengthened."[15] Having not grown up with a Christian worldview, new converts needed to be taught biblical basics, like who God is and what sin is.

Today, too, it may be good to wait till we are sure a person has truly given up his or her past life and embraced Christianity fully. In pluralistic cultures, where people follow many religious traditions at the same time, persons may "pray the sinner's prayer" or "pray to receive Christ," without any intention of giving up their former religion or way of life. For this reason, many churches choose to wait a little after conversion before baptizing them. Some have the new believers follow a short course of study on the basics of Christianity before they are baptized. Of course, we cannot make a rule out of this, given the scriptural precedent of baptizing soon after conversion.

The time and place of the baptism needs to be carefully chosen. It can be done in a public place—like a river near where the church meets. However, there may be hostile reactions in a small town where people view this as their "territory." Because of this, some churches baptize people at a river or the sea some distance away from their meeting place. Some churches have baptismal facilities within their own premises, which averts the problem. Some churches without such facilities perform their baptisms in a nearby church that has them.

---

15. Philip Schaff, *History of the Christian Church*, vol. 1, *Apostolic Christianity* (New York: Charles Scribner's Sons, 1910; repr., Grand Rapids, MI: Eerdmans, 1994), 468.

If family members take a relatively tolerant stance toward the conversion, it would be wise to invite them to the baptism. Doing so includes family members in this important event in the life of the new Christian. In our church the family members are accorded a place of high honor during baptisms. They are introduced to the whole congregation, and everyone is encouraged to welcome them as honored guests. The ideal situation in Acts was the baptism of whole households at the same time (16:15, 33). What a refreshing contrast this is to the customary family hostility accompanying baptism.

As Youth for Christ is a parachurch organization, we do not perform baptisms. Our mission is to feed local churches with new believers, and the churches decide when to baptize them. But we encourage youth not to be baptized until they have reached the legal age of adulthood, which is eighteen years in Sri Lanka. In some countries there is prosecution for baptizing underage youth.

Donald McGavran, the father of the modern church growth movement, popularized the idea of "conversion with a minimum social dislocation."[16] That is always our aim with new converts. So long as we do not compromise biblical principles, we should try to ensure that all unnecessary hostilities with one's original community are avoided.

Making Peace with One's Relationship with Family Members

Whether the parents of a believer are Christians or not, it is very important for children to make peace with their relationship with family members. By that awkward phrase I mean that they need to do everything they can to have a harmonious relationship with them and then be at peace with the outcome.

Some parents may not approve of their child becoming a Christian; some may not even want to have any relationship with him or her. But Christian children should do all they can to establish and maintain a loving relationship. I have encountered a few Christians who have had a bad relationship with their parents and siblings and done nothing to improve it. This often results in warped growth in the Christian's life. Children who do not seek a meaningful relationship with their parents

---

16. See Donald McGavran, *Understanding Church Growth*, 3rd ed., ed. C. Peter Wagner (Grand Rapids, MI: Eerdmans, 1990).

often end up having unhealthy relationships with their own children. I have seen this especially with father-son relationships.

It is sometimes painful to talk about difficult issues with family members. Because of that, Christians may not want to risk opening wounds. But disciplers need to keep urging their disciplees to pursue peace with their family members. One simply cannot ignore or set aside relationships that are so much a part of one's essential identity. Those who do not try to heal these relationships could live with a nagging sense of guilt. Even if their efforts fail, those who try to resolve issues live with the knowledge that they tried. And there is a healing that comes from knowing that they have done everything possible. After all, Paul also left room for failure in relationships when he said, "If possible, so far as it depends on you, live peaceably with all" (Rom. 12:18).

Involvements in the Wider Community

The year 2004 saw widespread attacks on Christians and churches in Sri Lanka, especially in places where people had converted to Christianity from other faiths. As Christian leaders discussed this issue, one concern that surfaced was that people disengaged unnecessarily from their communities when they became Christians. A pastor told me that when people became Christians, they immediately became bad neighbors. Earlier they participated in community activities. But once they became involved in Christian activities, going to church most days of the week, they didn't have time for the community. Numerous false stories were being spread about Christians, and because the people had minimal contact with Christians, they had no way to correct the false impressions made by those reports.

This social disengagement contradicts the call for Christians to be "the salt of the earth" and "the light of the world" (Matt. 5:13–14). Indeed, we reject a lot of what we see in the world; but we cannot bear effective witness for Christ unless we are engaged with the communities in which we live. The call of Christ is for Christians (1) to be holy by living according to the Word of God, (2) to not conform to the sin of the world, and (3) to go into the world as God's agents. Jesus presents these three emphases in his great High Priestly Prayer:

"I do not ask that you take them out of the world, but that you keep them from the evil one. They are not of the world, just as I am not of the world. Sanctify them in the truth; your word is truth. As you sent me into the world, so I have sent them into the world" (John 17:15–18; see also 1 Cor. 5:9–13).

We must encourage our disciplees to develop healthy relationships with people in the communities around them. This requires wisdom and sensitivity, because it was with the non-Christian society that many sinned before their conversion to Christ. Immediately after the man from the country of the Gerasenes was delivered, Jesus told him, "Go home to your friends and tell them how much the Lord has done for you, and how he has had mercy on you" (Mark 5:19). Perhaps we would not say the same thing to a former alcoholic about his friends in the bar. In Jesus's High Priestly Prayer, before saying that he was sending the disciples into the world, he said that he "guarded them" (John 17:12). But because he was going back to the Father, it was time for them to go into the world without the protection of his physical presence with them. We too must be sensitive to the need to protect our people, but sooner or later they must go into the wider community. Of course, the Holy Spirit, whom Jesus called "the Helper," provides his immediate and constant presence, making it advantageous for Jesus's disciples that he has left them (John 16:7).

The members of the communities in which Christians live should recognize Christians as friendly, faithful, and helpful neighbors who are committed to the welfare of the community. Once they sense that Christians are part of them, then Christianity can take on a legitimacy in their community. It is usually after this recognition that persecution subsides. But in many unreached areas it may take the church's people as much as five to ten years of patient involvement before they are considered legitimate entities in a community. Christians must not lose heart in this effort to identify with their surroundings.

Here are some distinct ways in which Christians can be involved in their communities:

- We need to get involved in community-run projects as fellow citizens. To overtly share the gospel at such times may be a breach of etiquette. There will be other opportunities for that. After the Indian Ocean tsunami of 2004, our ministry was involved in helping schools get back to normalcy. We worked very hard, but we had to abide by the condition placed upon us that we would not preach the gospel. However, it was very clear to the people that what we did came out of our Christian commitments, and doors of receptivity to the gospel were opened.

- When Christians do social projects, they can inform local authorities and seek their advice and help in deciding who might benefit from the projects and how they should be done.
- We can make our facilities (like a church hall) available for social events in the community, so long as those events do not contradict Christian principles. In Youth for Christ centers, we provide sports facilities for youth and playgrounds with things like swings, seesaws, and mat slides for children in the neighborhood. These have been appreciated by the communities, though it is a challenge to ensure that the facilities are used responsibly.
- We should encourage our children to be involved in voluntary service projects and sports and musical events during festivals such as a New Year festival. Adults and youth might take part in organizing and implementing these projects and events.
- We might seek membership in community groups, such as funeral aid committees, school committees, and committees for the protection of peace and security in the neighborhood.
- Christians who are celebrities in sports and other forms of entertainment, or leaders in politics and government, can exemplify how Christians are genuine members in their communities.
- Sometimes Christianity is associated with things that have no necessary connection with the gospel. For example, some people today associate Christianity with the United States. They may presume Christians believe that the United States is superior to all other countries. That could result in resentment by those considered inferior, and become an obstacle to gospel witness. We should distinguish Christianity from the agenda of any country or culture. Christianity stands above all nations

and cultures, and challenges every nation to conform to the values of the Creator of the world.

- Christians can actively participate in public dialogues on television, radio, or the Internet on issues facing the nation, such as sexuality and marriage, corruption, drug addiction, and racism. They can use such forums while agreeing to the limitations imposed for involvement (such as no overt evangelism). The Christian gospel has clear and very relevant answers to the problems facing the world today. Christians can present these answers with great effectiveness without using Christian jargon.

———

Does all this have a place in a book on discipling? Yes! Because disciplees must live out their Christianity in their families and in the wider world to which they belong. Disciplers must help them to meaningfully engage with the contexts in which they live.

5

Facing Suffering, Persecution, and Loss of Honor

Indeed, all who desire to live a godly life
in Christ Jesus will be persecuted.

2 Timothy 3:12

In the last chapter we wrestled with the need to be wise and sensitive in matters relating to earthly structures and, where possible, to affirm them. Yet our sensitivity, wisdom, and affirmation will not insulate us from opposition and persecution. Jesus warned: "'A servant is not greater than his master.' If they persecuted me, they will also persecute you" (John 15:20). Paul said, "Indeed, all who desire to live a godly life in Christ Jesus will be persecuted" (2 Tim. 3:12). If this is so, disciplers need to bring up this topic with disciplees. Persecution is not limited to those who come from non-Christian backgrounds. The statements of Jesus and Paul quoted here have no such restriction.

Though this discussion on suffering is only indirectly related to parenting, I include it within the section on spiritual parenthood because of its connection with the previous chapter. Besides, it is a responsibility of parents to prepare their children for suffering.

It Goes with Being Like Jesus

Any Christian who wants to faithfully follow Christ will face persecution and suffering. Some years ago, I did a study on the passages in which Jesus is presented as our example in the New Testament. I found twenty-eight of them; and in eighteen he is presented as an example of suffering.[1] To be Christlike is to suffer like he suffered. We often quote the discipleship text "Let us run with endurance the race that is set before us, looking to Jesus, the founder and perfecter of our faith" (Heb. 12:1b–2a), and we stop there. But that verses goes on to say, "who for the joy that was set before him endured the cross, despising the shame, and is seated at the right hand of the throne of God. Consider him who endured from sinners such hostility against himself, so that you may not grow weary or fainthearted" (Heb. 12:2b–3). We focus on running the race and looking at Jesus. And what do we see when we look at Jesus? He "endured the cross, despising the shame. . . . [He] endured from sinners such hostility against himself."

This truth must be drilled into the minds of new believers: if we are Christians, we will suffer because of it. Then, when suffering comes, we won't be disillusioned by it or tempted to give up Christianity. When a scribe came to Jesus and told him, "Teacher, I will follow you wherever you go," Jesus responded, "Foxes have holes, and birds of the air have nests, but the Son of Man has nowhere to lay his head" (Matt. 8:19–20). That is not what we would expect to hear in an evangelistic situation! But he did not hold back in warning of the difficult times ahead. When we do not talk of the cost of discipleship to a prospective follower of Christ, we may be justly accused of being untruthful in our presentation of the gospel We are like an insurance salesman who skips the fine print when trying to sell a policy.

Often the gospel presentation that people hear is all about blessings that come from Christ. The blessings are real. But in the Christian understanding of life, suffering is also a blessing, as we will see below. The Bible does not look at suffering as an end itself. When suffering is mentioned, usually the blessings that come from suffering are in view. The passage from Hebrews quoted above says that

---

1. See Ajith Fernando, "Jesus: The Message and Model of Mission," in *Global Missiology for the 21st Century*, ed. William D. Taylor (Grand Rapids, MI: Baker Academic, 2000), 209–10.

Jesus endured the cross and shame "for the joy that was set before him" and that he "is seated at the right hand of the throne of God" (Heb. 12:2b).

Another study I did some years ago revealed that suffering and joy are mentioned together eighteen times in the New Testament.[2] Many Christians think that when they suffer, they will lose their joy. But in Christianity suffering can coexist with joy and is sometimes a means to joy (see Rom. 5:3; Col. 1:24; James 1:2). In fact, Paul describes suffering as a privilege gifted to us when he says, "For it has been granted to you that for the sake of Christ you should not only believe in him but also suffer for his sake" (Phil. 1:29). The word translated "granted" (*charizōmai*) as used here means "give freely as a favor, give graciously."[3] In Paul's understanding, suffering is a gracious gift from God.

Strength for Suffering

Since the Bible mentions so often that suffering is an essential feature of the Christian life, we would be wise to let our disciplees know early in their walk with Christ about the biblical attitude toward suffering. While the Bible does not dwell on the *why* of suffering, it often talks about *how* we should face suffering. It teaches many things that give us strength to face suffering.

Fellowship of Suffering with Jesus (Phil. 3:10)

One of the most beautiful consequences of suffering is that it brings us closer to Christ. Paul says that he wishes to know "the fellowship of His sufferings, being conformed to His death" (Phil. 3:10 NASB). There is a depth of oneness with Christ that we can experience only through suffering. Our key teaching to and desire for our people is related to their knowing Christ and growing deeper in that knowledge. Suffering is a means through which this happens. We teach this to them as part of their basic training.

---

2. See Ajith Fernando, *The Call to Joy and Pain: Embracing Suffering in Your Ministry* (Wheaton, IL: Crossway, 2007), 19.

3. Frederick William Danker and Walter Bauer, *A Greek-English Lexicon of the New Testament and Other Early Christian Literature*, 3rd ed. (Chicago: University of Chicago Press, 2000), 1078.

Sometimes people have an amazing experience of intimacy with God during periods of suffering. But not all Christians come out of suffering and persecution sensing that it brought them nearer to Christ. The nearness may not be felt emotionally. Being assaulted or humiliated or insulted really hurts. But if what the Bible says is true, even these experiences will help believers to draw closer to Christ. If they know this, and if they consider closeness to Christ one of the greatest riches in life, that will give them strength to go through the dark periods. So we must arm new believers with this vital truth about Christianity.

Fellowship with Believers (Acts 4:23)

The first time the church faced anything like persecution was when Jewish leaders told Peter and John that they could not preach the gospel anymore (Acts 4:18). Their response teaches us many lessons on how to face persecution (Acts 4:23–31).[4]

The moment they were released "they went to their friends and reported what the chief priests and the elders had said to them" (4:23). The word translated "friends" (*idios*) means "one's own" and is translated by the NASB as "their own companions." Luke may be suggesting that they went to a close group of their friends. This shows us how important it is to get close to believers when they are persecuted or suffering in some way. When disciplees are under attack, disciplers should contact them immediately, possibly by phone, and make arrangements to be with them as soon as possible.

After hearing stories of heroic endurance amidst persecution, we may be tempted by a romantic attitude and a rosy mental picture about it. The reality is that most people struggle deeply when persecuted. The battle with evil is draining. Some even give up on Christianity or on evangelism because of the threat. Even John the Baptist began to have doubts about Jesus as he languished in a prison (Matt. 11:2–3). Some end up bitter over the way they were treated or over other Christians failing to help them in their time of need. Some become proud and consider themselves superior to others because they have suffered.

---

4. For a full exposition of Acts 4:23–31, see Ajith Fernando, *Acts*, NIV Application Commentary (Grand Rapids, MI: Zondervan, 1998), 167–78.

Often people wonder why the powerful God does not intervene to help in terrible situations. Being abused physically and verbally is an assault on the identity and significance of a person and is difficult to bear. All suffer from the pain of being attacked. Christians love all people, and to be hated by some is a painful experience to those who make love their aim. The pain is intensified when the hateful behavior comes from family members whom they deeply love. We know that even Jesus struggled deeply as he faced the prospect of his saving death. Usually the heroic responses to suffering come as a sudden infilling of boldness by the Holy Spirit, as happened to Stephen in Acts 7:55, or after a major inner struggle, as happened often with the psalmists (see, e.g., Psalm 73).

A key to victory in this struggle is the part played by friends. In 2 Corinthians 1 Paul talks about a severe problem he had and how God comforted him (1:3–10). But we must wait till 2 Corinthians 7 to find out how this comfort came. Paul explains his situation like this: "For even when we came into Macedonia, our bodies had no rest, but we were afflicted at every turn—fighting without and fear within" (7:5). Then he says, "But God, who comforts the downcast, comforted us by the coming of Titus" (2 Cor. 7:6). The brave, rugged warrior for the gospel, Paul, was comforted by the coming and ministry of his spiritual child!

The comfort of friends is one of the great antidotes to bitterness. When we share our pain, fears, and disappointments with sympathetic friends and experience their comfort and solidarity, the slide into bitterness is arrested through the experience of loving, healing concern. One of the greatest contributions disciplers make in the lives of disciplees is helping stem the growth of bitterness. Life is tough, and we will often face unkind blows. When the discipler is committed enough to give time sacrificially to the disciplee in need, the disciplee experiences the security and warmth of being loved and affirmed. Few things help combat bitterness as effectively as the experience of such love. Therefore, when we sense that someone we are discipling is going through a rough time, we try to meet the person, however inconvenient that might be. Having to carve out unscheduled time for disciplees in need is one of the most tiring and costly aspects of discipling.

We can help people avoid making rash and foolish decisions when they are under attack. Some hit back and aggravate the situation. Some lose heart and wilt under the strain. Some proclaim something unnecessary that inflames their opponents, or they write a letter they should never have written. Some are ignorant of the legal protections they can have in the situation they face. All these needs should be addressed through the wisdom of another coming to assist a person who is under attack.

God's Sovereignty (Acts 4:24–28)

The next thing Peter, John, and their friends did was to pray, and their prayer was primarily an affirmation that God is sovereign over history. They addressed God as "Sovereign Lord, who made the heaven and the earth and the sea and everything in them" (Acts 4:24). "Sovereign Lord" translates one Greek word (*despotēs*) used typically of a powerful master and used only six times for God in the New Testament.[5] The disciples then described God as the Creator of everything. The implication is that God is the sovereign Lord over these people who have prohibited evangelism; in fact, they have been created by him.

Next, they quoted Psalm 2:1–2, which talks of the powerlessness of the powerful people who tried to oppose God's anointed person in history (Acts 4:25–26). The disciples confessed that all the powers available in Jerusalem were arrayed against Christ (4:27). But these powers ultimately did "whatever your hand and your plan had predestined to take place" (4:28). The greatest tragedy became the greatest triumph in history. Through the death of Christ salvation was won for the world. The disciples' prayer is a ringing affirmation of the sovereignty of God over difficult circumstances. Having lived amidst war and persecution for over three decades, I can testify that nothing has helped us persevere in our work as much as the vision of God's sovereignty.

Such a vision of sovereignty may not come at once. There is a place in biblical religion for lament and groaning amidst hardship (Rom.

---

5. The usual word in the New Testament for "Lord" when referring to Jesus or God is *kyrios*.

8:20–23). Between one-third and half of the songs in the Psalms have been classified as laments. We do not glibly ask people to rejoice in the midst of suffering, even though rejoicing in suffering is something taught in the Bible. Instead we may let them groan, and we ourselves may groan with them, trying to share in their pain. Amazingly, Paul says that the Holy Spirit groans with struggling people (Rom. 8:26). As struggling people seek God, the vision of his sovereignty will break through, and they will be able to look at the situation with hope. The sequence of bitter groaning giving way to joyous praise for God's sovereignty is beautifully illustrated in Psalm 73.

This vision of sovereignty enables the Christian to have peace during the storm and respond to the crisis without breaking Christian principles. Fundamentalism has a bad name today because it is associated with harsh and impolite responses to opposition. It betrays a lack of peace in the hearts of the respondents. Christians don't have to be uncivil in their responses to attacks on them. Because we believe in God, we don't give up on the truths found in God's Word about how to answer attacks. The Bible tells us, "Love your enemies, do good to those who hate you, bless those who curse you, pray for those who abuse you" (Luke 6:27–28). It says, "Bless those who persecute you; bless and do not curse them" (Rom. 12:14). The vision of God's sovereignty gives us the strength to respond this way to our opponents. We are at peace because we know that God is in control, and we respond out of that peace.

A government captor once challenged a person arrested because of the gospel, "What can your God do for you now?" The Christian replied, "He can give me the strength to forgive you!" How different that is from the combative replies of Christians who give voice to fundamentalist insecurity. Harsh answers dishonor God and hinder the progress of the gospel. Because we believe in the sovereignty of God, we believe that we don't need to break biblical principles in our battle for truth. To help young Christians facing attacks, disciplers should demonstrate the peace of believing in God's sovereignty. Their lives should remind disciplees of the truth of the saying "When the outlook is bleak, try the uplook!"[6]

---

6. Cited in Warren W. Wiersbe, *Be Comforted* (Wheaton, IL: Victor, 1996), 29.

I believe God permits disciplers to go through painful situations to help those they disciple. One of the hardest lessons for new Christians to learn is to remain hopeful and at peace when they face serious crises. When we tell them this, their response often is, "You can say that because you haven't gone through troubles like we have."

When my wife was diagnosed with a fairly serious cancer, everyone in our church was shocked. As former Buddhists, they still had vestiges of the attitude that such misfortunes happen to people who have not lived righteous lives. One of the first things my wife said after hearing of the diagnosis was, "Now we can talk to our suffering people, because we too have experienced hardship." We thank God that she is well now. But I believe the way she faced the cancer was an encouragement to many.

God's Commission (Acts 4:29–30)

After affirming the sovereignty of God, the disciples asked for the ability to be faithful to the Great Commission: "And now, Lord, look upon their threats and grant to your servants to continue to speak your word with all boldness, while you stretch out your hand to heal, and signs and wonders are performed through the name of your holy servant Jesus" (Acts 4:29–30). They asked God to help them to be faithful to the evangelistic task given to them and to intervene with miracles that would attest the truthfulness of their message. When the leaders "charged them not to speak or teach at all in the name of Jesus" (Acts 4:18), their immediate response was, "Whether it is right in the sight of God to listen to you rather than to God, you must judge, for we cannot but speak of what we have seen and heard" (Acts 4:19–20). They simply had to share the gospel.

The Great Commission is compelling because it was given by the Lord Christ. Matthew's version of the commission begins, "All authority in heaven and on earth has been given to me" (Matt. 28:18). Only after that does he say, "Go." It is the sovereign Lord of the universe who has commissioned us. You can imagine how this would strengthen God's servants under attack.

It is said that when the great British military and political leader the Duke of Wellington was asked whether Christians should be involved in missions, he replied with a counter question: "What has your commander-in-chief said." The answer was, "He has asked us to go." He is said to have replied, "Then there is no question. Now you have to obey."[7] If God is sovereign, then the thing to fear most is disobedience of God, not the power of those attacking us.

As our people face the prospect of persecution, it is easy for them to lose the evangelistic momentum, saying that the climate is not ripe for evangelism. There are churches in Sri Lanka that adopted that approach as things began to get difficult. Others refused to be deterred from their task despite all the problems. They have seen great fruit for the kingdom. Disciplers always keep before their people the challenge that the Lord of the universe has given them a commission. A discipler's heart must burn with a passion for sharing the good news of Christ. (I will say more about this in the next chapter.)

God's Intervention (Acts 4:31)

After the disciples had prayed, "the place in which they were gathered together was shaken, and they were all filled with the Holy Spirit and continued to speak the word of God with boldness" (Act 4:31). God had intervened, showing his power by causing the place to shake. Sometimes, in the book of Acts, when things grew tough and discouraging, God visited his servants in some supernatural way. They saw Jesus or were spoken to by him (Acts 7:55–56; 18:9; 23:11). Paul was visited by an angel during his dreadful two-week ordeal in a massive storm (27:23–24). In the same way, we can pray that when our disciplees face opposition and pain, they will experience a clear divine intervention on their behalf. That too will brace them to face up to the challenge before them.

God knows how much we can bear. He will never permit us to bear a burden that is too heavy. He will give us sufficient evidence that he is with us, so that we can pursue the path of faithfulness. It could be something we read that day during our time with God. It could be a letter or email message. It could be a sudden provision of funds. It could be the conversion of a person who had long resisted the gospel. Such things remind us that God is with us. That gives us the courage persevere.

---

7. Cited in John T. Seamands, *Harvest of Humanity: The Church's Mission in Changing Times* (Wheaton, IL: Victor, 1988), 24–25.

Present Loss of Honor and the Coming Honor

What I have said above does not address a major issue that arises among converts to Christianity. I will explain in chapter 11 how many who come to Christ today are from backgrounds where there is a strong sense of community solidarity and where acting outside the community's accepted values is considered a serious violation. In these cultures, some of the most important values are honor and shame. Leaving the family religion and embracing Christianity brings a serious loss of honor to the person and his or her family. This is one of the hardest things for a new Christian to bear. The Bible is very much aware of this problem. Let's look at some biblical teachings that we need to teach new believers in this regard.

Discipleship, Suffering, and Future Honor (Mark 8:34–38)

Jesus's basic call to discipleship recorded in the three Synoptic Gospels understood the reality of suffering and shame. Consider Mark's Gospel. First, the call to discipleship was a call to a cross: "If anyone would come after me, let him deny himself and take up his cross and follow me" (8:34). Second, it included losing one's "life for [Christ's] sake and the gospel's" (8:35). And third, it called for people not to be "ashamed of [Christ] and of [his] words in this adulterous and sinful generation" (8:38). All these statements imply persecution, and the third also implies loss of honor.

But included in this same discourse is the promise of the final reward for those who take up the cross. It is described first as saving one's life as opposed to losing it (8:35). Second, it means not "forfeit[ing] his soul" (8:36). Third, the result of discipleship is that the "Son of Man [will not] be ashamed [of the disciple] when he comes in the glory of his Father with the holy angels" (8:38). When Jesus returns, he will come with glory and honor, and we will share in that honor. In John's Gospel, after calling every disciple to die like a grain of wheat and hate his life in this world, Jesus says, "If anyone serves me, *the Father will honor him*" (John 12:26).[8]

---

8. For detailed study of this theme, see Ajith Fernando, "Heaven for Persecuted Saints," in *Heaven*, ed. Christopher W. Morgan and Robert A. Peterson, Theology in Community (Wheaton, IL: Crossway, 2014), chap. 10.

It is very clear from the above that the call of Christ to discipleship is a call to suffering and shame; but it is also a call to real life and honor. Those who reject it are going to be destroyed and shamed. This dual emphasis on shame and honor also appears in the book of Hebrews: "So Jesus also suffered outside the gate in order to sanctify the people through his own blood. Therefore let us go to him outside the camp and bear the reproach he endured. For here we have no lasting city, but we seek the city that is to come" (Heb. 13:12–14). These are basic truths that new believers should be exposed to. Yet dishonor is hard to endure!

Earthly Honor Is Rubbish (Phil. 3:5–8)

Paul, who endured great dishonor for Christ, spoke to this issue as well. He was very conscious of the fact that conversion resulted in a loss of social honor for him. Writing to the Philippians from prison, he describes the honor that he once had as a Jew in this way: ". . . circumcised on the eighth day, of the people of Israel, of the tribe of Benjamin, a Hebrew of Hebrews; as to the law, a Pharisee; as to zeal, a persecutor of the church; as to righteousness under the law, blameless" (Phil. 3:5–6). He mentions things considered high honors among the Jews. And he had to give all of that up when he became a Christian. Rejection by his people, whom he loved, would have been a bitter pill to swallow.

Yet Paul says that he gave it all up because of the surpassing worth of knowing Christ: "But whatever gain I had, I counted as loss for the sake of Christ. Indeed, I count everything as loss because of the surpassing worth of knowing Christ Jesus my Lord. For his sake I have suffered the loss of all things and count them as rubbish, in order that I may gain Christ" (Phil. 3:7–8). "Rubbish" is a strong word! That is the disdain with which he looked at earthly honor he gave up to follow the gospel way. We must warn people of this loss of honor, and we must also introduce people, with even more emphasis, to the new honor they have in Christ.

Adoption, Inheritance, Experience, Hope, and Patience (Rom. 8:16–28)

But it is not easy for people suffering shame to accept that they have an honored position. Fortunately, Paul has more to say about that in

Romans 8. In verses 16 and 17 he says, "The Spirit himself bears witness with our spirit that we are children of God, and if children, then heirs—heirs of God and fellow heirs with Christ, provided we suffer with him in order that we may also be glorified with him." The key to our honor is our *adoption* as children of the King of kings and the Lord of lords. There is real status here. When we struggle with loss of honor on earth, we remind ourselves that we have the high honor of being princes and princesses in the kingdom that will ultimately rule the universe. Paul adds that as children we are heirs, fellow heirs with Christ.

Significantly, Paul gives a condition for receiving these blessings: ". . . provided we suffer with him in order that we may also be glorified with him." When we think of our shame, our rejection as insignificant people, and the feelings of poverty all this brings, we remind ourselves that a great *inheritance* awaits us and that our suffering is a condition for receiving this honor.

But is that enough to give us strength to endure the dishonorable present? Inheritance relates to the future. How about our present pain? Verse 16 shows how we can *experience*, here and now, the reality of our adoption as God's children and heirs: "The Spirit himself bears witness with our spirit that we are children of God." The Christian response to suffering is based not only on a set of beliefs that we are compelled to accept. We experience God and the reality of the truths we believe. The Holy Spirit speaks to our own spirit in different ways reminding us that we are God's children. In our discussion on God's intervention, above, we saw some of these ways that the Holy Spirit witnesses to us. While we face the humiliation of dishonor, the Holy Spirit, by witnessing to our spirit, keeps hammering into our consciences that we are princes and princesses of the eternal kingdom.

When the great Indian evangelist Sadhu Sundar Singh (1889–ca. 1929) became a Christian as a teenager, he was poisoned by his brothers and sent out of his home. After being miraculously healed, he devoted himself to proclaiming the gospel. Once he was preaching near his family home, and he decided to visit his father. It broke his heart of see his father treating him like an outcaste. His father made him sit at a distance so that he would not pollute the family or their vessels. When his father gave him water, he poured it onto Sundar's hands, keeping the jug high above.

This is how Sundar Singh responded: "When I saw this treatment I could not restrain the tears flowing from my eyes that my father, who used to love me so much, now hated me as if I was untouchable." Yet while he was going through the pain, the Holy Spirit gave him an experience that reminded him of who he was. He recalls: "In spite of all this, my heart was filled with inexpressible peace. I thanked him for this treatment also . . . and respectfully I said good-bye, and went away. In the fields, I prayed and thanked God, and then slept under a tree, and in the morning continued my way."[9] The dishonor he experienced from his father was counteracted by the witness of the Spirit, who reminded him of his riches in Christ. Incidentally, Sundar Singh's father became a Christian shortly before his death.[10] (I will say more about the witness of the Spirit in the section "Assurance of Salvation," in chap. 12, p. 237.)

This combination of belief in our adoption and inheritance, with the assurances that come through the witness of the Spirit, helps us to look at life with *hope*. A little later in Romans 8, Paul says that hope is a basic aspect of the gospel: "For in this hope we were saved. Now hope that is seen is not hope" (8:24a). By embracing our identity as God's children and experiencing this reality through the Spirit, we have the strength to look at life with hope. Hope is looking for something wonderful when things are not going well. A little later Paul will say, "And we know that for those who love God all things work together for good, for those who are called according to his purpose" (Rom. 8:28). Again, you can see the element of hope.

This hope gives us the strength to be *patient* amidst hardship. Paul goes on: "For who hopes for what he sees? But if we hope for what we do not see, we wait for it with patience" (Rom. 8:24b–25). Biblical patience is not what comes from a "pie in the sky in the world by and by" kind of religion, as some claim. They see it as acquiescing to inaction while experiencing injustice. Such a religion produces bitter people

---

9. Cited in A. J. Appasamy, *Sundar Singh: A Biography* (Madras: Christian Literature Society, 1966), 27.

10. Appasamy, *Sundar Singh*, 117. This story about Sundar Singh is also related in Fernando, *Call to Joy and Pain*, 61.

in the here and now. But our hope spurs us to action. In the Bible, patience is an active virtue. Leon Morris says this about the Christian understanding of patience: "Paul's word denotes not so much a quiet acceptance as a positive endurance (cf. NASB, 'perseverance'). It is the attitude of the soldier who in the thick of the battle is not dismayed but fights on stoutly whatever the difficulties."[11] The comprehensive hope that we have gives us courage to be actively serving God amidst humiliation and difficulties, looking forward to the good and the glory that will surely come out of the situation. It is essential that new Christians understand that this perseverance-producing hope is a basic aspect of the gospel.

A Religion of Postponed Honor

Christianity, then, is a religion of postponed honor. That was the perspective that drove Jesus. Paul says that we should have the "mind" of him who "emptied himself, by taking the form of a servant, being born in the likeness of men. And being found in human form, he humbled himself by becoming obedient to the point of death, even death on a cross" (Phil. 2:7–8). But this shame opened the door to ultimate honor: "Therefore God has highly exalted him and bestowed on him the name that is above every name, so that at the name of Jesus every knee should bow, in heaven and on earth and under the earth, and every tongue confess that Jesus Christ is Lord, to the glory of God the Father" (Phil. 2:9–11).

The writer to the Hebrews had the same perspective. He urges us to "run with endurance the race that is set before us, looking to Jesus, the founder and perfecter of our faith" (Heb. 12:1–2a). But as we saw above, when we look at him, we see one "who for the joy that was set before him endured the cross, despising the shame, and is seated at the right hand of the throne of God" (12:2b). Jesus despised the cross because of the coming glory. "Despising" conveys the same resolve as Paul's word "rubbish" in Philippians 3:8. We teach our people to despise the shame that comes with faithfulness to God. That is the Christian response to dishonor borne because of the faith.

---

11. Leon Morris, *The Epistle to the Romans*, The Pillar New Testament Commentary (Grand Rapids, MI: Eerdmans; Nottingham, UK: Apollos, 1988), 325.

Before I move on, let me point out that three times the New Testament says, "whoever [or "everyone who"] believes in him will not be put to shame" (Rom. 9:33; 10:11; 1 Pet. 2:6). This must have been an important idea to communicate to believers in those days of persecution and opposition to the gospel. The discipler, then, has an important body of truth to introduce to the disciplee:

- Things are going to be tough.
- Worse than that, we are going to be dishonored.
- But the reality is that we are already honorable people.
- We know Jesus personally.
- And we experience in real life what it means to be children of God.
- Further, an incredibly honorable future awaits us with an inheritance that has been reserved for us.
- So we persevere in hope without giving up.

This is the stuff out of which heroism is born.

Taking Action against Persecutors, Especially within the Family

Biblical thinking about persecution is loaded with paradoxes, not least in how we should respond to those who persecute us. On the one hand, Paul says, "Bless those who persecute you; bless and do not curse them" (Rom. 12:14). On the other hand, Paul's actions sometimes seemed to contradict that. When he was told that the magistrates had ordered his and Silas's release from prison in Philippi, his response was: "They have beaten us publicly, uncondemned, men who are Roman citizens, and have thrown us into prison; and do they now throw us out secretly? No! Let them come themselves and take us out" (Acts 16:37). On hearing this, the magistrates were afraid that they had broken the law in the way they had treated a Roman citizen. "So they came and apologized to them" (Acts 16:39). Here Paul was acting for the benefit of the gospel cause. He wanted to win legal protection for Christianity and to keep his arbitrary arrest from becoming a precedent for the treatment of Christians. Sometimes, then, we must go to the law to seek the protection of the right of people to practice and propagate Christianity. We need to assess the situation and decide what is the best route to take. Situations differ, so the decision must be made on a case-by-case basis.

This issue becomes very important when the persecution comes from family members. It is an especially sensitive matter in cultures where shame and honor are important values (see above and chap. 11). It is a huge blow to a family when a Christian publicly exposes unkind things that others in the family are doing to him or her. But there is no denying that Christians are hurt by their own family members. Therefore, to provide comfort and healing of their hurts, it is necessary for Christians to share their pain confidentially with other trusted Christians. It is usually best not to make public the unkind things done by one's family members. If abuse is happening, one may need to go to the authorities. But such a step should be taken only after serious thought. Familial love is something that never leaves a person. Living with the guilt of knowing that one brought shame to one's own family is a painful burden to bear.

This principle applies to sharing testimonies and prayer requests also. Generally, we recommend that converts avoid saying humiliating things about their family members in public. If non-Christians hear that a family member has been saying bad things about them, the resulting wounds could make them even more hostile to the gospel. For example, a Christian yearns for the day when a non-Christian family member will come to church. If this family member knows that bad things have been said about him in the church, it is unlikely that he will want to enter the church.

When responding to persecutors, then, we must think of the progress of the gospel and the welfare of the persecutor. In keeping with the call to bless persecutors, we will always keep their ultimate welfare in the back of our minds. If talking publicly about them hinders them from being receptive to the gospel, we may be wise not to do so. This should makes us reluctant to commercialize reporting on persecution. Some people love to hear stories of persecution. They need to know what is happening so that they can pray. But caution needs to be exercised. Publicizing persecution also makes non-Christian citizens or family members look at Christians as having betrayed their nation or family and brought shame upon it. Then they will think of Christianity as an alien religion intent on hurting the nation or family. Responding to persecution calls for wisdom and sensitivity.

Following Christ as Insiders within Pre-Christian Religious Communities?

Sometimes non-Christians identify Christianity with Western culture or with people who once oppressed them. They can associate Christianity with things they find repulsive, like colonial domination, radical Western individualism, and the open sexual promiscuity portrayed in Western media. All this makes it very difficult for some people who come to Christ. Sensitive Christians have been acutely aware of the difficulties encountered by new converts in places hostile to followers of Christ.

Alongside this hostility, we find a universal admiration of Christ among non-Christians. They admire Jesus, but they are repulsed by what they understand as "Christian culture." These competing realities have resulted in much fresh thinking and experimenting about how one should incorporate converts into the church while eliminating unnecessary stumbling blocks to commitment.

Some have gathered converts into churches that use many of the cultural features of the communities to which those converts belonged. Timothy Tennent describes what a church with converts from Islam might look like. They may use words like *Allah* for God, *salat* for prayer, and *injil* for the gospel. These Arabic words are parts of the vocabulary of their Muslim past. If an outward practice normally associated with Muslim faithfulness is not explicitly prohibited in Scripture, they may adopt it. So these Christians would avoid eating pork, abstain from alcohol, and remove shoes when coming for worship. Though they retained a lot of the practices of their former religion, the Islamic community would not recognize them as being Muslims. But a lot of things that the Muslims find offensive would be eliminated. There is much to commend in this approach.[12]

Another development that has gained prominence in missiological circles is the phenomenon known as "insider movements." This term

---

12. Many points in this paragraph were drawn from Timothy C. Tennent, *Invitation to World Missions: A Trinitarian Missiology for the Twenty-First Century* (Grand Rapids, MI: Kregel, 2010), 304.

refers to groups of followers of Jesus, mostly from Muslim and Hindu backgrounds, who nevertheless do not leave their former religious communities. They would not call themselves Christians or identify themselves with the Christian church. Some of these Christ followers from Muslim backgrounds even continue to worship in the mosque. These followers of Christ inside the Muslim community have also been called "Messianic Muslims." Devotees of Jesus remaining within the Hindu community have been called "Jesus Batkta," that is, devotees of Jesus.[13] They seek to follow the teachings of the Bible, but they do not leave their original religious communities. There are reputedly hundreds of thousands of such followers of Christ from Muslim and Hindu backgrounds.

Many articles[14] and books have been written for[15] and against[16] this phenomenon. It is beyond the scope of this book to evaluate this approach. I do wonder whether, by not associating and identifying with the existing expressions of the church, Christians violate the strong biblical teaching about the body of Christ. I stated in chapter 3 that evangelicals have generally been weak in their understanding of this doctrine. Yet I do not want to downplay the pain that people experience when they leave the strong communities that religions like Islam have. I have seen people from Muslim backgrounds who have accepted the truth of the gospel and responded in faith to Christ, only to return to the Islamic fold, mainly because of the power of the Muslim community (known in Arabic as *Ummah*[17]). I also know that it is sometimes expedient for persons who have received Christ not to associate openly with the church, even though they are being discipled by Christians, until the time is appropriate for them to "come out." We have seen this happening with Buddhist monks who have come to Christ.

---

13. Cited in Tennent, *Invitation to World Missions*, 499.

14. See Tennent, *Invitation to World Missions*, 500n10, for a survey of articles written for and against.

15. See Herbert H. Hoefer, *Churchless Christianity* (Pasadena, CA: William Carey Library, 2001). For a comprehensive anthology on this issue, see *Understanding Insider Movements: Disciples of Jesus within Diverse Religious Communities*, ed. Harley Talman and John Jay Travis (Pasadena, CA: William Carey Library, 2015).

16. See Jeff Morton, *Insider Movements: Biblically Incredible or Incredibly Brilliant* (Eugene, OR: Wipf and Stock, 2012).

17. For a comprehensive look at the various issues related to Christianity and the Muslim community, see *Longing for Community: Church, Ummah, or Somewhere in Between*, ed. David Greenlee and Bob Fish (Pasadena, CA: William Carey Library, 2013).

The presence of thousands of secret believers in cultures known to be hostile to Christianity is surely a sign that God is working among these people. I think Tennent is right in saying that this could be "a temporary, transitional bridge over which some Muslims will be able to cross into more explicit Christian identity."[18] I am reluctant to say that we should build a theology of the church to justify the insider-movement phenomenon. But this topic does highlight the seriousness of the issue of leaving one's original community.

We await the day when there will be a great turning to Christ among resistant groups like the Muslims. It will probably be preceded by severe persecution, including martyrdom; but it could lead to waves of positive responses to Christ that will be difficult to suppress. We hope that the present turning to Christ that we are seeing is but the firstfruits of this coming harvest. And we stand in solidarity with them, especially through prayer, that God would sustain and protect them as they face persecution.

———

The last beatitude of Jesus holds out this hope:

> Blessed are those who are persecuted for righteousness' sake, for theirs is the kingdom of heaven.
>
> Blessed are you when others revile you and persecute you and utter all kinds of evil against you falsely on my account. Rejoice and be glad, for your reward is great in heaven, for so they persecuted the prophets who were before you. (Matt. 5:10–12)

---

18. Tennent, *Invitation to World Missions*, 305.

6

Mission, Ambition, and Exhortation

Follow me, and I will make you become fishers of men.

Mark 1:17

This charge I entrust to you, Timothy, my child, in accordance with the prophecies previously made about you, that by them you may wage the good warfare, holding faith and a good conscience.

1 Timothy 1:18–19

Along with the story of the creation of the first humans comes God's commission to them to look after his creation (Gen. 1:28), a commission that remains part of our calling. In another of the epochal events in human history, God's call to Abraham, the father of the faithful, was accompanied by a promise that Abraham would be a blessing to the nations (Gen. 12:3). This was realized with the coming of the second Adam, who was God's answer to the mess that the world had become. He was the Savior of the world, and he called his followers to represent him in taking that blessing to others, as expressed in the multiple statements of the Great Commission he gave before he left the world. It should not surprise us, then, that his call to his first disciples was also a call to mission: "Follow me, and I will make you become fishers of men" (Mark 1:17).

Discipling within a Mission Team

Mission Teams

The first disciples of Jesus were a ministry team, and that is the ideal context for discipling. Sometimes when mentoring more mature Christians, a mentor may not be part of the same ministry team of the mentee. Mentees ideally have their own teams and have already grown into an understanding of the place a team ministry has in the Christian life. But when discipling newer believers, it is ideal that the discipler and the disciplees serve together in a ministry team. There will, of course, be exceptions, depending on the situation one is in. I have had some relationships that included no ministry involvement with the persons I was discipling, and I always sensed the limitations of that model. Generally, growth in the Christian life through discipling is growth in service together. If both service and body life are indispensable parts of Christianity, then discipling should include an experience both of service and of relating to other Christians. An ideal discipleship group then would also be a mission team.

Paul summarized his desire for the Philippians, saying, "Only let your manner of life be worthy of the gospel of Christ, so that whether I come and see you or am absent, I may hear of you that you are standing firm in one spirit, with one mind striving side by side for the faith of the gospel" (Phil. 1:27). He looked for two things: the unity of the group and their striving side by side for the gospel. This biblical pattern needs to be burned into every Christian leader: discipleship groups are mission teams—people growing in their love of God and each other, and serving God together.

The discipler should find ways in which the discipleship group can minister together by getting the members involved in ministry assignments. Jesus traveled with his disciples when he was serving the masses. The benefit I as a young person had from traveling on ministry assignments with Sam Sherrard, my leader in Youth for Christ, was incalculable. Sometimes I went as a singer; sometimes I just accompanied him when he went to the printer or a place of ministry. Sometimes I handled the publicity table after meetings. I think I learned most about ministry by helping in a youth club or an evangelistic camp. Praying for the programs, planning out ways in which we could fulfill our dreams, and grappling for the souls of other young people were key to our growth. Seeing people come to Christ was exhilarating. Etched also in my memory are the times when, as a seminary student, I accompanied Robert Coleman as he went to preach. I may not have had any major responsibility, but it was a thrill to be involved in something great. The conversations on the journeys to and from the venues were priceless.

A Learning Process

James Edwards points out that in Jesus's call in Mark 1:17, "the Greek wording is actually more nuanced" than the familiar "I will make you fishers of men," which leaves the word *genesthai* (from *ginomai*, "become") untranslated. This is corrected in the ESV translation: "I will make you become fishers of men" (see also the NASB). As Edwards puts it, "The process of becoming disciples of Jesus is a slow and painful one for the Twelve."[1] Jesus taught them and involved them in his ministry, gradually giving them more responsibilities.

Being involved in ministry is not the same as being in leadership. When Paul gives qualifications for overseers in the church, he tells Timothy, "He must not be a recent convert, or he may become puffed up with conceit and fall into the condemnation of the devil" (1 Tim. 3:6). Sometimes we are tempted to put enthusiastic and capable people into leadership before they are spiritually mature. That could inhibit their growth in the Christian life. They may think they are already mature and become "puffed up," which will make learning difficult.

In our drug rehab ministry, it is very important that we help recovering drug dependents become active in serving God as soon as possible. However, we have to be cautious about the danger of their substituting addiction to drugs with addiction to service. They will be part of a ministering team that is active in Christian service. They will help organize programs, which requires a lot of demanding work. But we are reluctant to encourage them to share their testimonies at public meetings soon after they experience freedom from the habit. Usually their testimonies are so spectacular that they can soon become

---

1. James R. Edwards, *The Gospel according to Mark*, The Pillar New Testament Commentary (Grand Rapids, MI: Eerdmans; Leicester, UK: Apollos, 2002), 50.

celebrities in the Christian community, getting numerous invitations to share. But they have a lot of important issues to sort out along the path to wholeness. They especially need to repair and nurture their relationships with the members of their families who suffered much because of their addiction. It is tempting for a former drug dependent to compensate for the unpleasantness of his home environment by being more and more active as a star in the Christian circuit. The guilt of an unhappy home situation is assuaged by the pride of being a Christian celebrity. But, as the Proverb says,

> Pride goes before destruction,
> and a haughty spirit before a fall. (Prov. 16:18)

Sadly, I have seen some people fall back into sin this way.

Passionate Leadership

Will people stay motivated about mission if we do not give them leadership positions? Yes, if we give them the sense that what they are doing is significant and of lasting value. The leader of the discipleship group is the key. Leaders must burn with passion for the task at hand. That passion is transmitted to the others. Augustine wrote in his *Confessions*, "Love in one person is infectious in kindling it in another."[2] That fire of love in a leader can turn what others consider drudgery into an exciting assignment. Passion for mission is a basic aspect of discipleship and is, therefore, a prerequisite for discipling.

If leaders lose their passion, they should either step down or (much better) grapple with God until the passion returns. This may mean taking time off to recuperate after years of hard work has left body, mind, and spirit exhausted. It could mean spending time with God and grappling with him until one is ignited by the fire of the Holy Spirit. E. Stanley Jones, an American missionary to India, tells the story of a young preacher who said, "I've been perjuring myself. I've been preaching things not operative within me. I'm through with this unreality. I'll give God till Sunday to do something for me. And if he doesn't do something for me before Sunday, someone else can preach.

---

2. Saint Augustine, *Confessions*, trans. Henry Chadwick (Oxford: Oxford University Press, 1991), 65. The most popular translation of this quote is "One loving spirit sets another spirit on fire."

I won't." The young preacher took Saturday off as a day of retreat. God met him, and the preacher went into the pulpit a new man. That Sunday the congregation got the shock of their lives. They had a new minister! The congregation found itself seeking what their young minister had found.[3] A contagious urgency had been triggered by an experience of God and his truth. God is still active in this world; and his Word is still like a fire (Jer. 20:9). He can restore passion in a listless soul.

Holistic Learning

Christian responsibility encompasses a lot of areas, and disciplers should try to ensure that the team has a holistic experience of at least a little of each different area. The passion that drove Jesus resonates in his mission statement, "For the Son of Man came to seek and to save the lost" (Luke 19:10). But his disciples were actively involved with him in a wide variety of things. They were with him as he preached, healed, exorcised, fed the multitudes, debated with leaders, went to homes for meals and for funerals, and suffered at the hands of enemies.

Similarly, the members of a discipleship group should burn with a desire to see lost people being found by the Savior. People need the Lord more than anything else, and the group should always be dreaming about how the lost can be found. But the group should also be exposed to many other different kinds of service. They can visit lapsed Christians and help restore them, or visit people who have not come to church for some time. With some experience, they could be assigned the care of a few Christians and themselves become disciplers. When there is a need in the life of a member of the church, they can take it on as an assignment. Recently, my discipleship group helped build a fence around the home of a single mother in our church. In the time of a catastrophe like a flood, a tsunami, or an earthquake, they can become actively involved in relief operations. They can help ensure that the poor receive justice by filling out forms for them, representing them in government departments, or giving them educational help.

---

3. E. Stanley Jones, *The Word Became Flesh* (Nashville: Abingdon, 1963), 149.

All the above activities come within the responsibilities of Christians. People may specialize in specific areas as they grow. But all need to have some experience in the different areas of involvement as a part of their growth to healthy Christianity.

Discovering and Using Gifts

While Christians should be taught the importance of the gamut of Christian responsibility, with time they will discover that they are better at some activities than at others. This was addressed in the early church when Paul and Peter gave a body-life structure to the missional life of believers by talking about gifts. From Romans 12:3–8, 1 Corinthians 12:1–31, Ephesians 4:7–16, and 1 Peter 4:10–11, we can get a comprehensive picture of how gifts operate in the body:

- It is clear that all Christians have one or more gifts that have been given by God for use in his service.
- These gifts are carefully apportioned to each person according to the plan of God for the body of Christ.
- The gifts give each Christian a significant role in God's plan so that no one can consider himself or herself inferior or superior to another.
- The gifts operate within the context of the body of Christ and not in an individualistic manner.
- Christians are to be sensitive to recognize the callings of others.
- The body is enriched through the operation of each gift, and when the gifts are used according to God's plan, the body grows and matures.

If gifts are so important, we should be helping disciplees discover what their gifts are. We will look at this in the next section.

I need to add that healthy Christians do much more than use their distinct gifts. Jesus and Paul served in a variety of ways, and so must we. Otherwise we will become unbalanced individuals. Often, we learn most by doing things we are not very good at. Those things provide the background experiences that help us use our gifts effectively. So while we help people discover and use their gifts, we should not give them the sense that using their distinct gifts is all they do for the kingdom. Most of us are generalists who devote some extra time for our specialization. Christians shouldn't feel they are wasting their time and being unfulfilled when they do things they are not exceptionally good at. We are servants, and we do what the body needs us to do, even though we may not like to do it. We need to communicate such an attitude regarding service early in the life of disciples of Christ, so that servanthood becomes an admired cultural value in the group.

Senator Mark Hatfield was a fine Christian and a US Senator from Oregon for many years. He had a long and distinguished career in politics. Howard Hendricks tells of an incident that took place when he spoke at an early morning father-son breakfast at the Fourth Presbyterian Church in Washington, DC. There were many prominent and not-so-prominent people there. Hendricks says, "After I had finished speaking and the meeting was dismissed, I looked over to my right, and there was Senator Mark Hatfield, stacking chairs and picking up napkins that had fallen on the floor." Hendricks comments, "Ladies and gentlemen, if you are impressed that you are a United States senator, you don't stack chairs and pick up napkins."[4] That was not Hatfield's primary gifting, but serving where needed was part of his primary calling.

Ambition

Areas of Ambition

A characteristic feature of parenting is having ambitions for children. Covering three areas, Dennis McCallum and Jessica Lowery helpfully describe the goals one should have in discipleship:

- **Character** (having a good personal walk with God, becoming a loving person with successful relationships . . . manifesting the fruit of the Spirit, a relatively stable emotional life, etc.).
- **Understanding** (a thoroughly developed Christian worldview, good theology, knowledge of the Bible, and ability to use the Bible in ministry, wisdom, discernment, resistance to false teaching, etc.).

---

4. Howard Hendricks, "The Problem of Discrimination," *Preaching Today*, tape 76, www.PreachingToday.com.

- **Ministry capability** (ability to successfully minister in evangelism, pastoring others, personal discipleship, teaching or discussion leading. . . .).[5]

In addition to the three areas mentioned above, I would add familial, vocational, and social thriving—areas outside the programs typically associated with a church. Disciplers want disciplees to be devoted family members and to do well in their education, their jobs, and their other activities in society. When they meet, disciplers need to discuss with their disciplees how they are faring in each of these four areas.

We have looked at different goals of disciplers in numerous places in this book. Here we will look at ambitions we have for what McCallum and Lowery call "ministry capability." But first let me say that earthly parents, even Christians, often have worldly ambitions for their children. We must balance the desire to see them do well in life economically and socially with our desire to see them as radically obedient children of God. As we think of them and ourselves, we should always keep in our minds the statement of Jesus "But seek first the kingdom of God and his righteousness, and all these things will be added to you" (Matt. 6:33). As this is a countercultural approach to life, we need to constantly remind ourselves of this regarding our ambitions for both ourselves and our disciplees.[6]

Desiring to See Disciplees Become Great People

We must always look at people through eyes aware of the possibilities of grace to make them great people. When Jesus called Peter, he first told him that he would become a fisher of men. Even before that, when Peter first came to Jesus with Andrew, "Jesus looked at him and said, 'You are Simon the son of John. You shall be called Cephas' (which means Peter)" (John 1:42). Jesus saw beyond the impulsive and somewhat unstable person that Peter was and prophetically described him as a rock. As Bruce Milne says, "It is striking how regularly Jesus approached people from the perspective of their potential" (see Luke

---

5. Dennis McCallum and Jessica Lowery, *Organic Discipleship: Mentoring Others into Spiritual Maturity and Leadership* (Columbus, OH: New Paradigm, 2012), 23. The authors expand on this in pages 267–77.

6. I am grateful to my friend at Trinity Evangelical Divinity School, Jeffrey Stevenson, for alerting me to this factor as a key aspect of good parenthood.

5:10; 18:22; John 1:47; 4:7; 6:70).[7] His ambition for Peter was evident even when he predicted Peter's denial. Jesus said, "Simon, Simon, behold, Satan demanded to have you, that he might sift you like wheat, but I have prayed for you that your faith may not fail. And when you have turned again, strengthen your brothers" (Luke 22:31–32). His restoration after the denial was a recommissioning to service. Three times Jesus told him: "Feed my lambs. . . . Tend my sheep. . . . Feed my sheep" (John 21:15–17).

Paul's ambition for Timothy was stimulated through a prophetic word given about him. He said, "This charge I entrust to you, Timothy, my child, in accordance with the prophecies previously made about you, that by them you may wage the good warfare" (1 Tim 1:18). Thomas Lea and Hayne Griffin comment, "The 'prophecies' probably represent promising comments concerning Timothy's spiritual usefulness spoken at earlier occasions in his ministry."[8] Here Paul strongly urges him about his personal life. But he does so "in accordance with the prophecies." The wording suggests that the prophecies will help him to wage the good warfare. God has, through prophecies, affirmed that he has great potential. Now Paul reminds him of this potential. He uses his belief in Timothy's potential to urge him to grow in his ministry. Elsewhere Paul tells him, "Do not neglect the gift you have, which was given you by prophecy when the council of elders laid their hands on you" (1 Tim. 4:14). Paul tells Timothy to persevere in fulfilling the tasks assigned to him so that he will progress in the exercise of his ministry: "Practice these things, immerse yourself in them, so that all may see your progress" (1 Tim. 4:15). How many times Paul reminds Timothy of his potential!

You can imagine how Peter and Timothy would have been encouraged when great people like Jesus and Paul looked at them with prophetic vision. Commenting on Peter's name change, Bruce Milne says, "The vision of future potential can be a deeply effective means to the realizing of that potential."[9] The statement in 2 Timothy 1:7, "For the

---

7. Bruce Milne, *The Message of John: Here Is Your King!*, The Bible Speaks Today (Downers Grove, IL: InterVarsity Press, 1993), 59.

8. Thomas D. Lea and Hayne P. Griffin Jr., *1, 2 Timothy, Titus*, The New American Commentary (Nashville: Broadman & Holman, 1992) 80.

9. Milne, *Message of John*, 59.

Spirit God gave us does not make us timid, but gives us power, love and self-discipline" (NIV), suggests that Timothy seems to have been a timid person.[10] Paul's frequent reminders of his bright potential must have encouraged him immensely.

When I was about fifteen years old, I sensed that God was calling me to the ministry, but I dared not tell anyone. I was so shy and lacking in confidence to open my mouth in front of others that I must have thought people would laugh at the prospect of me being a preacher. One day my pastor, the Rev. George Good, asked me whether I had ever thought of going into the ministry. What a boost that was to me in confirming that I did indeed have a call from God! Disciplers learn to look at disciplees with prophetic eyes that see the possibilities of grace in their lives. By communicating that vision, they spur them on to reach out for God's best for their lives.

Ambitions Become the Focus of Our Prayers

When we have ambitions for people, it is natural to mention those ambitions often in our prayers. Praying for disciplees is such an important topic that I have devoted almost a whole chapter to it (see chap. 9).

Opening Doors for Disciplees

Jesus sent his disciples on ministry assignments. Paul did all he could to help Timothy to flourish in ministry. In his second letter to Timothy, he says, "For this reason I remind you to fan into flame the gift of God, which is in you through the laying on of my hands" (2 Tim. 1:6). This shows how a leader proactively pushes for others to use their gifts in the life of the church. Paul went further, using his credibility as an esteemed leader to recommend Timothy to the churches (1 Cor. 4:17; 16:10; Phil. 2:19–24). Several times he sent him as his representative to churches (1 Cor. 4:17; 16:10; Phil. 2:19–24; 1 Thess. 3:2–6). He mentions Timothy six times as a coauthor of his letters (2 Cor. 1:1; Phil. 1:1; Col. 1:1; 1 Thess. 1:1; 2 Thess. 1:1; Philem. 1). Pushing junior people forward is an aspect of good Christian leadership.

---

10. See William D. Mounce, *Pastoral Epistles*, Word Biblical Commentary (Dallas: Word, 2000), 478.

Paul was following a pattern set by Barnabas. When Paul made his first visit to Jerusalem after his conversion, the church there was suspicious of him, wondering whether he was a spy. Barnabas stuck his neck out for Paul and took him to the inner circle of the church, the apostles. And not only did Barnabas take him there; he also told Paul's story to the apostles (Acts 9:27). Here was a reversal of roles typical of our "upside-down kingdom."[11] In society, the junior people act as public-relations officers for the senior people. In God's kingdom, the senior people talk about the junior people to help them progress in life and ministry.

I do not know how it is in other parts of the world, but in Asia many younger leaders complain that senior leaders are not really committed to their progress and welfare. In chapter 2 I mentioned a survey a friend did on relationships between senior and junior pastors. He found that junior pastors generally considered senior pastors their heroes when they joined staff. But some of those heroes became demons after a time. Junior pastors can feel like pawns used to carry out programs, not as trainees under pastoral care.

According to the biblical teaching on gifts outlined above, God equips people within the body to benefit the body. God's best for the individual should dovetail with his best for the group. Leaders must believe this and work on that premise, investing in the welfare and progress of the individuals in the group. Sometimes the body may adjust its program to use a newly discovered gift that may benefit the body. Sometimes the group may release the person with its blessings to go elsewhere, as God leads. This may be a difficult decision as the group may have invested in that person's training and development. But if he or she is going to be working for the kingdom, then our overall aim to glorify God is being fulfilled. The group has contributed to the growth of the kingdom by giving of its wealth to another unit within the kingdom. If they refuse to release the person, there could be unpleasant and hurtful conflict and a departure that does not honor God.

Indeed, some trainees will abuse the help given to them. In Sri Lanka there is a saying: "When I'm given food I will eat. I will eat and

---

11. This expression comes from Donald B. Kraybill, *The Upside-Down Kingdom* (Harrisburg, VA: Herald, 2011).

run away!" People will unethically take advantage of our kindness. This is a hurt that comes with personal ministry. But there are others who make the effort worthwhile.

When Disciplees Overtake Disciplers

In chapter 2 I told of how disciplees may end up as leaders of their disciplers. Sometimes the discipled persons may become more prominent than the disciplers. Barnabas was a good preacher. That is why the church gave him the name Barnabas, meaning "son of prophecy" (which I prefer to "son of encouragement").[12] After ministering together for some time, however, it was Paul and not Barnabas who was preaching. The team is named as "Paul and Barnabas" (Acts 13:43; 13:50; 15:2, 22, 35, 36) rather than the earlier "Barnabas and Saul" (Acts 11:30; 12:25; 13:2, 7). Paul seems to have become the acknowledged leader in the team. But at the Council of Jerusalem, where Barnabas was an esteemed leader, the order changes back to "Barnabas and Paul" (Acts 15:12, 25). This shows that what is important is the agenda of the kingdom, not our position in it. If it is good for the kingdom's progress that the junior person becomes prominent, godly leaders will let it happen.

Of course, this is not as easy as it may seem. Commenting on this exchange of leadership roles, F. F. Bruce cites the rhymester,

> It takes more grace than I can tell
> To play the second fiddle well.[13]

Feeling defeated when someone else takes the place of prominence that we once had is a natural human reaction. Sadly, there are many stories describing the bad ways leaders respond to that change and hurt capable young leaders. This is where our theology addresses our natural inclination. First, our theology says that the kingdom of God benefits from this change and that our primary commitment is to the kingdom, not to our name. Second, our theology tells us that in the kingdom, the first will be the last and the last will be first (Mark

---

12. See Ajith Fernando, *Acts*, NIV Application Commentary (Grand Rapids, MI: Zondervan, 1998), 196.

13. F. F. Bruce, *The Pauline Circle* (Grand Rapids, MI: Eerdmans, 1985), 19.

9:35; 10:31). If that is so, we are gaining by losing our position of prominence! I feel this is one biblical teaching that many do not really believe, even though they claim to hold to the full authority and inspiration of the Bible. Their reaction to reversals like this show that they see the reversals differently than Jesus did.

On the other hand, biblical disciplers are thrilled to see the progress of those they disciple. Robert Coleman often says, "The glory of the teacher is to sit at the feet of the student and learn from him." Talking about the prospect of dying, Paul says, "My desire is to depart and be with Christ, for that is far better" (Phil. 1:23). But he chooses the option of staying on in the world for the benefit of others: "But to remain in the flesh is more necessary on your account. Convinced of this, I know that I will remain and continue with you all, for your progress and joy in the faith" (Phil. 1:24–25). The "progress and joy" of our spiritual children is our passion! And that comes from within the wider passion for the growth of God's kingdom. Jesus considered John the Baptist the greatest person in his era (Luke 7:28). Following the logic of Jesus that the last shall be first, we can conclude that one reason for John's greatness was the attitude expressed in his statement "He must increase, but I must decrease" (John 3:30).

Those Whom Jesus Chose

It is interesting to note that the twelve disciples Jesus chose were not people who had high positions in society. Later he did choose such a person, Paul, which shows that God can use the noble backgrounds of people to contribute significantly to the cause of Christ. God uses all kinds of people to do great things for him. Among the Twelve were two people from despised groups: Simon the zealot and Levi the tax collector. One of Jesus's disciples would betray him. We should be careful of the temptation to choose those we disciple based on worldly criteria. I know that some Christian organizations especially target those with leadership potential. That may be God's leading in some groups; but it is not a pattern to be universally followed.

The following statement by Paul is so powerful that I will quote it in full:

For consider your calling, brothers: not many of you were wise according to worldly standards, not many were powerful, not many were of noble birth. But God chose what is foolish in the world to shame the wise; God chose what is weak in the world to shame the strong; God chose what is low and despised in the world, even things that are not, to bring to nothing things that are, so that no human being might boast in the presence of God. (1 Cor. 1:26–29)

In a subsequent letter, Paul wrote, "But we have this treasure in jars of clay, to show that the surpassing power belongs to God and not to us" (2 Cor. 4:7). Rather than handicaps, our weaknesses can be seen as advantages for the kingdom agenda because they exhibit vividly the marvels of God's grace.

In forty-one years of working in a youth organization, I have seen hundreds of youth come to Christ. I must confess that when I see some coming to Christ, I am tempted to be a little happier than when others come. Some seem to have much more potential. How wrong I am in making such value judgments. The key to usefulness in the kingdom of God is not one's background, or talent, or looks, or educational qualifications. It is grace. The great Paul himself said, "Therefore, having this ministry by the mercy of God, we do not lose heart" (2 Cor. 4:1). That is the key—mercy—pity extended to a helpless person. Those who realize they are helpless are open to God's grace, and that makes them powerhouses through which grace flows. Many of the people in our ministry who have gone on to do great things for God were not at first thought to have much potential.

Besides, in God's plan for his body, not all will be leaders. Our celebrity culture focuses on the talented, and some of them will become superstars. Recent history has shown how dangerous this is. When they behave badly, God's name is greatly dishonored. Besides, others feel that they are not significant, even though the Bible says that all Christians are equally significant (see especially 1 Cor. 12:14–26). I am indebted to the classic book by A. B. Bruce *The Training of the Twelve* for stimulating thoughts that resulted in this section. He says:

Three eminent men, or even two (Peter and John), out of twelve, is a good proportion. . . . Far from regretting that all were not Peters and Johns, it is rather a matter to be thankful for, that there were diversities of gifts among the first preachers of the gospel. As a general rule, it is not good when all are leaders.[14]

In his book about shepherds, Timothy Laniak presents a fascinating insight that applies to discipling people who are weaker and needier that the rest. "When [Jacob] and Esau were reconciled after years of estrangement, Jacob still insisted on traveling at the pace of his needy ones."[15] Jacob's response to Esau's proposal to travel with him was, "My lord knows that the children are frail, and that the nursing flocks and herds are a care to me. If they are driven hard for one day, all the flocks will die" (Gen. 33:13). Some "weak" ones in the group may slow us down. Some soldiers, wounded from the battle, may need special care. But it does not harm the group to slow down for the sake of others. That is what body life is like. Our addiction to efficiency could make us miss some of the great blessings of body life in which patience is a great source of enrichment.

All this is to say that when we choose someone to disciple, the key is whether God has called us to be involved in this person's life. Looking for outward qualifications, we may miss God's chosen people. Of the Twelve, only Peter, James, and John are mentioned in Acts. But the great Savior of the world discipled nine others, and nothing in the Bible says that Jesus made a mistake in choosing those nine. We must, with much prayer, seek God's will about whom to disciple. This is not a decision to be taken lightly or made quickly. Sometimes, of course, the decision is made for us, as when people come under our care because of their position in the organization or church. We take that as God's will and do our best to help them. But as for our goals in discipling, they should be kingdom goals. We seek to help people find their place in God's plan and help them to fulfill that role as faithfully and happily as they can. It may not be in a place of prominence. But it is surely in a place of significance if it is God's place for that person.

Leaders need to demonstrate by their lives that non-prominent roles are also significant in the kingdom of God. Then those who get

---

14. (1894; repr., Grand Rapids, MI: Kregel, 1971), 39.
15. Timothy S. Laniak, *While Shepherds Watch Their Flocks: Forty Daily Reflections on Biblical Leadership* (n.p.: ShepherdLeader, 2007), 72.

no public recognition will learn not to resent it. After all, we follow a servant Lord who washed the feet of his disciples—a servant's task—and asked his followers to do the same (John 13:15). After he rose from the dead as glorious Lord, we find him one morning preparing and serving breakfast to his hungry disciples after they have spent a night in a boat fishing (John 21:9–13). As Jesus said, "Whoever would be great among you must be your servant, and whoever would be first among you must be slave of all" (Mark 10:43–44). When disciplers demonstrate that attitude in their own service, their disciplees will grasp the biblical principle that servanthood is nobility.

When Disciplees Reject Our Ambitions for Them

Sometimes our disciplees do not accept the ambitions we have for them. There are many reasons for this. One reason is fear. They have seen so much disappointment in life that they balk at leaving their comfort zone and launching into unfamiliar territory for fear of failure. Some will not accept an offer of training for fear of being obligated to the church or group offering it. We must persevere in such situations, doing all we can to help them change their minds. But we cannot force our ideas on them. In fact, our ambition may not be God's will for them. Yet, sometimes a sensitive nudge from a discipler can change one's perspective and help him or her progress in life.

Victor was living in very poor housing and, to earn a living, doing menial labor that left him extremely tired. To wash away his weariness, he resorted to strong drinks and became an alcoholic. Then he came to Christ and joined a discipleship group in his church. He stopped consuming alcohol and was set on a path of upward social mobility. But he did not have a National Identity Card. In his country, without that card he would find it difficult to get a job. His discipleship group leader kept pushing him to get his card, but Victor kept evading the issue. Then his discipler realized that Victor was uncomfortable with having to fill out all the necessary forms and having to face the authorities in the government registration office. His discipler pushed him to proceed with the application and helped him with the process. Victor did get a card, and with that came a new job. Now decades later, he would be considered middle-class, and his children have all done well spiritually and vocationally. What he needed was a little push from his discipler.

Exhortation
Exhorting out of Ambition (1 Tim. 1:18–19)
Exhortation in its different forms is an important aspect of working to achieve our ambitions for disciplees. Consider this exhortation of Paul: "This charge I entrust to you, Timothy, my child, in accordance with the prophecies previously made about you, that by them you may wage the good warfare, holding faith and a good conscience" (1 Tim. 1:18–19). Paul says that prophecies drove him to give Timothy a charge. Timothy was waging a good warfare. That is serious business. So his leader gave him an urgent "command" (NIV). Disciplers must sometimes give stern advice and rebuke to disciplees. But as the great fourth-century expositor Chrysostom said, "He charges him as his son, not so much with arbitrary or despotic authority. Rather as a father, he says, 'My son, Timothy.'"[16] We also see that behind that charge was the ambition framed by "the prophecies previously made about" him. It was done not to devastate, but to lift Timothy up so that he would strive to achieve the great goal ahead of him.

Even scolding disciplees, when needed, must be done in a way that lifts them up and makes them want to do well. I have heard stories about disciplers who scolded disciplees in insulting, humiliating, and devastating ways. This is not the biblical way of rebuking. Paul's advice is "Fathers, do not provoke your children, lest they become discouraged" (Col. 3:21). Fathers can discipline their children in ways that do them great harm. Both spiritual and physical parents need to be led by God when they correct their children. Luke records that before Paul rebuked the sorcerer Elymas in Cyprus, the apostle was "filled with the Holy Spirit" (Acts 13:9). We need the Spirit's fullness for rebuking people. When we scold people, we pray, "Lord, anoint me; fill me with your Spirit, so that I can rebuke in a way that will help this person." That help includes the following four forms.

---

16. From John Chrysostom, "Homilies on 1 Timothy," homily 5 in *Colossians, 1–2 Thessalonians, 1–2 Timothy, Titus, Philemon*, ed. Peter J. Gorday, New Testament vol. 9 of *Ancient Christian Commentary on Scripture*, ed. Thomas C. Oden (Downers Grove, IL: InterVarsity Press, 2000), 148.

Protection. Disciplees are in a war against a dangerous and powerful enemy. Protecting them from harm is an urgent necessity. In his High Priestly Prayer, Jesus said: "While I was with them, I kept them in your name, which you have given me. I have guarded them, and not one of them has been lost except the son of destruction" (John 17:12). A newer Christian may not be able to handle a powerful opponent and may need to be protected from having to face that opponent.

A relatively new Christian I was discipling came to our group and announced that he had been visited in his home by some Bible teachers. As a new believer, he was eager to learn from them. On questioning him, I realized that these visitors were Jehovah's Witnesses. I told him as strongly as I could that he must have nothing to do with those people. A new believer could easily be led astray by such people, who can seem to have a good knowledge of the Bible. He needed to be protected from this danger.

Warning. Colossians 1:28, one of Paul's great discipling verses, states the goal of discipling: "that we may present [probably at the second coming] everyone mature in Christ." Just before that statement Paul describes one of the ways in which he works toward that end: "Him we proclaim, warning everyone." The verb translated "warning" (*noutheteō*) appears eight times in Paul's writings and teaching in the New Testament with this idea of warning believers.[17] The noun form appears three times (1 Cor. 10:11; Eph. 6:4; Titus 3:10). Jesus uses two other Greek words in the Gospels twenty times to express "warning." The first word, *prosechō*, appears ten times and means "pay close attention to . . . , be on guard, watch, be careful." The other word, *blepō* appears sixty-six times in the Gospels, and it usually means "see," but it can take the meaning "beware of," and it appears in this sense ten times. These twenty references show us that Jesus often warned people about the dangers they would face in this sinful world.[18] Clearly both Jesus and Paul considered warning people of danger to be an important aspect of nurture.

---

17. Acts 20:31; Rom. 15:14; 1 Cor. 4:14; Col. 1:28; 3:16; 1 Thess. 5:12, 14; 2 Thess. 3:15.

18. These last four sentences echo my book, *Jesus Driven Ministry* (Wheaton, IL: Crossway, 2002), 172.

A discipler finds that a young woman she disciples is spending too much time with a young man who is not a believer. She warns the young woman of the dangers of falling in love with an unbeliever. A young Christian is not doing his studies as he should even though his exams are close. His discipler warns him of the consequences of failing his exams. A believer is buying too much on credit and is destined to get into serious financial trouble if he doesn't change the habit of such indiscriminate buying. His discipler warns him of these dangers.

We need to warn people about false teaching that comes into the church in attractive ways. Paul warns us, "For the time is coming when people will not endure sound teaching, but having itching ears they will accumulate for themselves teachers to suit their own passions, and will turn away from listening to the truth and wander off into myths" (2 Tim. 4:3–4). Sometimes in our desire to be polite and civil with all people, we may not react as severely as Paul would have when he encountered false teaching. But accommodating falsehood is not a biblical attitude. Some fundamentalists, by their harsh and unreasonable opposition to questionable teaching, have brought disrepute to the biblical call to "contend for the faith that was once for all delivered to the saints" (Jude 3). But that should not cause us to abdicate this call. If our people are being misled, that is a grave concern. Love for them would compel us to do all we can to rid the church of the false teaching.

Rebuking. In 2 Timothy 4:2, after giving Timothy the "charge" to "preach the word," Paul specifies three ways Timothy should do so: "reprove, rebuke, and exhort." The first two words have a similar meaning—rebuking people when they have done wrong. The word rendered "reprove" here (*elenchō*) is translated elsewhere in the ESV as "rebuke" (1 Tim. 5:20; Titus 1:9, 13; 2:15). These references tell us that there are times when disciplers need to rebuke Christians for doing wrong. A Christian spreads unnecessary gossip about another believer and that causes some tensions in the group. Another gets angry and scolds a sister publicly, using bad language. A Christian is caught copying on an exam. A young woman refuses to help her sick mother with her work at home, preferring to enjoy fellowship with her Christian friends. These are all times when believers need to be rebuked.

Exhorting. After saying, "reprove, rebuke" in 2 Timothy 4:2, Paul adds, "and exhort." Sometimes what people need is positive exhortation on what they should do. A person who has been irregular with his devotions or with his church attendance should be clearly exhorted to set aside laziness and do what he must do to delight in the Lord.

I was discipling a young man who often got angry with his mother and sometimes scolded her in bad language. I used to meet him weekly, and we would do some ministry together. One day when I asked him how things were at home, he told me that he had spoken very badly to his mother. I told him that he must apologize to her and that I would ask him whether he had done so when we met the next week. Yet he did not apologize to her for the whole week. But just before leaving home to meet me, he went to his mother and said, "Ajith asked me to apologize to you; so I am apologizing," and quickly left home. It was a small start, but his relationship with his mother gradually improved as he learned to apply his Christianity at home.

With Patience and Teaching (2 Tim. 4:2)

Paul adds a caution to his call to rebuke and exhort. He says, "Reprove, rebuke, and exhort, with complete patience and teaching" (2 Tim. 4:2). We have a responsibility to rebuke people when they do wrong and to clearly instruct them about what they should do. But this must be done with self-control. Paul says elsewhere, "Be angry and do not sin" (Eph. 4:26). We get angry when our disciplees do foolish things because of our love for them, and we respond with rebuke. But this must always be tempered by "complete patience," which is also an aspect of love. Paul also says that the reproving and rebuking are to be done "with . . . teaching." Not only do we tell disciplees that they have done wrong; we also teach them why something is wrong and how Christians think and act in such situations. We may need to do some homework to find out more about the issue in order to be able to teach them correctly.

Winning a Hearing

Many Christians today resist warnings, rebuke, and exhortation from Christian leaders. They have seen or heard of the abuse and excessive control exerted by leaders in cultic groups. People are so eager to guard their independence today that they don't like the idea of others interfering with their lives. They are open to rebuke in a business setting, where people are paid for the work they do. But they think it has no place in a church or Christian organization, where people are supposed to be volunteers.

A key way to overcome this obstacle is to prove our concern for people through paying the price of commitment to them. In the first chapter we spoke about commitment as the key to parenthood. Such commitment gives leaders credibility, which encourages others to receive strong words of rebuke, when necessary.

Of all Paul's epistles, Galatians was the one in which he adopted his fiercest tone of rebuke. Would the people accept such sharp rebuke from Paul? Toward the end of the letter he says, "From now on let no one cause me trouble, for I bear on my body the marks of Jesus" (Gal. 6:17). Paul is saying, "Listen to me; take my words seriously; I have suffered for the gospel." He uses a similar argument in Ephesians: "I therefore, a prisoner for the Lord, urge you to walk in a manner worthy of the calling to which you have been called" (Eph. 4:1). Paul was writing from prison because of his commitment to the gospel. That gave him the credibility to "urge" the people.

This is how to overcome the effects that a selfish, individualistic culture can have on us: by being committed to our cause and to our people. Costly commitment nurtures trust, which gives disciplers the credibility to warn, rebuke, and exhort. Of course, such credibility may take time to develop. But those who persevere in loving, costly concern for their disciplees will see many reciprocate with trust that opens the door to disciplers frankly speaking into their lives.

———

The order of this chapter is important. There is passion in the discipling relationship—a passion for mission. Disciplers burn with the sense that they are involved in a great work. And they know that the persons they disciple have a vital role in that great work. So they are fired by ambition to help these people to become great for God. That ambition drives them to do all they can to help them to achieve the ambition. Disciplers protect them, warn them, rebuke them, and exhort them. But in presenting a model of greatness, they never forget that, in the kingdom of God, greatness is servanthood.

Part 2

HOW CHRISTIANS
CHANGE

7

The Change Process

But that is not the way you learned Christ! . . . you . . .
were taught . . . to put off your old self, which belongs to
your former manner of life and is corrupt through deceitful
desires, and to be renewed in the spirit of your minds, and
to put on the new self, created after the likeness of God in
true righteousness and holiness.

Ephesians 4:20–24

Indramany Somapala was a devout Buddhist who saw the dramatic
change in her brother's life after he was converted to Christianity after
attending a Youth for Christ evangelistic camp. She was so impressed
that she decided to come to our church. As someone devoted to acts
of kindness she found the life of Jesus irresistibly attractive. She became a "Christian" and was baptized in our church. Having suffered
several nervous breakdowns, she was not immediately freed from this
struggle with anxiety. If we noticed her coming close to a breakdown,
we would sometimes have her come to our home. She became one of
my wife's closest friends.

Soon we realized that, even though she had been baptized, Indramany had not fully understood the heart of the gospel of salvation
by grace through faith. She had replaced her Buddhist practices, like

going to the temple, meditating, giving alms to the poor, and showing kindness to the elderly, with Christian practices, like going to church, praying, tithing, and showing kindness to the needy. I think it took about seven years of exposure to the gospel for her to really understand the Christian idea of grace.

I do not know when she was really born again into the family of God. But once the gospel got hold of her, she became a radiant woman of God. Her weakness, which would trigger nervous breakdowns, became an ally, driving her to trust in God and develop a powerful life of prayer—especially intercessory prayer. She intensified her ministry of kindness to others, including our family. She continued to take her psychiatric medicine until she died, but she lived a vibrant Christian life of loving service. She died in her sixties a few years ago, after being run over by a bus while walking on the road. Like the funeral of Tabitha (Dorcas) in Acts, Indramany's funeral saw many testify to her life "full of good works and acts of charity" (Acts 9:36).

The Need for Change

When Paul described the change that takes place at salvation, he said: "If anyone is in Christ, he is a new creation. The old has passed away; behold, the new has come" (2 Cor. 5:17). But he knew that after salvation all Christians have many thoughts and actions that they still need to give up, and many they need to take on, as the quotation from Ephesians 4 at the beginning of this chapter indicates. There needs to be a massive shift in thinking in many areas. Jesus faced the same challenge with the disciples. A. B. Bruce says of the disciples, "At the time of their call they were exceedingly ignorant, narrow-minded, superstitious, full of Jewish prejudices, misconceptions, and animosities."[1] These wrong ideas did not leave them at once. Peter, for example, after Jesus's ascension to heaven, had to be jolted into realizing that Gentiles too could be saved through a vision and accompanying experiences. Jesus's method of effecting change in the thinking of the disciples is instructive to us, and I will refer to it often in this book.

---

1. A. B. Bruce, *Training of the Twelve* (1894; repr., Grand Rapids, MI: Kregel, 1971), 14.

Christian anthropologist Paul Hiebert explains that the "biblical view of transformation" includes "both a point and a process; this transformation has simple beginnings (a person can turn wherever he or she is), but radical, lifelong consequences." Hiebert continues, "It is not simply mental assent to a set of metaphysical beliefs, nor is it solely a positive feeling towards God. Rather it involves entering a life of discipleship and obedience in every area of our being and throughout the whole story of our lives."[2]

Some basic *beliefs* must change. Most people who come to Christ, whether from Christian backgrounds or not, previously depended on their good works to justify themselves. Just like Indramany, they too may take some time to understand the Christian teaching of salvation through grace mediated through the work of Christ. Some ingrained *practices* also must change. Many people come to God because they see him as an answer to their problems. While they may have understood that coming to Christ includes a change of lifestyle, they may not realize how dramatic that change needs to be. In the context of the Ephesians passage quoted above, Paul goes on to urge his readers to put off lying, sinning when angry, stealing, bitterness, and a few other sins (4:25–31). And he calls them to put on a lifestyle of kindness (4:32–5:2).

Christians in the West find that the community solidarity and commitment of Christianity clash with the individualism they have grown up with. In non-Western countries, some might consider it wrong to refuse to lie or take revenge in situations where the family honor is involved. All over the world, race and class prejudice is common among people who claim to have had a born-again experience, even many years after their spiritual rebirth.

In the verses quoted above, Paul writing to Ephesian Christians tells them that they should put off the things that characterized their former life and put on things that characterize the Christian life. Among the things to put off are their "manner of life" and their "desires" (4:22). And they are to "put on the new self, created after the likeness of God in true righteousness and holiness" (4:24). This comprehensive change does not take place automatically, right after conversion. If we do not

---

2. Paul G. Hiebert, *Transforming Worldviews: An Anthropological Understanding of How People Change* (Grand Rapids, MI: Baker Academic, 2008), 310.

address these areas in people's lives, there could be disastrous consequences. History is loaded with shameful examples of "born-again" Christians who have behaved corruptly when in power or have acted out of racial, caste, or class prejudice. Such areas of unholiness must be addressed early in the life of a new believer.

Three Agents of Change

There are three primary agents in the character formation or sanctification of a Christian. Within these three categories come several other means that God uses to change Christians.

The Word of God. The first agent is Scripture, as is shown in Jesus's statements "Sanctify them in the truth; your word is truth" (John 17:17) and "Already you are clean because of the word that I have spoken to you" (John 15:3). As we read the instructions of the Bible, we are urged to obey them, and resolving to do so, with God's help, makes us grow in holiness. Being exposed to the Scriptures also exposes us to the nature of God. When we spend time with God in prayer and in the Word, his nature permeates us, causing us to change without our even realizing it. When I got to know my wife and her family, they would use some expressions that I found strange. I would laugh when I heard these expressions. After a few years I found myself using the same expressions. It happened unconsciously. Paul said: "And we all, with unveiled face, beholding the glory of the Lord, are being transformed into the same image from one degree of glory to another. For this comes from the Lord who is the Spirit" (2 Cor. 3:18).

The work of the Spirit. The verse just quoted introduces the second source of character formation: the work of the Holy Spirit in our lives. Christian character is described as "the fruit of the Spirit" (Gal. 5:22–23). Peter talks of "the sanctification of the Spirit, for obedience to Jesus Christ" (1 Pet. 1:2). And Paul declares, "If by the Spirit you put to death the deeds of the body, you will live" (Rom 8:13). Sometimes this work of sanctification is attributed simply to God. Paul says to the Thessalonians, "Now may the God of peace himself sanctify you completely, and may your whole spirit and soul and body be kept blameless at the coming of our Lord Jesus Christ" (1 Thess. 5:23).

The life of holiness may involve giant leaps forward through powerful works of the Holy Spirit in what may be called crisis experiences. The apostles' experience at Pentecost is an example. Many Christians testify to a new level of holiness following a specific act of faith or surrender or rededication. But change generally takes place as a process. Martin Luther is credited with having described the growth of a Christian after conversion in this way: A person is rapidly declining in health because of a disease, and the doctors do not know its cause. Then the doctors correctly diagnose the disease and prescribe the appropriate medicine. He is not completely healed immediately upon starting to take the medicine. But from that point on, he improves until he is completely well. In the same way, after we experience conversion, there is a decisive turn in our lives, after which the movement is in the direction of holiness rather than sin and death.

The fellowship of believers. The third agent in character formation is fellowship with other Christians. Paul says, "So flee youthful passions and pursue righteousness, faith, love, and peace, along with those who call on the Lord from a pure heart" (2 Tim. 2:22). The writer to the Hebrews says, "And let us consider how to stir up one another to love and good works" (Heb. 10:24). The flight from evil and the pursuit of holiness occur with the aid of other Christians. Under the category of fellowship, we can also include the disciplers and the discipleship groups to which Christians belong. It is in community with them that some of the most marked changes take place. In the chapters that follow, we will see how God uses means like prayer, worship, chatting, and teaching in community, along with the understanding and affirmation of friends, to help Christians to grow and experience healing from wounds.

Three Kinds of Transformation

Hiebert talks of three kinds of transformation that take place when a person is converted.[3]

First, there is *cognitive transformation*, where a person's belief system changes. Certain facts about the gospel must be understood

---

3. See Hiebert, *Transforming Worldviews*, 312–14.

in order to exercise saving faith and to continue living the Christian life. We must believe these facts if we are to become open to receiving God's salvation and growing. The preaching and teaching of the Word and personal and group Bible study are among the means used in this kind of transformation.

Second, there is *affective transformation*, where we personally experience God. He speaks personally and specifically to our situation, he guides and comforts us in clearly recognizable ways, he assures us of our salvation through experiences that affirm our identity in Christ, and he intervenes in our lives and the lives of people near to us in miraculous ways. We change as we learn about God through these experiences, and we experience new depths of love, joy, peace, and freedom from guilt.

Third, there is *evaluative transformation*, where we evaluate the beliefs and practices of the prevailing culture. Those in keeping with the gospel (like honoring parents) are retained with a Christian flavor, and those which contradict the gospel (like sexual indulgence, prejudice, and dishonesty) are rejected. It would be good for Christians to discuss these cultural factors and see how they square with biblical teaching. When my children were young, we would sometimes watch television together and discuss from a Christian perspective what we saw in the programs and the commercials.

So our minds believe the truth of God; our hearts experience the love and power of God; and our wills obey the ways of God. It is sad that individual churches usually major on one of these three kinds of transformation and do not give sufficient emphasis to the other two. How health-giving is a church that demonstrates God's commitment to impacting believers completely! Below I will show how changes take place in disciples of Christ as God uses all three areas: their beliefs, their feelings, and their behavior.

The Role of the Discipler

God uses parents to play a key role in developing the character of children in earthly families. In a comparable way, spiritual parents play an important part in the development of the Christian character of their children. Parents mediate many of the blessings that come through the Word and the Spirit. Paul addressed the Galatians as "my little children, for whom I am again in the anguish of childbirth until Christ is formed in you!" (Gal. 4:19). He was comparing his role in the character-forming process of the Galatians to that of a mother going through labor pains to deliver a child!

———

The Scriptures tell us of several ways in which people change through entering into a discipling environment. That should not surprise us, considering that the change process is a complex one, involving our beliefs, feelings, and behavior. I will present some of these ways in the next few chapters.[4]

---

4. The sequence of the following chapters is not meant to imply an order of importance.

8

Learning the Truth

Sanctify them in the truth; your word is truth.

John 17:17

Most people initially *come to* Christ because he meets their personal needs. Soon they discover that some of their personal requests for which they earnestly pray are not granted. They may be tempted to turn away from Christ and seek refuge elsewhere, and some do. But they will *stay with* Christ if they realize that he is the truth.

After many of Christ's disciples turned back and stopped following him, Jesus asked the Twelve whether they also would "go away." Peter's response was, "Lord, to whom shall we go? You have the words of eternal life, and we have believed, and have come to know, that you are the Holy One of God" (John 6:68–69). The knowledge of the truth about Jesus kept them faithful to him. Jesus himself prayed, "Sanctify them in the truth; your word is truth" (John 17:17).

It is vitally important to get the truth of the Word into the lives of believers. As we saw in the last chapter, that is not an easy task. In this chapter we will look at some keys to teaching the truth to believers. But before that, we will look at the importance of helping Christians develop the practice of learning the truth by reading the Bible themselves.

Personal Reading of the Word

Today many people read the Bible to receive an inspiring word that lifts them up and gives them strength to face life. This is indeed one of the ways in which the Bible blesses us. But the primary reason for reading the Bible is to get God's thoughts into our lives so that we can become more Christlike people. Paul says, "All Scripture is . . . profitable for teaching, for reproof, for correction, and for training in righteousness, that the man of God may be complete, equipped for every good work" (2 Tim. 3:16–17). This is something we should drill into the minds of believers: we read the Bible to learn how to think and act. Psalm 1:2 shows how this happens by describing a righteous person:

> His delight is in the law of the LORD,
>   and on his law he meditates day and night. (Ps. 1:2)

A quotation variously attributed to John Wesley's mother, Susanna; to John Bunyan; and to D. L. Moody says, "This book will keep you from sin, or sin will keep you from this book." As the psalmist puts it,

> I have stored up your word in my heart,
>   that I might not sin against you. (Ps. 119:11)

As we are constantly exposed to God's Word, our lives change without our realizing what is happening. I mentioned above that after a few years of living with my wife, I found myself using expressions of hers that I once considered odd. I had unconsciously imbibed them through constant exposure to her. One of the surest ways to behold the glory of the Lord is to expose ourselves to his Word. Paul's words in this regard are worth quoting again: "And we all, with unveiled face, beholding the glory of the Lord, are being transformed into the same image from one degree of glory to another" (2 Cor. 3:18).

A thirst for the Scriptures is a good sign that a person is truly converted. As I have said, most people initially come to Christ because they believe he will meet their needs. Prayer is natural in such an approach to Christianity. But that is not the only sign that a person is really committed to Christ. A desire to be fed by the Word may be a surer sign that someone is truly born again. A spiritual life needs and wants feeding. Peter describes this hunger: "Like newborn infants, long for the pure spiritual milk, that by it you may grow up into salvation—if indeed you have tasted that the Lord is good" (1 Pet. 2:2–3).

A Christian leader once told me that a person he discipled was not reading the Word, despite constant reminders to do so. The leader, who had given him a guidebook to help him read the Bible, finally resorted to sending him a text message every day to remind him. Even that did not help. He finally came to the sad conclusion that, even though this person enjoyed fellowship and activities with other Christians, he might not be truly committed to Christ.

We need to give new believers some guidance on how to read the Bible and possibly give a daily devotional book that introduces them to the practice of reading the Bible. With time, they may develop their own methods of learning from the Bible. I like to recommend that they write down what God has taught them from their reading each day. I do this during my devotions and find it very helpful. I also recommend that they take a pencil to the Scriptures and underline or write notes as they read.

Today's digital generation, which gravitates more naturally to digital Bibles, needs to develop methods that help people harvest riches from the Word, as my generation does with paper Bibles. This could be one of the most important challenges facing advocates of Bible reading today. I challenge tech-savvy students of Scripture to devote themselves to this task and pave the way for a new generation of diligent digital Bible students.[1] Many Christians today are listening to Scripture using audio Bibles. Many do this when driving to and from work. Though this may have limitations in terms of concentrated learning, it is certainly a welcome development. The main thing is to ensure that we get the message taught in the text and meditate on it.

Leading Means Feeding

Jesus preached often to crowds. But he gave an important place in his schedule to teaching his twelve apostles. In this way, as in others, Jesus is a model to all leaders. Peter's public preaching, immortalized

---

1. I am grateful to the Rev. Renny Khoo of Kota Kinabalu, Malaysia, for alerting me to this need.

in his speeches recorded in Acts, had a massive influence on the history of Christianity. He was the leader of the first church. When Jesus restored him to ministry following his denial, Jesus summarized Peter's call with the words "Feed my lambs" (John 21:15). As Timothy Laniak says, "The Lord was emphasizing to Peter that *leading means feeding.*"[2]

Paul's list of qualifications for overseers in the church are very different from most lists used when selecting leaders today. Of the fifteen qualifications in 1 Timothy, only one has to do with ministerial ability. The rest have to do with reputation, character, and family life. Paul says, "An overseer must be . . . able to teach" (1 Tim. 3:2). The Greek verb *episkopeō*, corresponding to the noun translated "overseer" here (*episkopē*), "means to 'watch over' or 'look after' those in one's care."[3] We saw in chapter 1 that this is the job of the discipler. The best way a Christian leader can look after others is to help them find and do God's will for their lives. A key to achieving that is to direct them to God's Word through teaching. Anyone who wants to be a leader of others in the kingdom of God must learn skills in teaching.

Friendship-Building Teaching

In his final discourse before he died, Jesus told his disciples, "No longer do I call you servants, for the servant does not know what his master is doing; but I have called you friends, for all that I have heard from my Father I have made known to you" (John 15:15). The Twelve had been comprehensively taught by Jesus, and that had become the basis of his friendship with them. The friendship grew over the three years he was constantly with them. A little later that same evening, Jesus said in his High Priestly Prayer, "I have manifested your name to the people whom you gave me out of the world" (John 17:6). Leon Morris explains that "to manifest the name of God is . . . to reveal the essential nature of God to people."[4] This is our great aim in discipling.

---

2. Timothy S. Laniak, *While Shepherds Watch Their Flocks: Forty Daily Reflections on Biblical Leadership* (n.p.: ShepherdLeader, 2007), 61 (italics his).

3. Linda Belleville, "Commentary on 1 Timothy," in Linda Belleville, Jon C. Laansma, and J. Ramsey Michaels, *1 Timothy, 2 Timothy, Titus, Hebrews*, Cornerstone Biblical Commentary (Carol Stream, IL: Tyndale, 2009), 66.

4. Leon Morris, *The Gospel according to John*, The New International Commentary on the New Testament (Grand Rapids, MI: Eerdmans, 1995), 640.

As A. W. Tozer has famously said, "What comes into our minds when we think about God is the most important thing about us."[5] That is what determines our actions.

Let's look at how Jesus did this friendship-building teaching about God.

Time Spent Together

Right at the start of Jesus's ministry, when John the Baptist was with two of his disciples, Jesus walked by, and they heard John say for the second time, "Behold, the Lamb of God!" (John 1:36). They began to follow Jesus, and when Jesus asked them what they were seeking, they asked him, "Where are you staying?" Jesus's answer, "Come and you will see," resulted in their going to the home where Jesus was staying. It was four in the afternoon, "and they stayed with him that day" (John 1:38–39). Scholars are not agreed on whether that meant they spent the night with him or they stayed with him till the end of that day. Either way, it was a foretaste of a pattern throughout the ministry of Jesus. The Savior of the world would spend time with people, especially his disciples. One disciple of John, Andrew, not only became one of the apostles; he also brought his brother Simon (Peter) to Jesus (John 1:40–42).

Three times in John 1:38–39 the Greek word *menō* is used to speak of Jesus and his two new friends "staying." Elsewhere in John (especially John 15) this word conveys the key concept of abiding in Christ.[6] John seems to be introducing that concept as he describes the first encounter Jesus had with prospective disciples. He was a teacher who was going to have deep relationships by spending extended times with his students. As Robert Coleman put it, "They were his spiritual children (Mark 10:24; John 13:33; 21:5), and the only way that a father can properly raise a family is to be with it."[7] It is not surprising, then, to find that the first reason given for Jesus appointing the Twelve was "that they might be with him." Their mission to "preach" and "cast out demons" is mentioned only after that (Mark 3:14–15).

5. A. W. Tozer, *The Knowledge of the Holy* (New York: Harper & Brothers, 1961), 9.

6. See D. A. Carson, *The Gospel according to John*, The Pillar New Testament Commentary (Grand Rapids, MI: Eerdmans; Leicester, UK: Inter-Varsity Press, 1991), 155.

7. Robert E. Coleman, *The Master Plan of Evangelism* (Grand Rapids, MI: Revell, 1993), 38.

As his ministry began to grow, Jesus intentionally took his disciples away from the crowds so that he could teach them. For this purpose, he sometimes went to Gentile territory, where he was relatively unknown. Mark records that he went to Tyre and Sidon, northwest of Israel (Mark 7:24). Then Mark reports that he was in the regions of Decapolis, on the eastern side of the Sea of Galilee (Mark 7:31). A little later, Mark says he was in the villages of Caesarea Philippi, on the northeast side of the Sea of Galilee (Mark 8:27). All these cities had largely Gentile populations. Later still Mark says, "They went on from there and passed through Galilee. And he did not want anyone to know, for he was teaching his disciples" (Mark 9:30–31).

The Gospels often report that Jesus was in the homes of his close friends, such as Simon, Matthew, and Lazarus. It was the same with Paul. Luke and Acts give special prominence to homes and hospitality.[8] There is something warm about being in one's house, especially when eating together. Being in the most important place in people's lives fosters an openness and depth in the relationship. I know that in the West, and now in the non-Western world also, people often go out to restaurants when they want to have a meal together. But there is something to be said about intimate friends, such as those in a discipling relationship, being in each other's homes. This is a warm setting for teaching.

I try occasionally to have my discipling appointments in the home of the disciplee. Then I can meet not only with the disciplee but also with his family members. In an article that describes how important hospitality was in the Bible, Christine Pohl says, "These shared meals provide an important setting for [Jesus's] teachings on divine and human hospitality."[9] Pohl's book *Making Room* seeks to show that "although hospitality was central to Christian identity and practice in earlier centuries, our generation knows little about its life-giving character."[10]

After his resurrection, Jesus's time on earth was almost exclusively spent with the disciples. And much of that time was spent teaching.

---

8. On this see Ajith Fernando, *Acts*, NIV Application Commentary (Grand Rapids, MI: Zondervan, 1998), 127–28.

9. Christine D. Pohl, "Hospitality," in *Dictionary of Scripture and Ethics*, ed. Joel B. Green (Grand Rapids, MI: Baker Academic), 379.

10. Christine D. Pohl, *Making Room: Recovering Hospitality as a Christian Tradition* (Grand Rapids, MI: Eerdmans, 1999). The quotation is from the publisher's publicity.

Luke says, "He presented himself alive to them after his suffering by many proofs, appearing to them during forty days and speaking about the kingdom of God" (Acts 1:3). On one beautiful occasion, the disciples came to the shore after fishing all night to find Jesus preparing breakfast for them (John 21:9–13). The gloriously risen Lord was still their friend.

The longer times that Jesus spent away from the crowds and with the disciples correspond to retreats that discipleship groups can spend together today. Away from the rush of life in ordinary society, the group can spend time talking and enjoying fellowship. I strongly recommend this as a regular practice for all discipleship groups. The place does not have to be high-class and costly. The main agenda is being with each other. The richness of the time is the richness of the fellowship and not the plushness of the facilities.

Here are some of the things my discipleship group at church does. Some days we eat dinner in the home of a member, sometimes inviting the other family members to join for the meal. At least once a year we go on a day-long retreat to chat, enjoy a river swim, study the Scriptures, share our needs, and pray for each other. We have gone as a group to have fun by the sea. Sometimes members of the group join me in visiting people connected with our church who are struggling with a need. In all these activities we act as friends enjoying being with each other.

Teaching by Example

When Jesus was with his disciples, teaching was taking place through his example. His basic call to them was "follow me," which included being with him, observing, and learning through that. Coleman notes that "the natural informality of this teaching method of Jesus stood in striking contrast to the formal, almost scholastic procedures of the scribes." He says, "The religious teachers insisted on the disciples adhering strictly to certain rituals and formulas of knowledge which distinguished them from others; whereas Jesus asked only that his disciples follow hm."[11] He projected his life to them as an example to follow. After the washing

---

11. Coleman, *Master Plan of Evangelism*, 33–34.

of the disciples' feet, he clearly told them that they should do as he did (John 13:15). On another occasion he said, "Take my yoke upon you, and learn from me, for I am gentle and lowly in heart, and you will find rest for your souls" (Matt. 11:29). On many other occasions the implication is clear that he intended them to act as he did.

Paul adopted a similar approach to ministry. Six times he asked his readers to follow his example (1 Cor. 4:16; 11:1; Phil. 3:17; 4:9; 1 Thess. 1:6; 2 Thess. 3:9). He once told Timothy, "You, however, have followed my teaching, my conduct, my aim in life, my faith, my patience, my love, my steadfastness, my persecutions and sufferings that happened to me" (2 Tim. 3:10–11). Donald Guthrie observes that the Greek word translated "have followed" (*parakoloutheō*) carries the meaning "to trace out as an example."[12] William Mounce explains that "almost every virtue . . . [mentioned in 2 Tim. 3:10–11] appears elsewhere in the [Pastoral Epistles] in an admonition to Timothy, either using the same word or the same concept."[13] Timothy was being told to behave in the way he had seen Paul behave. That is how Christian truth is communicated: both by word and by demonstration.

The knowledge that we are examples to those we disciple is a great incentive along the discipler's path to holiness. Sometimes when those I disciple tell me about the temptations they face, I realize that I too face the same temptations. I am spurred to ensure that I get my act together and be a model to those I disciple.

Learning by Experiencing Life Together

Many of the key teachings of Jesus emerged from events that took place in his ministry. A question or an event would present a teaching situation. The following examples are from the start of his ministry as recorded in Luke:

- On his first visit to Nazareth Jesus sensed a hesitancy of the people in his hometown to fully accept his authenticity. This prompted a discourse on how God worked with Gentiles like the widow of Zarephath and Naaman the Syrian (4:22–30).

12. Donald Guthrie, *The Pastoral Epistles: An Introduction and Commentary*, Tyndale New Testament Commentaries (Downers Grove, IL: InterVarsity Press, 1990), 178.
13. William D. Mounce, *Pastoral Epistles*, Word Biblical Commentary (Dallas: Word, 2000), 556.

- The next conversation was after the record haul of fish caught after the fishermen listened to Jesus. Seeing this, Peter responded in fear over his own sinfulness. Jesus allayed the fishermen's fears and told them that they would have a new vocation of catching men. Their response was to leave everything and follow him (5:4–11). Seeing the power of God at work and listening to a few words from Christ resulted in their making a total commitment to Christ.

- Next, Jesus demonstrated his ability to forgive sin by healing a paralytic. Jesus spoke only a few words but taught a profound lesson about who he was (5:18–26).

- The astonishment over Jesus partying with tax collectors started a conversation culminating in his saying that the righteous had no need of him and that he came to call sinners to repentance (5:27–32).

- A question about why his disciples didn't fast elicited a discourse about patching torn garments, and about new and old wineskins (5:33–39).

- A question about the behavior of the disciples on the Sabbath resulted in a proclamation that Jesus was Lord of the Sabbath (6:1–5).

These key teachings were not issues raised by the disciples themselves, but the disciples were with him each time. And each incident sparked teachings that the disciples preserved so that they were recorded as essential aspects of the truth about Christ in the Gospels. We must wait till the sixth chapter of Luke to find the first lengthy teaching discourse of Jesus (6:20–49).

This kind of learning while experiencing life together helps new believers grasp Christian principle that are difficult to practice. One such principle is that of not taking revenge. In our Sri Lankan culture, when one is insulted or hurt, it is considered dishonorable and wrong *not* to take revenge. Some three times in situations of conflict when my wife and I advised hurt Christians not to take revenge, we were told that not taking revenge may be acceptable to us mature Christians but was an impossible path for them to take. However, I found that as we stayed with them, sharing their pain and chatting lovingly, they gradually began to accept the Christian way of not taking revenge. The doctrine in the mind was put into practice in real-life situations and shown to be an acceptable way to live.

Verbal Instruction

I am sure you have heard people say, "Truth is caught and not taught." That clearly was not Jesus's philosophy of teaching. Truth was caught *and* taught in his ministry. The disciples caught truth by observing him. But Jesus also taught them verbally. His teaching took place through informal conversations and more-formal discourses.

Learning by Chatting

The classic text on conversational learning is Moses's instruction to families: "And these words that I command you today shall be on your heart. You shall teach them diligently to your children, and shall talk of them when you sit in your house, and when you walk by the way, and when you lie down, and when you rise" (Deut. 6:6–7). The picture here is that of a family constantly talking about things related to God's Word.

The informal teaching sessions of Christ show him to be a conversational teacher. The incidents we looked at above took place while Jesus was ministering in public. But there were other times in Luke when conversations among the disciples brought out great truths from their Master:

- Chapter 8 has important teaching in response to the request from the disciples for an explanation of the parable of the sower (8:9–15).
- Chapter 9 records Jesus giving the disciples instructions before they go out on a mission (9:1–6).
- In the same chapter, we have the famous conversation when, in response to a question by Jesus, Peter confesses that Jesus is the Christ. This leads to Jesus explaining the heart of his mission and the terms of being a disciple (9:18–27).
- Later in the chapter, the disciples argue as to who is the greatest. This unpleasant conversation results in great teachings about humble spirituality (9:46–48).

A discipler, then, is a conversational teacher. In chapter 6 I described how, in my youth, I learned so much from conversations had when traveling with Dr. Sam Sherrard and Dr. Robert Coleman on ministry assignments.

Some conversations among Christians are loaded with gossip and small talk. Shallow talk is inevitable with short meetings. That is why we need to ensure that we have opportunities for long conversations with a few people. I like to use the term "holy conversation" for this kind of chatting. The phrase has had different meanings in history and perhaps could be misleading. But I think you can get the idea I am trying to communicate: Christians having long talks from a Christian perspective. Few things in life are as pleasant as that. C. S. Lewis says of such conversations, "Life—natural life—has no better gift to give."[14]

We need to bring such conversations back into the life of the church. And they do not need to be confined to spiritual topics. Spiritual concerns, of course, are vitally important. It is also very important for us to converse on so-called "secular" topics like sports, politics, and economics. But these conversations are done against the backdrop of our Christian convictions. Then we learn to look at sports, politics, and economics from a Christian perspective. A failure to integrate ordinary life into Christianity would result in unhealthy and ineffective Christians.

Learning through More-Formal Teaching

Jesus also had longer, more-formal teaching sessions, like the Sermon on the Mount (Matthew 5–7) and the discourse about the future (Matthew 24–25). Longer discourses have been a time-tested way of teaching Christians and should not be neglected in our pursuit of more-interactive teaching methods. Biblical sermons, congregational Bible studies, and small group Bible studies should be key ingredients in the life of any Christian community.

The discipleship group I lead meets only once every three weeks. That frequency may be sufficient when one is mentoring a group of leaders. Our group has Christians who are not leaders. But we were

---

14. C. S. Lewis, *The Four Loves* (New York: Harcourt, Brace, 1960), 105.

forced into that pattern because of our schedules. Given the infrequency of our meetings, they are long—generally three to four hours. Usually we chat during the first hour. That conversation includes talk about ethical, political, and sporting issues and the like, as well as theological issues. We could spend our whole time doing this. But I need to make sure that we get to our Bible study time, which occupies our second hour. Here too we could get sidetracked on an issue and move away from the text. Unless I feel the issue is very important, I will strenuously endeavor to bring us back to the text. The third hour is given for sharing our individual experiences and needs and praying for each other and for other needs. Leaders must ensure that the Word has priority in the agenda.

It goes without saying that helping people discover what is in the Scriptures gets them actively involved in the learning process and increases the chances of their internalizing the truth. Questions that help them discover what the Scriptures say also help keep the participants alert. And such questions give them practice in how to handle the Scriptures, which they can use in their personal study. Always the Word is basic, but we can use various methods in helping people to get its message into their innermost being.

Generally, small group meetings today do not devote sufficient time to studying the Word. There will be time for chatting, for praising God, for testimonies, for presenting needs, and for praying. But with little time left for a study, usually only a short devotional is shared. People who come for a meeting may feel inspired, but a vital opportunity to teach the Word has been missed. And that teaching is essential for growth in the Christian life. Of course, having a Bible study makes demands on the leader. I usually go through a book with my group. This means I need to devote time to studying the passage and preparing the study. But I see this as an important aspect of my service to the group.

Culturally Appropriate Teaching Methods

The methods used in teaching must be creatively chosen by the teacher. The Word must be uppermost, but the unchanging Word can be presented in different ways, as the Bible itself presents its truth. This is particularly so with people who are not used to learning truth through reading. Today they are called oral learners. The International Orality Network defines oral learners as "people from all over the globe, from all walks of life and all levels of education who learn primarily or exclusively through oral, not textual means." It says, "While some oral communicators learn this way out of necessity because they cannot read or write with understanding, others simply prefer non-print forms of communication." The network claims, "Studies have shown that 80% of the world's population are oral communicators—that is approximately 5.7 billion people!" It asserts that the lives of people are "more likely to be transformed through stories, songs, drama, proverbs and media."[15]

The biblical prophets used many different methods to get their message across. Jeremiah and Ezekiel used rather striking enacted prophecies. Jesus's miracles were also occasions for people to learn truth. An esteemed lexicon explains that in the Gospel of John the commonly occurring Greek word *sēmeion*, meaning sign, used for Christ's miracles, does not mean "simply a miraculous event but something which points to a reality with even greater significance."[16] After the feeding of the five thousand, John presents Jesus's teaching about being the Bread of Life (John 6). After the healing of a man born blind, Jesus talks about being the Light of the World and about spiritual blindness (John 9).

People learn truth not only by logical argumentation. Sometimes they learn truth by sensing its reality through an experience they have or something they have observed. The unchanging truth of the Word is always foundational, but the way it is learned may vary. Because of this, the Bible is loaded with stories. The parables are characteristic of the teaching of Jesus. This method is particularly relevant in teaching the truth to people in non-Western cultures. Buddhist and Hindu doctrine is communicated mainly through stories. Postmodernists, with their emphasis on the subjective truth, are also more open to listening to stories.[17] We can use that means to lead them to the objective truth

---

15. "Who Are Oral Communicators," ION (website), accessed June 15, 2018, https://orality.net/about/who-are-oral-communicators/.

16. Johannes P. Louw and Eugene A. Nida, *Greek-English Lexicon of the New Testament: Based on Semantic Domains*, 2nd ed., vol. 1 (New York: United Bible Societies, 1996), 442.

17. For treatments on using story in evangelism, see Leighton Ford, *The Power of Story: Rediscovering the Oldest, Most Natural Way to Reach People for Christ* (Colorado Springs: NavPress,

in the Bible. The biblical method of using stories, then, is appropriate for converts all over the world, not only in evangelism but also in discipling.[18]

A number of chapter titles in Jay Moon's book *Intercultural Discipleship* helpfully challenge us to find the best way to communicate truth:

- Chapter 4. "Symbols Speak When Words Can't"
- Chapter 5. "Rituals Drive Meaning Deep into the Bone"
- Chapter 7. "Stories Portray It, Not Just Say It"
- Chapter 8. "Proverbs Are Worth a Thousand Words"
- Chapter 9. "Music, Dance, and Drama—We Become What We Hum"
- Chapter 10. "Holistic Discipleship Connects Word and Deed"[19]

We must discover how people best learn truth and see if we can use those methods appropriately in our teaching. We will discuss some of those methods in the remainder of this and the next few chapters.

Learning through Corporate Worship

Hymns as Teaching Tools

Worship is a wonderful way for people to learn truth because, ideally, in worship one's body, mind, and heart are actively involved. Such simultaneous involvement of different faculties can result in truth being more effectively internalized.

Hymn singing was so much a part of the Methodist revival in Britain in the eighteenth century that some Methodist hymnbooks began with the statement "Methodism was born in Song."[20] In an influential book on English hymnody written almost a century ago, Louis Benson says that the Methodist hymns were "the result of the

---

1994); and Christine Dillon, *Telling the Gospel through Story: Evangelism That Keeps Hearers Wanting More* (Downers Grove, IL: InterVarsity Press, 2012).

18. For the use of stories in discipleship see Christine Dillon, *Stories Aren't Just for Kids: Busting Ten Myths about Bible Storytelling* (2017); available at Kindle and free at ibooks, Barnes & Noble, and Kobo.

19. W. Jay Moon, *Intercultural Discipleship: Learning from Global Approaches to Spiritual Formation* (Grand Rapids, MI: Baker Academic, 2017).

20. *The Methodist Hymn Book* (London: Methodist Publishing House, 1933), v.

Revival experiences with the poor and unlettered."[21] The early Methodist leaders realized that with poorer, semiliterate people, hymns were a good way to communicate gospel truth and Christian doctrine. As I said above, many people who come to Christ today are not functionally literate and not used to learning through lecture-style presentations. While we must never downplay the importance of preaching and formal teaching, we can say that singing is a key to nurturing new believers today also.

In his preface to his hymnbook published in 1780, the founder of Methodism, John Wesley, said, "The hymns are not carelessly jumbled together, but carefully ranged under proper heads, according to the experience of real Christians. So that this book is in effect *a little body of experimental and practical divinity.*"[22] It was a book of theology! This kind of topical arrangement of hymns was a new development in English hymnody, though around the same time, evangelical Anglicans John Newton and William Cowper also published a topically arranged hymnbook called *Olney Hymns.*[23] Wesley knew that the experience of singing would be an effective way for people to learn and remember doctrines. Many people were not educated or literate, so they would find it difficult to learn doctrine through the more traditional types of formal education.

When people from other faiths were converted to Christ and joined our church, we primarily used songs that could be sung to a drum beat, rather than the translated hymns with an unfamiliar musical style. The drum is more important than other instruments to many converts in our context. But because I wanted them to get a taste of the wonderful heritage of hymns in the church, I tried to use at least one translated historic English hymn for each service. Some members would tell me that they couldn't sing those songs! Third- and fourth-generation Christians had no difficulty getting into the mood of these translated hymns. But not new Christians unaccustomed to eighteenth- and nineteenth-century Western tunes. This made me wish

---

21. Louis F. Benson, *The English Hymn* (London: Hodder and Stoughton, 1915), 248; cited by Oliver A. Beckerlegge, in the introduction to the bicentennial edition of John Wesley, *The Works of John Wesley*, vol. 7, *A Collection of Hymns for the Use of The People Called Methodists*, ed. Franz Hildebrandt and Oliver A. Beckerlegge, rev. ed. (Nashville: Abingdon, 1989), 62.

22. Wesley, *Collection of Hymns*, 74 (italics mine).

23. Beckerlegge, introduction, 27.

some of the great old hymns were translated in a way that they could be sung in our indigenous style of music. (I haven't attempted to do this, as this is not an area of personal giftedness.)

I also began to use a familiar concept to introduce a not-so-familiar concept during worship. For example, our people can naturally and lustily sing the Sinhala translation of the chorus "Is there anything too hard for the Lord. / No nothing is too hard for the Lord," using the Western tune, which lends itself to a drum beat. Most of our members came to Christ attracted by the power of God to heal or meet some other need. So the power of God was a key aspect of their belief system. After this song, I used the song by the great Salvation Army leader Albert Orsborn:

> Let the beauty of Jesus be seen in me,
> All his wondrous compassion and purity,
> O thou Spirit divine, all my nature refine,
> Till the beauty of Jesus is seen in me.[24]

This is a song about holiness, a theme our new believers do not necessarily associate very readily with their experience of Christianity. As we shall see below, many think holiness is a good thing in principle but impossible to practice. The earlier song proclaimed that nothing is too hard for the Lord—a theme they are familiar with. This song affirms that one of the things not too hard for the Lord to do is make us holy. Two strategically placed songs helped teach an unfamiliar doctrine.

I recommend that sometimes before singing, a brief introduction of about two or three sentences be given to the doctrine represented by the song. Then the people can orient themselves to engaging with the words being sung. Often the joy of worship in today's worship revolution is through emotionally stirring tunes that give an atmosphere of spiritual exhilaration. We can use this as an opportunity to teach vital truths about Christianity. But a song introduction must be brief. Otherwise, people will lose the momentum or attitude of worshipful

---

24. Albert Orsborn, "Let the Beauty of Jesus," accessed September 4, 2017, https://www.salvationist.org/songbook.nsf/vw_us_al/C127F2877A4CD2238025669B005043C2?Open Document. In public domain.

singing. We need to ensure that the people remain fully engaged (and music has a way of doing that). In this way a doctrinal lesson harnesses the emotional power of singing. It should be evident from what I am saying that I do not think being engaged emotionally during worship is a bad thing!

A case could be made that all the segments of public worship are means of teaching: the call to worship, the prayers, the announcements, the readings, the giving of offerings, the sermon, the Lord's Supper, the benediction, and even what happens after the benediction. Those who lead worship should plan the service in such a way that every element is a means of growth for the participants.

Bible Christians: An Alien Idea

A Different Attitude toward Scripture

We saw earlier that Paul described how the Word nurtures Christians to maturity: "All Scripture is . . . profitable for teaching, for reproof, for correction, and for training in righteousness, that the man of God may be complete, equipped for every good work" (2 Tim. 3:16–17).

Many people who come to Christ today have not had such an attitude toward religious scriptures. Buddhists and Hindus may rise up in anger if they feel that their scriptures have been insulted in any way. But most don't see their scriptures as containing absolute truth that they can and must follow scrupulously in daily life. Most Buddhists in Sri Lanka recite the *Pancha Sila* or the five precepts of Buddhism daily. One of them is that they will not lie. But lying is a part of the culture, as it is in most South Asian countries. Sadly, many Christians also view the ethical demands of the Bible in a similar way. They think that lying and taking revenge are "necessary evils" in today's world.

Or take the issue of abstinence from sexual relations before marriage. Many Westerners who come to Christ do so from a background that accepts extramarital sex as normal. Given the power of hormones experienced since the teen years, it would require a major change in their thinking to believe that extramarital sex is not acceptable. One news story reported that research has shown that teaching abstinence to teenagers is not effective and, in fact, can be harmful. That is because many Americans marry in their thirties and cannot wait till then to have sex. Therefore, the researchers said that teenagers need instruction not about abstinence but about methods of contraception.[25]

So we live in an age when society in general tends to think that obedience to absolute truths taught in religious texts is not necessary or desirable. Today's discipler faces a major challenge when presenting the Christian ethic of living under the Scriptures.

The Holy Spirit Will Change Our Attitudes

We must not be disheartened by this challenge. The first thing to remember is that we are working with people indwelt by the Holy Spirit. Jesus promises his disciples that the Holy Spirit will "teach you all things . . . , will convict the world concerning sin and righteousness and judgment . . . [and] he will guide you into all the truth" (John 14:26; 16:8, 13). Paul says, "The Spirit of God dwells in you . . . ," and the "sons of God" are "led by the Spirit of God" (Rom. 8:9, 14). Surely included in this work of the Holy Spirit in the believer is the orienting of our thoughts to see not only that the way of God is correct but also that it is desirable and possible to obey. We must not discount the significance of the direct work of the Holy Spirit in believers to convince them about the truth of God's ways and to guide and empower them to follow those ways.

Teach What the Word Says about Itself

Deuteronomy speaks often about the miraculous way in which God gave the Word to his people. Moses says that the people "came near and stood at the foot of the mountain, while the mountain burned with fire to the heart of heaven, wrapped in darkness, cloud, and gloom" (4:11). Then he says: "The LORD spoke to you out of the midst of the fire. You heard the sound of words, but saw no form; there was only a voice" (4:12). There are eleven references in Deuteronomy to God speaking his Word "out of the fire" (4:12, 15, 33, 36; 5:4, 22, 23, 24, 26; 9:10; 10:4). If the Bible repeats something so often, it must be important, even to us today. It tells us that God authenticated the

---

25. CBS Chicago WBBM News Radio, August 2017.

revelation he was giving in miraculous ways so that the people would know that the truth communicated was unique.[26] The intent was that people respect the Word and fear to disobey it. This attitude is well represented in Isaiah 66:2:

> But this is the one to whom I will look:
>> he who is humble and contrite in spirit
>> and trembles at my word.

Mature Christians have an attitude of penitent humility that makes them look at disobedience to the miraculously given Word with fear.

This attitude is sadly rare among Christians today. We are perplexed when children of evangelical parents, children who grew up in the church, respond to some of the contemporary controversial issues in ways at odds with Scripture. For example, many children of evangelicals would not be upset about legalizing homosexual marriage. They may themselves prefer heterosexual marriage but concede that if someone wants to "give full expression to his sexual orientation," they are not going to oppose it. The Bible, of course, is clear that homosexual relations are sinful. But they don't seem afraid to support a view contradicted in the Bible.

How did this happen? I think one reason is that people have not looked at the Bible as the clear guide for assessing what is right and what is wrong. They have gone to the Bible for inspiration, not for instruction. Sermons and Bible studies have "blessed the people" but not helped inculcate a fear of God and of disobedience to the Word. When the issue of homosexual marriage came up, the children of evangelicals did not look to the Bible as the primary place to find out whether it was right or wrong. We need to nurture people who will view the Bible the way John Wesley did when he said, "My ground is the Bible. . . . I follow it in all things, both great and small"[27]—people who tremble at God's Word (Isa. 66:2).[28]

---

26. The preceding sentences are adapted from my book, *The Family Life of a Christian Leader* (Wheaton, IL: Crossway, 2016), 196.

27. A. Skevington Wood, *The Burning Heart: John Wesley, Evangelist* (Grand Rapids, MI: Eerdmans, 1967), 212.

28. This section grew out of a conversation I had with Pastor Mike Woods of the Xenos Fellowship in Columbus, Ohio.

Let People See the Word Applied

Disciplers can also demonstrate how the authority of Scripture is applied in their lives and ministries. When people see us letting the Bible drive our thinking and acting, they will see the practical applicability of the Scriptures demonstrated in real life. Robert Coleman observes that "in the Gospels, there are at least ninety separate instances in which Jesus referred to the [Old Testament], either by direct quotation, allusion to an event, or language similar to biblical expressions." That would expand to 160 references "counting duplication in parallel accounts."[29] The disciples would have soon realized how important the Old Testament was to the thinking and acting of Jesus. They themselves adopted a similar approach to truth. Coleman also observes, "References to the Old Testament, either by direct quotation, synopsis of a passage, or allusion to some event, occur nearly 200 times in the Acts, mostly in the apostles' sermons."[30] The early Christians grew up seeing the Word applied to daily life.

I consider my mother to be the most important Bible teacher in my life. She was converted to Christ from Buddhism in her teens and never had any formal biblical training. But she was a woman of the Word. It was clear to us that her actions were directed by Scripture. The importance of the Bible and its authority and of being obedient to it was burned into our hearts. At that time the church in Sri Lanka was strongly influenced by a liberal attitude toward the Bible. But my four siblings and I have not wavered from the commitment to the Scriptures that we saw in our mother.

In the same way, if we want to see our disciplees develop healthy attitudes toward Scripture, we too should model living under its authority in the way we live and minister. When I was about twenty years old, a friend—after hearing me preach—advised me that whenever I preach, all my major points should come from the Scriptures. Still, almost fifty years later, I try to follow that principle. We should let our disciplees know that whenever we are asked a question, the primary thing we look for to answer it is what the Bible says. When we talk about things happening in society and about what we see in

---

29. Robert E. Coleman, *The Mind of the Master* (Shippensburg, PA: Destiny Image, 2000), 54.
30. Robert E. Coleman, *The Master Plan of Discipleship* (Old Tappan, NJ: Revell, 1987), 105.

the media, we should model evaluating them by biblical criteria. It would encourage disciplees to hear about recent discoveries we have made and lessons we have learned when reading the Bible in our daily devotions. If they see such an attitude toward Scripture in us, they will almost unconsciously incorporate it into their own lives.

——

The atmosphere we create of submitting to the Word and the accountability we ask of our disciplees regarding their personal exposure to the Word will help them become people of the Word. I know a vibrant, witnessing Christian who cannot read. I once saw him at a camp, all by himself, in what seemed to be deep thought. His leader told me that he was having his devotions. Though illiterate, he would listen carefully to the Scripture lessons and sermon on Sunday and use what he remembered for his devotions during the week. He was a Bible Christian.

9

Praying

When you get to heaven and realize all that prayer did on this earth, you will be ashamed that you prayed so poorly.
William E. Sangster[1]

The British Methodist preacher William E. Sangster has telling words about intercessory prayer (above). The Bible presents prayer as an important means of influencing people. Paul mentions praying for his readers in ten of his thirteen letters, and he asks for prayer from his readers in eight of his letters. Peter asks that the apostles be released from some administrative tasks so that they can "devote [themselves] to prayer and to the ministry of the word" (Acts 6:4). One aspect of this life of prayer would be praying for the people they lead. Samuel told the people of Israel, "Moreover, as for me, far be it from me that I should sin against the Lord by ceasing to pray for you, and I will instruct you in the good and the right way" (1 Sam. 12:23). As in Peter's statement, here too, teaching the Word and prayer are presented as two primary roles of a leader.

Praying for Disciplees
While prayer for the people we lead in general is very important, so is prayer for those we are particularly discipling. Twice Paul uses the

---

1. William E. Sangster, *Teach Me to Pray* (1959; repr., Nashville: Upper Room, 1999), 29.

phrase "night and day" in connection with his praying. Once it is about his earnest desire to visit the Thessalonians (1 Thess. 3:10). The other time it is about his prayers for Timothy, to whom he says, "I remember you constantly in my prayers night and day" (2 Tim. 1:3).

The twenty-six-verse-long High Priestly Prayer is the longest prayer of Christ recorded in the Gospels (John 17:1–26). In seventeen of these verses he is praying for his disciples. The only time the Gospels report Jesus talking about his prayer life is when he tells Peter, shortly before Peter denies Christ: "I have prayed for you that your faith may not fail. And when you have turned again, strengthen your brothers" (Luke 22:32).[2] These two prayers of Jesus are "discipling prayers," that God would change the way his disciples think and act.

The name Scudder has a prominent place in South Asian Christian history. John Scudder came to Ceylon (Sri Lanka) in 1819 as the first medical foreign missionary sent from the United States. After several years in Sri Lanka, the Scudder family moved to Madras (now known as Chennai), India. The Scudders had thirteen children, nine of whom lived to adulthood. Of these, seven became medical missionaries and pastors in India.[3] Their grandchild Ida is the best known of the Scudders. After seeing women "who were deprived of medical services due to the lack of female physicians,"[4] she gave up her determination not to be a missionary and started a hospital and medical school that are now two of the most prestigious medical institutions in India.

John Scudder has said that his children were literally prayed into the kingdom by their mother. She had a practice of spending the birthday of each child praying for that child.[5] Praying is one of the most important things parents do for their children. This is true of both physical and spiritual parents.

We noted in the first chapter that Paul used the word *agōnizomai*, meaning wrestling, fighting, battling, or struggling, for discipling (Col. 1:29). He used the same verb when he told the Colossians,

---

2. Robert E. Coleman makes this point in *The Mind of the Master* (Shippensburg, PA: Destiny Image, 2000), 38.

3. Gary J. Bekker, "Scudder, John, Sr. (1793–1855)," in *Dictionary of Christianity in America*, ed. D. G. Reid et al. (Downers Grove, IL: InterVarsity Press, 1990).

4. Ruth A. Tucker, "Scudder, Ida Sophia (1870–1959)," in Reid, *Dictionary of Christianity in America*.

5. I recall reading this many years ago, though I no longer have the source.

"Epaphras, who is one of you . . . , [is] always struggling on your behalf in his prayers, that you may stand mature and fully assured in all the will of God" (Col. 4:12). The NIV translates this verb (a participle) here as "wrestling." Epaphras was "a Christian from Colossae and co-worker of Paul whose evangelistic work helped start the church in Colossae."[6] Now he is with Paul in Rome wrestling in prayer for the Colossian Christians. The next verse says, "For I bear him witness that he has worked hard for you and for those in Laodicea and in Hierapolis" (Col. 4:13). He was living far away from them, but he "worked hard" for them. Some commentators believe that the hard work Epaphras was doing was combating the heretics who were causing damage in the church. This may indeed have been included in his work. But considering that he was probably far away from them in Rome, it is more likely that Paul was talking about his prayer for them. As F. F. Bruce says, "Praying is working; and by such fervent prayer Epaphras toiled effectively on behalf of the churches of Colossae."[7]

Prayer is the most effective means of spiritual warfare. After Paul's lengthy listing of armor for spiritual warfare in Ephesians 6:10–17, we would have expected him to say something like, "Now, go and fight." Instead he urges the Ephesians to be "praying at all times in the Spirit, with all prayer and supplication. To that end, keep alert with all perseverance, making supplication for all the saints, and also for me, that words may be given to me" (Eph. 6:18–19). Christian parents can tell you of the earnest battle in prayer waged on behalf of their children. We wage a similar war on behalf of our spiritual children. When they go for job interviews or are doing major assignments like preaching, leading a meeting, or sitting for an exam, we battle for them at home in prayer. Moses did this when his assistant Joshua was fighting the Amelekites. He prayed with his hands held up by Aaron and Hur (Ex. 17:10–13). Then, too, when our disciplees are moving in a way that could be injurious to them, we wage a battle against that.

6. "Epaphras," in *The Lexham Bible Dictionary*, ed. D. Barry et al. (Bellingham, WA: Lexham. 2016), Logos Bible Software version.

7. F. F. Bruce, *The Epistles to the Colossians, to Philemon, and to the Ephesians*, New International Commentary on the New Testament (Grand Rapids, MI: Eerdmans, 1984), 181.

Once when I was abroad, I sent a text message to Sri Lanka, pleading with a young man to return to his church and to the Lord. It was the culmination of days of sad and earnest praying for his soul. Interestingly, the text message never reached him. But after several months this brother had gone to church on Sunday one or two days after I sent the message. Perhaps the wrestling in prayer for him bore fruit!

When I was a student at Asbury Seminary, I had a few opportunities to preach in chapel. Always before I went to preach, my teacher and mentor Robert Coleman would say, "I'll be there in the Amen Corner." I still remember where he used to sit: about halfway down the chapel toward my right. If ever I got nervous, all I needed to do was to look in his direction. Seeing his beaming face, I would be encouraged to persevere. It means a lot to our disciplees when they know that we are praying for them. This is how Joshua must have felt while he was leading the Israelites in a battle against the Amalekites. Moses had given him instructions and then gone to a hill and battled in prayer (Ex. 17:10–13).

While on sabbatical in the United States, one day just before going to have my time with the Lord I saw a heated chain of WhatsApp text messages where a disciplee was being scolded for something he had done. Usually I don't keep my phone near me when I am having my devotions. But that day I did, so that I could stand in solidarity with my brother in Christ. I told him that I was reading all the messages and waging war on his behalf in prayer halfway around the globe. Knowing that others are standing with them, Christians under attack are helped to have God's peace and stability so that they can act wisely without overreacting. But more than that, our prayer unleashes God's power into their lives.

The Content of Paul's Prayers for His Spiritual Children

An analysis of the prayers of Paul will help us learn some of the secrets of discipling prayer.

Thanksgiving and Joy

In eight of the ten letters where he mentions praying for his recipients, Paul says he thanks God for them:

- Twice he gives thanks for God's grace to them and their salvation (1 Cor. 1:4–9; 2 Thess. 2:13).
- Six times he thanks God for their faith and spiritual maturity (Eph. 1:15–16; Col. 1:3–5; 1 Thess. 1:2–3; 2 Thess. 1:3; 2 Tim. 1:3–5; Philem. 4–6).
- Four times he thanks God for their love for other Christians (Eph. 1:15–16; Col. 1:3–12; 2 Thess. 1:3; Philem. 4–6).
- Once he thanks God for their partnership with him in the gospel (Phil. 1:3–5).

There was joyous thanksgiving in Paul's heart when he thought of his spiritual children. Sometimes we find disciplers looking down on their disciplees. They don't admire them. They don't give the impression that they are thankful to God for them. Disciplers may even give the sense that discipling them is a burdensome duty, and that unworthy disciplees should be indebted to them for so great a sacrifice. Apart from God's overriding grace, such disciplers will not nurture people to greatness. Thank God, there are many examples of the overriding grace of God when disciplees have become great servants of God, even though the discipler's attitudes were an obstacle. Disciplers must discipline themselves to rejoice over their disciplees.

Indeed, some of those we disciple bring us a lot of pain. This is what the church in Corinth did to Paul. But he thanks God for them too. He thanks God for their conversions, for changes in their lives, and for the knowledge that God will keep them faithful till the end (1 Cor. 1:4–9). He does not mention warm memories of fellowship and service together as he does in other letters. But he mentions the most important thing about them: they are recipients of God's salvation. I think it is significant that even though there are hardly any Christians in many of the towns mentioned in the New Testament, there has always been a church in Corinth, even today. Paul's faith in what God had done and will do among the Corinthians was not unfounded.

Of course, the side effect of admiration by the discipler is a joyous relationship. Paul tells Timothy, "I long to see you, that I may be filled with joy" (2 Tim 1:4). How burdensome a deep relationship would be without joy, and how enjoyable relationships are when flavored with joy over one another!

When the Israelite pilgrims traveled up Mount Zion on their way to the festival in Jerusalem, they sang what are now known as the Songs of Ascents, which cover Psalms 120 to 134. One of the psalms describes the joy of the pilgrims over each other that characterizes them as they climbed the hill:

> Behold, how good and pleasant it is
>   when brothers dwell in unity!
> It is like the precious oil on the head,
>   running down on the beard,
> on the beard of Aaron,
>   running down on the collar of his robes!
> It is like the dew of Hermon,
>   which falls on the mountains of Zion!
> For there the Lord has commanded the blessing,
>   life forevermore. (Ps. 133:1–3)

A happy band of lovers of God who love and enjoy each other! This is the kind of fellowship that should characterize the discipler-disciplee community.

I must say, as a person in his late sixties with the privilege of investing in much younger people, that discipling is a delight that brings freshness to my life. Yes, there are those dark days of battling for their souls. There are the tiring visits that must be made when someone is facing a crisis. There is the pain of seeing some fall away or exploit the kindness shown them. But those are compensated by the joy we can have as a group.

Kinds of Petitions

Paul's petitions for his readers can be classified in several categories. (We will also look at one petition from Jesus's High Priestly Prayer.)

Paul's ministry to his readers. Paul prays for himself, the discipler, that he might visit his readers and be a blessing to them: ". . . always in my prayers, asking that somehow by God's will I may now at last succeed in coming to you. For I long to see you, that I may impart to you some spiritual gift to strengthen you" (Rom. 1:10–11); ". . . as we pray most earnestly night and day that we may see you face to face and supply what is lacking in your faith" (1 Thess. 3:10). And that is the prayer of all disciplers: "O that I may be able to meet those in my care as frequently as I should and know how best to help them!" Discipling is a great responsibility. We wish we had the time to care for them adequately and knew what we should do. But we realize that we are inadequate and in need of God's help. So we plead for God's help. Before and all through our appointments with an individual or meetings with a group, we pray, "O God, help me!"

Their godliness. The theme that appears most often by far is Paul's prayer that his readers would be godly. He wishes for them to be strong and mature (Eph. 3:14–19). He prays often that they may be more holy and loving in their character and behavior (Rom. 15:5; 2 Cor. 13:7; Eph. 3:19; Phil. 1:9–11; Col. 1:9–10; 2 Thess. 1:11–12). Even though godliness may be a person's most important need, how rarely this request comes up in prayer bulletins! This goal is a challenge to the discipler too. Our desire for our people's godliness challenges us to be examples of godly living. As I said before, sometimes when a disciplee shares with me some of the temptations he is struggling with, I realize that I face the same temptations. That brings with it a firm resolve to get my act together!

Their joy. This request is from Jesus. Twice during the discourse at the Last Supper Jesus mentions his desire that his disciples will have the joy he has. He says, "These things I have spoken to you, that my joy may be in you, and that your joy may be full" (John 15:11). The need for joy is expressed in the High Priestly Prayer also. "But now I am coming to you, and these things I speak in the world, that they may have my joy fulfilled in themselves" (John 17:13). Notice that in both these places the joy Jesus wishes for his disciples is his joy, and his joy is connected to his teaching. Jesus is a joyous person, and his teaching is intended to ignite joy in his disciples. The same should be true of all disciplers.

Their growth in understanding. Coming back to Paul, we find him praying that his readers may grow to understand the truth of God and experience its riches (Eph. 1:16–23; 3:18–19; Phil. 1:9–10; Col. 1:9–10; Philem. 6[8]). This is in line with Jesus's prayer that the disciples would be sanctified in the truth (John 17:17). Connected to this is the need to teach disciplees the Scriptures and show them how to study, apply, and obey the Scriptures. I have dealt with this elsewhere in this book, but here let me reiterate that our deep desire for our people is that they become people of the Word. Paul connects this growth to experiencing the riches God intends for his people. So he writes of "the riches of his glorious inheritance in the saints, and what is the immeasurable greatness of his power toward us who believe" (Eph. 1:18–19). This is an aspect of sanctification—that people have a rich experience of God.

Their fruitfulness. Paul also prays that his readers will bear fruit in the service of God (Col. 1:9–10; see John 17:18). As we have seen elsewhere, an essential aspect of discipleship is service. We want to see our disciplees effective as servants of God. I devoted chapter 6 to this key aspect of discipleship.

Their spiritual unity. Paul says, "May the God of endurance and encouragement grant you to live in such harmony with one another, in accord with Christ Jesus, that together you may with one voice glorify the God and Father of our Lord Jesus Christ" (Rom. 15:5–6). We saw above that four times Paul thanked God for the love his readers had for each other. In Ephesians 4:1–6, using the language of urgency, he appeals to the Christians to be "eager to maintain the unity of the Spirit in the bond of peace" (4:3; see also Phil. 2:1–11). This was a major point in Christ's High Priestly Prayer for his disciples (John 17:21–23). Any leader of a group of Christians would soon recognize that one of the most absorbing challenges he or she has is to help the group maintain its unity. Selfishness, misunderstanding, hurt, differ-ent ideas on an issue, a feeling of betrayal, and a whole heap of other things can cause disunity. Striving for unity is often an unpleasant task involving unpleasant confrontations; and we may be tempted to avoid it. But that would be dangerous to the health of the group. Over the

---

8. This seems to be the thrust of Philem. 6, which is very difficult to translate.

years, during times of disunity and not knowing what to do, I have sung, over and over again, the prayerful words of Rick Ridings's song "Father, Make Us One."

Their ultimate salvation. Three of Paul's prayers are that his readers may be saved in the last day. He writes, "And it is my prayer that your love may abound more and more . . . and so be pure and blameless for the day of Christ" (Phil. 1:9–10). Colossians 1:11–12 is less direct. There Paul's prayer is that the Colossians would be strengthened, and he says, God "has qualified you to share in the inheritance of the saints in light." Of Onesiphorus, who cared for Paul when others shunned him during his imprisonment, he says, "May the Lord grant him to find mercy from the Lord on that day!" (2 Tim. 1:18).

We are always aware that people have an eternal destiny. Our lives and the lives of those we disciple are always looked at from that perspective. The seventeenth-century Scottish preacher Samuel Rutherford once told someone, "I would lay my dearest joys in the gap between you and eternal destruction."[9] As we saw in our discussion of Colossians 1:28–29 in chapter 1, our dream is to present our people to God when we see our Master face to face. When we think of the welfare of a person, the highest priority is his or her eternal destiny.

Their endurance in hardship. Paul knows that people can abandon their faith in the face of hardship. So he wishes that the Colossians may endure hardship with joy, thanks, and hope: "[May you be] strengthened with all power, according to his glorious might, for all endurance and patience with joy; giving thanks to the Father, who has qualified you to share in the inheritance of the saints in light" (Col. 1:11–12). Often when Christians face problems, they do not respond with "endurance and patience with joy." It is easier to respond to crises in unchristian ways. That in turn results in larger spiritual challenges. People can easily go deeper into discouragement or disobedience. So we pray for them and, as we saw in chapter 5, we get alongside them and encourage them.

9. Cited in *The Letters of Samuel Rutherford*, ed. Frank Gaebelein (Chicago: Moody Press, 1980), 22.

Their forgiveness. When we work closely with people, we get hurt. The first battle we have is to forgive them. Paul goes one step further when he thinks of how he was abandoned by the Christians in Rome. He wishes for those who hurt him to be forgiven: "At my first defense no one came to stand by me, but all deserted me. May it not be charged against them!" (2 Tim. 4:16). Paul was following the example of Jesus and Stephen here (Luke 23:34; Acts 7:60). Ministry, especially the ministry of discipling, brings with it a fair share of hurt. We dare not let that turn to bitterness. And one of the best ways to solve that problem is through forgiveness. The failure to forgive can result in disillusioned people who give up on discipling after a time. We must pray that God heals the disappointments we all face.

———

Isn't it interesting that many of these requests of Paul are not the usual prayer requests that people make? That shows how far we may be from Paul's priorities.

But this is not a comprehensive list. We pray for all the needs of those we love: their health, their vocations, their finances, their families, and many other needs. Paul gave Timothy advice about how to treat his "frequent [physical] ailments" (1 Tim. 5:23). He urged Timothy to pursue excellence in his vocation as a pastor, as the two epistles to him show. Jesus told Peter: "I have prayed for you that your faith may not fail. And when you have turned again, strengthen your brothers" (Luke 22:32). This also is a prayer relating to his vocation. We can extend this to praying for excellence in so-called secular vocations also. Most of the people discipled in a typical church serve God in secular jobs. All the exhortations given in the Bible can become subjects of prayer.

Organizing Our Prayer Lives

Despite our good intentions to pray for people, many of us Christian leaders don't pray as we would like to. Therefore, it is helpful for us to develop organized routines for our prayer lives. W. E. Sangster says, "Praying without method is not serious prayer."[10] The first thing I recommend is developing a prayer list. Sangster says that the various problems associated with prayer, like not remembering to pray for people and praying in too general a way, "can all be overcome by a prayer list kept up to date and used daily."[11]

Because I see prayer as my primary job as a Christian leader, I see working on my prayer list as one of my most important responsibilities. It has evolved over the years, and I try to use my creativity to find the best way to pray for others at this stage of my life. This has been one of the most exciting adventures in my life. I have used cards, my paper diary, and photos. These days I have a digital prayer list in my tablet and computer. The value of this is that it can be revised as needs change. I spend a considerable amount of time revising my prayer list and finding ways to improve its usefulness.

A prayer list helps us remember the people we want to pray for. It helps us come back to focusing on praying amid the numerous distractions we have during prayer. I have struggled with wandering thoughts all through my journey with prayer. But the visual prayer list before me helps me refocus on the job at hand. One could write down specific things that need to be prayed for in a person's life. I find it helpful to jot down in my diary special events in the lives of those I disciple—like exams, job interviews, and medical procedures. This helps me pray for them before and during those events.

It is also helpful to have a system that ensures a regular frequency of particular prayers. I try to pray daily for my family members and the people I closely disciple. Most days these prayers are fairly brief. But once a week I try to pray for them comprehensively. I pray one or two times a week for those whom I mentor in a less intense manner. This frequency may increase if someone is facing a crisis.

All this can sound too complicated and legalistic. Indeed, prayer is challenging work. And getting down to it may involve a firm resolve to stop other, more appealing activities. But it can become the most refreshing thing we do. When we pray for others, we are letting love go out of us. However, because we are connected to God, the

10. Sangster, *Teach Me to Pray*, 29.
11. Sangster, *Teach Me to Pray*, 30.

inexhaustible source of love, through prayer, love is always coming into our lives. Love keeps coming in and going out; and the result is that we glow with the love of God. We are refreshed!

Helping Others Become People of Prayer
Setting an Example

If prayer is so important to the Christian life, we should do all we can to help our disciplees to become people of prayer. The Gospels give a prominent place to the prayer life of Jesus. In *The Mind of the Master*, Robert Coleman says, "Prayer shines through the Gospels like a dominant color in a painting, giving the whole picture of Christ a characteristic hue."[12] Coleman shows how we find record of Jesus praying "during crucial moments in his redemptive mission," like his baptism (Luke 3:21–22) and the selection of the twelve apostles (Luke 6:12–13). After a long list of such events steeped in prayer, Coleman says, "Significantly, the disciples knew Christ was praying in each of these instances." Coleman reminds us that "it was [seeing the priority of prayer in his life] which led them to ask the Master to teach them to pray."[13]

I can testify to such influences in my life too. As a child, if I got up early in the morning, I would always see my mother kneeling and praying. When I stayed at my grandparents' home during my childhood, some days I got up very early while it was still dark to go to the bathroom. I had to walk through my grandparents' room. My grandmother would be kneeling behind her bed, with her head covered, praying. Later I found out that she had been praying for me every day. Both my mother and grandmother were converted to Christ from Buddhism. They had no opportunities for structured Christian education like Sunday school. But they were masters in the school of prayer.

One night when I was fourteen years old, I was trying unsuccessfully to communicate with God in prayer, and after a long struggle I went to my mother, woke her up, and told her about my struggle. It was the right time for her to tell me about my need for the Savior. That day, with my mother kneeling beside me, I experienced the peace

---

12. Coleman, *Mind of the Master*, 37.
13. Coleman, *Mind of the Master*, 38.

in the heart that comes with salvation. During the fifty-five years since then, even though I am not a person who takes to the discipline of daily routines naturally, there are two things I have tried to do daily, and that is to read my Bible and pray. The examples of my mother and grandmother were too important to ignore.

Urging Disciplees to Pray

We also find Jesus and Paul urging people to pray and advising them about prayer. Jesus "told . . . a parable [of the widow and the unjust judge] to the effect that they ought always to pray and not lose heart" (Luke 18:1). He advised his disciples, "Watch and pray that you may not enter into temptation" (Matt. 26:41). When his disciples asked him why they had failed to heal a possessed boy, he told them, "This kind cannot be driven out by anything but prayer" (Mark 9:29). Many times he told his hearers to "ask" God in prayer for their needs (e.g., Matt. 7:7, 11; 18:19; 21:22). Paul also urged people to pray. In eight of his letters he asks for prayer for himself. He tells the Thessalonians to "pray without ceasing" (1 Thess. 5:17), the Colossians to "continue steadfastly in prayer" (Col. 4:2), and the Ephesians to be "praying at all times in the Spirit, with all prayer and supplication" (Eph. 6:18). If Jesus and Paul urged people to pray, we should similarly urge our disciplees also.

Namal Weerasinghe is one of the senior leaders in our ministry. He lived in a little house in a high-crime neighborhood. Several members of his family were involved in illegal activity. In his teens, he came to two of our evangelistic camps. He debated with our leaders about the Christian faith and finally, at the second camp, decided to leave Buddhism and follow Christ. Shortly thereafter, a godly Christian lady took an interest in him. She told him that he must give priority to prayer in his life. And every day she would come at about 5:00 a.m. and knock at his window to wake him up so that he would pray. It is not surprising that Namal also became a prayer warrior.

It is good for us to ask our disciplees regularly how their devotional life is going. Some groups of youth in our ministry contact each other by phone daily to alert each other to pray. When I ask young Christians how their prayer and Bible study discipline are going, and they say, "Not well," that question sometimes helps them to snap back into a disciplined devotional life. When a single inquiry does not result in success, more needs to be done. There was a time when I sent text messages almost daily reminding a disciplee about his devotional life. These are all applications of the exhortation "Let us consider how to stir up one another to love and good works" (Heb. 10:24).

———

Let me end this chapter, as I started, with a quote from W. E. Sangster: "The great intercessors remain men and women of secret influence in all communities. To be mentioned in their prayers is incomparably more enriching than to be mentioned in their wills."[14]

---

14. Sangster, *Teach Me to Pray*, 39.

10

Confronting Guilt and
Receiving Forgiveness

If we say we have no sin, we deceive ourselves, and the truth is not in us. If we confess our sins, he is faithful and just to forgive us our sins and to cleanse us from all unrighteousness. If we say we have not sinned, we make him a liar, and his word is not in us. My little children, I am writing these things to you so that you may not sin. But if anyone does sin, we have an advocate with the Father, Jesus Christ the righteous.

1 John 1:8–2:1

In the Bible and in today's culture, people respond to issues of right and wrong along three lines: (1) guilt and forgiveness, (2) honor and shame, and (3) fear/bondage and power/liberation. In this and the next two chapters, we will look at how growth can take place through the operation of these values. I believe these three value systems are representative of responses to felt needs of humans. If that is so, we should expect the Word of the Creator of human life to say something about each. Thankfully it does. As Jayson Georges asserts, ours is a three-dimensional gospel, and God ministers to us comprehensively with all the three kinds of value systems that humans exhibit.[1]

This chapter will focus on the first, guilt and forgiveness.

Guilt and Forgiveness: Illustrating a Strange Idea

After I experienced salvation at the age of fourteen, my first major struggle was with getting angry. This tendency did not automatically leave me with my newfound experience of Christ. I would especially lose my temper with my mother and brothers. I knew that it was wrong and that I needed to go to those I was angry with and ask their forgiveness. Doing this was very humiliating, but God used the humiliation to help me overcome the habit. I still get angry, but hopefully most often it is not in the sinful way that I did as a youth.

I grew up in a Christian family where confession was considered an important value. God's Word told me that certain things are wrong and, as one who had learned to value the Bible, I knew I had to do something about my sin. From childhood I was taught that Jesus had done all that was necessary to forgive my wrongdoing. What I needed to do was to confess it. The freedom of having my guilt erased through forgiveness was a huge motivation for me to confess sin. The process of understanding guilt and receiving God's forgiveness is a key aspect of growth in the Christian life.

But many people who come to Christ today do not have such a background of exposure to the absolute truth of the Bible telling them they are guilty before God. In most Asian religions people seek their salvation through their works. They overcome the effects of the wrong they have done (bad karma) by earning merit through good works. Given this way out of guilt, they do not think it is necessary to confess sin, unless their wrongdoing is exposed, in which case confession would reduce the adverse consequences of that exposure. Most Eastern religions and New Age groups in the West follow the law of cause and effect through the outworking of the law of karma. People can erase the consequences of their wrongdoing by doing good works. A similar resistance to confession is found in the West among those

---

1. Jayson Georges, *The 3D Gospel: Ministry in Guilt, Shame, and Fear Cultures* (n.p.: Timē Press, 2016).

whose religion centers on self-effort. Its focus on performance produces a cultural block to admitting helplessness and relying on Christ's performance on their behalf.

Christianity also says, "Do not be deceived: God is not mocked, for whatever one sows, that will he also reap" (Gal. 6:7). Justice requires that wrong is paid for. But the gospel says that knowing that we cannot pay for our own wrongdoing, God sent Jesus to die to bear the punishment for our sin. Justice was thus satisfied. What we must do is to repent of our sin, confess it, and seek God's forgiveness. This attitude of living under grace does not come to new believers immediately.

In fact, in many cultures, people first come at Christ attracted by features other than the atoning death of Christ. The idea of one dying to pay the penalty for sin is difficult for them to understand. We must labor by all creative means in our reach to explain it and make it understood. I talked about such means in the discussion of "Culturally Appropriate Teaching Methods" in chapter 8 (p. 158). I generally use numerous stories from daily life and history to illustrate how different aspects of substitution work. The idea is to show that it is not as strange as people think when they first hear about it.[2]

Let me take just one aspect of many in the death of Christ for our sin to show how we can demonstrate its believability: the idea of salvation through the sacrifice of another. The principle of sacrifice is found and admired throughout life, even among those who revolt against the idea that Christ sacrificed his life for us. The whole of creation breathes the idea of one dying to save another. E. Stanley Jones puts it like this:

> The cross is in our blood. The white corpuscles circulate through the blood looking for infection. When they find it they absorb it, if possible. If not, they throw themselves against the infection and die that the rest of the body might live. The pus that comes off is the corpses of the white corpuscles which have died that the rest might live.[3]

2. I am grateful to my teachers Robert Coleman and J. T. Seamands for introducing me to this approach. This method is well described in Coleman, *The New Covenant: A Devotional Study on the Blood of Christ* (Carol Stream, IL: NavPress, 1985); and Seamands, *Tell It Well: Communicating the Gospel Across Cultures* (Kansas City, MO: Beacon Hill, 1981). I have used this approach in *The Supremacy of Christ* (Wheaton, IL: Crossway, 1995).

3. E. Stanley Jones, *The Word Became Flesh* (Nashville: Abingdon, 1963), 109.

Jones talks of the mother bird that throws herself into the open jaws of the serpent to save her young. We regard as heroes those who die in battle fighting for the freedom of their nation. We think it is normal for a mother to stay awake night after night sacrificing to care for a sick child.

Once I was speaking on the cross of Christ and the mother of a Buddhist youth who had come to Christ was present. It was her first time in a Christian meeting. The youth had suffered from polio as a child. I asked her if she would consider it unusual for her to make great sacrifices to care for her son when he was sick. She said no and, at the end of the meeting, said that the message of the cross did make sense to her. Some months later it was my joy to be at a service where she and her son were baptized as Christians. Now, decades later, she continues to follow Christ.

Jones concludes, "The Cross is inherent. It is not merely written in the Scriptures; it is plowed into the facts of life." J. T. Seamands, after a similar line of argumentation, says: "Now if this is a universal law—and it seems to be—then when we come to God, the highest being, we would expect to find in him the greatest and noblest expression of sacrificial love in the whole universe. Otherwise the creature would be greater than the Creator."[4] In a similar way we can show how other aspects of the substitutionary death of Christ make sense. I have done this in some detail in my book *The Supremacy of Christ*.[5]

Confession of Guilt, and Grace That Forgives

The Meaning of Confession

The Bible was written in a culture where the other two values regarding right and wrong—honor and shame, and bondage and liberation—were highly regarded. Yet the Bible presents a strong case for the appropriateness and necessity of confessing wrongdoing by those guilty of sin. Two words are translated "confess" in the New Testament, *homologeō* and *exomologeō*. Though these verbs appear a total of thirty-six times, only five times are they used in the sense of confession

---

4. Seamands, *Tell It Well*, 161–62.
5. Fernando, *Supremacy of Christ*, chaps. 9–11. The three paragraphs above are quoted mainly from chap. 10.

(Matt. 3:6; Mark 1:5; Acts 19:18; James 5:16; 1 John 1:9). In each of these five occurrences the "confession of sin was public, not private (i.e., not just between the individual and God)."[6] The idea of private confession is more prevalent in the Old Testament. There we have both confessing alone, as David did in Psalm 51:3–4, and confessing in the presence of others, as David did before Nathan (2 Sam. 12:13) and the whole congregation did on the Day of Atonement (Leviticus 16).

Most of the other thirty-one New Testament occurrences of the two Greek words for confessing refer to public proclamations or acknowledgments. The word *homologeō* itself literally translates as "same word," which gives us the idea "to say the same thing [about]."[7] As Warren Wiersbe explains, "To confess sin, then, means to say the same thing about it that God says about it."[8] James says, "Therefore, confess your sins to one another and pray for one another, that you may be healed" (James 5:16). The context of this verse shows that the prayer described here refers primarily to prayer for healing from sickness, so that the confession probably means confessing the sin that holds back healing. But I believe we are justified in inferring a more general principle that confession can be a means of healing after all kinds of sin.

First John 1:9 says that when we confess our sins, God will "forgive us our sins and . . . cleanse us from all unrighteousness." One aspect of this is the cleansing of our conscience. As Hebrews 9:14 puts it, "the blood of Christ [will] purify our conscience." The result is the freedom of knowing that our guilt has been taken away. While guilt may not be a prominent public feature in many cultures today, it is a human trait that all possess to a lesser or greater extent. Confession clears that guilt, resulting in forgiveness through the blood of Christ. People in Sri Lanka have told me of the freedom they felt after they confessed long-hidden sin. David said,

> Blessed is the one whose transgression is forgiven,
> whose sin is covered. (Ps. 32:1)

---

6. Colin G. Kruse, *The Letters of John*, The Pillar New Testament Commentary (Grand Rapids, MI: Eerdmans, 2000), 68. I am indebted to Kruse for many points in this paragraph.

7. Warren W. Wiersbe, *The Bible Exposition Commentary*, vol. 2 (Wheaton, IL: Victor, 1996), 482.

8. Wiersbe, *Bible Exposition Commentary*, 2:482.

Then he added:

> For when I kept silent, my bones wasted away
> through my groaning all day long.
> For day and night your hand was heavy upon me;
> my strength was dried up as by the heat of summer.
> (Ps. 32:3–4)

In the next verse he continued,

> I acknowledged my sin to you,
> and I did not cover my iniquity;
> I said, "I will confess my transgressions to the LORD,"
> and you forgave the iniquity of my sin. (Ps. 32:5)

Confession, then, is a key to the path to freedom from guilt.

I do not think that a person must publicly confess every sin he or she has committed. But if a sin affects the collective body of believers, or is related to a person's obvious weakness, or is a more damaging sin like adultery or fraud, then confession to others would help the person recover. Many Christians are trapped in a web of sin and seem unable to escape. It may be a sinful affair, or addiction to pornography, or addiction to work, causing them to neglect family. In each of these cases, early confession can help prevent a major scandal. As Ecclesiastes 4:9–10 says, "Two are better than one. . . . For if they fall, one will lift up his fellow. But woe to him who is alone when he falls and has not another to lift him up!" Confession to another could start the process of being lifted up after a fall.

We must nurture our disciplees to value a culture of confession of sin. Then it will be easier for them to confess sin. And through that, not only will they be healed after sin; they will also grow through the process. As someone said, "Our sins are handles by which God gets hold of us." They expose a weakness, and by dealing with that, we grow spiritually.

The Need for a Grace Orientation

Many people come to Christ today with a magical view of God. They realize that the Christian God is most able to meet their needs, and they accept him as their God. They pray the sinner's prayer; but that is more like a mantra that they feel they need to recite to become a Christian. Their worldview—the way they look at life and the world, the beliefs that make them think and act the way they do—has not had a major change. They still see religion as a list of dos and don'ts. What they *do* has changed. Now they pray, read their Bible, go to church on Sundays, tithe, and get involved in service. But those activities do not represent the heart of Christianity.

The Christian life is essentially not a list of things we do or avoid doing. Everything has been done for our salvation by Christ. The loving God has loved us in sending his Son to win our salvation through his death on the cross. The holy God has let Jesus bear the punishment of our sin. Now it is our privilege to be forgiven, to be reconciled to God, and to enter a Father-child relationship with him. Everything in life springs from that relationship, which is a gift of grace. These ideas are strange to someone who has come from outside a Christian background.

Today when many think of the death of Christ, the focus is on how much he lovingly suffered for us in his heroic death. They have seen films like *The Passion of the Christ*, and they are deeply moved by the intensity of his suffering. Their own sin is not a major factor in their thinking. But the Bible teaches that sin mars their relationship with God. When those who understand grace commit a sin, they are eager to confess sin and to be quickly restored in their communion with God through grace. When Jesus taught his disciples an ideal prayer, he included in that a request for forgiveness (Matt. 6:12).

When we approach life from the perspective of grace, we are not afraid of sin. We are afraid *to* sin, but not afraid *of* sin. We know that "where sin increased, grace abounded all the more" (Rom. 5:20). John puts it beautifully. He first says, "My little children, I am writing these things to you so that you may not sin" (1 John 2:1a). There is no excuse for sinning. "But," says John, "if anyone does sin, we have an advocate with the Father, Jesus Christ the righteous. He is the propitiation [the sacrifice that takes away God's wrath] for our sins" (1 John 2:1b–2a). Those who understand this are eager to see sin cast aside through forgiveness, with the resulting restoration of their love relationship with God. They are eager to confess so that they can be free, and they are afraid of concealing their sin. As Proverbs 28:13 says,

> Whoever conceals his transgressions will not prosper,
> but he who confesses and forsakes them will obtain mercy.

Confession opens the door to that gift of grace without which we are empty and unhappy.

What if God accepted people based on what they did? That is how people approach religion before they become Christians. They think that the most important thing for a Christian is doing the things Christianity prescribes, like going to church, tithing, and showing kindness to others. Thinking that way would not encourage anyone to confess sin; to do so would be to say that one is not a genuine Christian. Sometimes "converts" transfer their ideas about the gods to the Christian God, whom they now accept as the best, the supreme God. What they really need is not to *transfer* old views of the gods but to *transform* their belief according to the biblical view of God.

In our discipling we must explain the gospel in such a way that people realize the primacy of grace and the futility of works for salvation. This is a big challenge. Sadly, because people from non-Christian backgrounds find the atonement so difficult to understand, many Christian leaders don't spend much energy trying to explain it to converts. That is suicidal! I will present some requirements for developing a relevant follow-up course with new believers in appendix 3. There I recommend the chronological approach to presenting Christian truth, which begins with creation and the fall before talking about the sacrificial systems and then introducing Jesus. Such an approach can help people to develop a Christian worldview in which sin, grace, forgiveness, and a loving and holy relationship with God are key elements.

So we must help our disciplees to understand the biblical teaching about guilt and forgiveness by helping them to understand the biblical doctrine of grace. Often when teaching young Christians, our Youth for Christ staff exhorts them firmly about Christian behavior. That is necessary, especially with youth. But I tell our staff to balance that teaching with the marvels of grace so that the most important thing to the youth will not be their performance as Christians but the amazing grace of God to them.

During this whole process we are encouraged by the truth that the Holy Spirit "will convict the world concerning sin and righteousness and judgment" (John 16:8). We do all we can to help people realize the seriousness of sin and the glory of grace. The Spirit will use our feeble efforts to bring about the life change he desires for God's children.

Disciplining for Sin

Discipline Is for Healing

Sometimes discipline is needed for Christians to be healed of failings that hinder their progress. While God forgives our sins, forgiveness does not ensure that someone has been healed of the weakness that caused the sin. Disciplining can be part of the process of bringing healing from the weakness. As Hebrews 12:11 says, "For the moment all discipline seems painful rather than pleasant, but later it yields the peaceful fruit of righteousness to those who have been trained by it." Not everyone comes out of it with "the peaceful fruit of righteousness." Some come out of a disciplining process bitter and angry over how they were treated. But it brings the desired result in "those who have been trained by it."

Let's take the case of a worship leader in a church. He confesses to his discipler that he often gets annoyed with his wife and scolds her with language that hurts her greatly. At discipling sessions, the discipler always asks how his relationship with his wife is. It becomes clear that the young man is continuing this pattern of scolding. He confesses to God, receives forgiveness, only to fall again. The discipler decides that disciplining him would be helpful in bringing healing to him. He tells him to step back from leading the worship in church for three months. For three months, the young man suffers on Sundays. The person who replaces him cannot sing in tune. People ask the young man why he is not up there as usual.

After three months, he is back to leading worship. One day when he returns from work, his wife has done something that annoys him greatly. Bad language wells up in him. But just before he spews it out, he remembers his three months of agony and stops. The psalmist prays,

> Set a guard, O LORD, over my mouth;
>   keep watch over the door of my lips! (Ps. 141:3)

The memory of the discipline serves as such a guard, preventing the unkind words from spilling out of his mouth.

It is unfortunate that today many Christians think of discipline as relating only to what we may call "major sins." Discipline can also be a great means of moving toward Christlikeness by addressing our weaknesses before they cause big problems.

Disciplining Is Costly for Leaders

Exercising discipline is a very costly activity for leaders. Many members don't realize what a huge strain their sin puts on leaders. Most leaders are busy, and when a person under their care sins in a way that needs immediate attention, they must respond. Delaying the process of confrontation makes the person who sinned vulnerable to temptation, or discouragement, or bitterness. Often leaders simply don't have the time to attend to this. But they must find the time—however costly—pay the price, meet the person, and go through the painful process of confrontation, forgiveness, and discipline. I think one of the hardest aspects of servanthood is the way it assaults our schedules. Servants often must change their plans because of the needs of the master. And in this case the master is the one we disciple.

Leaders must be very sensitive to the dynamics at work in a discipline situation. Other Christians aware of the discipline often react negatively to it. Some say it is too harsh. Others say it is too lenient. If the person who fell had responsibilities in the church, some blame the leaders for having entrusted responsibilities to this "untrustworthy" person. The disciplined person struggles with bitterness as he tastes the bitter pill of humiliation. Sometimes others do not know what to say to him, so they avoid him. The disciplined person takes that as rejection and becomes more hurt. No wonder Hebrews 12:11 says, "For the moment all discipline seems painful rather than pleasant." Yet if the process is done lovingly and firmly, there is great hope that the individual and the group will come out of it with "the peaceful fruit of righteousness."

Many leaders avoid taking necessary disciplinary steps because of the unpleasantness of the process. Others make a quick decision without thinking of the welfare of the church or the struggling person. Still others ask the sinner to leave. All these reactions hinder the healing of the person. Some who face the prospect of discipline leave the group to avoid the unpleasantness, or simply out of anger. And sadly, when they leave, other fellowships might recruit them, especially if they are gifted in ministry. Then the healing process is short-circuited. I have seen people who did not go through an adequate process of discipline after committing serious sins (such as with money and sex) falling into the same sins somewhere else.

While staying in the group where one is disciplined is usually the best environment for healing, sometimes it is best that the person move on. Sometimes the embarrassment and humiliation are just too much to bear, even with repentance. Sometimes the disciplining church has been abusive, or unfair, or too harsh in its disciplining. The person is too deeply hurt by the treatment he or she has received to go back there. In such situations, the best place for healing may be in another fellowship, provided its leaders are aware of the individual's need for restoration.

Disciplers think of the welfare of each disciplee and do what they think is best for the person, however costly that may be. We are followers of the Good Shepherd, who died for his sheep (John 10:11–15). Such commitment to our people makes us pay the price and endure the inconvenience that the discipline process entails.

Confidentiality

We need to be careful about how much of what people confess should be shared with others. The biblical passages on public disciplining should be balanced with this statement by Peter: "Above all, keep loving one another earnestly, since love covers a multitude of sins" (1 Pet. 4:8). The general practice is to keep things confidential when possible.

Sometimes it may be necessary to tell a specific group about it, like the leaders of the church. This helps the discipler to be accountable for the discipline prescribed. The sin should be shared with some group within the church if the church needs to take an action like suspending a worship leader's activities for some time. If the whole body is affected, then it may be necessary for the body to be informed through its leaders. This must be done with utmost discretion, seeking to find the best way to facilitate the recovery of the church and the individual from the sin. If the person disciplined has a spouse and children, then the harm to them must also be considered.

Generally, however, the rule is that we keep such things confidential as long as they can effectively be addressed on that level. As Jesus said of a somewhat similar situation: "If your brother sins against you, go and tell him his fault, between you and him alone. If he listens to you, you have gained your brother" (Matt. 18:15). Sadly, several Christians have told me that they don't want to share things with their leaders because the leaders don't keep what they share confidential. They may joke about it in public; they may mention something relating to it in passing at a team meeting or in a sermon. Such behavior is totally unacceptable for disciplers.

Our Motivation

In all this our major motivation is the welfare of the person who has stumbled and the surrounding believers. When a disciplee sins, the first questions the discipler asks are, "How can I help him/her recover?" "How can I help the church recover?" That is what drives us. It is a challenging task and, as I said, the discipler will face criticism. But the most important motivation is the welfare of the sinner and the health of the church. I have found that when conscientious, loving discipline is exercised, even though the ones disciplined may at first be very upset with the leadership, ultimately, they appreciate the commitment and stay on in the group that disciplined them. This helps them heal. Some rebel against the discipline and leave the group but come back after a time away, realizing that those who offered the discipline were the ones who truly cared for them.

It bears repeating that Christians are afraid *to* sin, but are not afraid *of* sin. This is because grace is greater that sin. How important it is to give our people this vision of grace! This is why praise and meditation on grace are so important in a Christian group. This is why grace should always be uppermost in what disciplers want to communicate to their disciplees. This is one of the most important lessons I learned from Robert Coleman, my mentor in seminary. Sometimes when I went to his office, I would find him singing praise to God. By his teaching and his example, he always made us look up to God and revel in his grace.

11

Understanding Biblical Honor and Shame

And the son said to him, "Father, I have sinned against heaven and before you. I am no longer worthy to be called your son." But the father said to his servants, "Bring quickly the best robe, and put it on him, and put a ring on his hand, and shoes on his feet. And bring the fattened calf and kill it, and let us eat and celebrate."

Luke 15:21–23

Helping Christians face up to their sin, as discussed in the last chapter, has been one of the biggest ministry challenges I have had in the past few decades. Why do Christians deny rather than confess their wrongdoing? Why do Christians lie to get out of an unpleasant situation? Why do Christians find it so difficult not to take revenge when someone has humiliated them? I had heard about the importance of honor and shame in our cultures and in the culture of the Bible and always thought that I must read up a little more about it. The opportunity arose when I was asked in 2007 to write an endorsement for *Theology in the Context of World Christianity*, by Timothy C. Tennent. This book has an excellent summary of the issue of honor and shame, with biblical reflections on it and hints on how it impacts ministry.[1] That

---

1. (Grand Rapids, MI: Zondervan, 2007), 77–103.

gave fresh impetus to my study of this topic, and to my observation of how it is expressed in ministry and how we should minister in an environment where these are highly valued.

How These Values Operate

In most cultures today, the shame of being known to have done wrong is considered more serious than the sin itself. This is particularly strong in honor-and-shame-oriented cultures in the non-Western world, which are more communal rather than individualistic in the way they decide on right and wrong. (I am using the order "honor and shame" rather than the more common "shame and honor," as I feel the latter order can have a negative connotation, implying that shame and honor are unhealthy motivations. I also use the word "oriented" because no culture follows this value system to the exclusion of other systems.)[2] The minority non-Caucasian and Hispanic populations in North America are also generally honor-and-shame oriented. An action is evaluated more in terms of how it affects the community than in terms of whether it breaks the laws of a supreme God or institution. An action is particularly significant if it brings honor or shame to the community. If confession of wrongdoing brings shame, it is considered wrong.

A teenage girl is sexually abused by her uncle, and she tells her mother about it. The mother rebukes the child, accusing her of bringing shame to her family and even accusing her of triggering the abuse by her "loose" behavior. A Christian leader is late for a meeting at church because he slept too long. But he lies, saying that he got caught in a traffic jam. Most people in the group know that he is not telling the truth. But because he is their leader, they don't want to shame him. They choose to pretend that they believe him. Accepting that one has done wrong is so shameful that in East Asia (and even in the West) public figures have committed suicide after having to publicly accept their wrongdoing.

This outlook is growing rapidly in the West also. A majority of people in the Western world have abandoned the idea of relating to a supreme God to whom they are accountable and whom they will face at a final judgment. That idea is what helped cultures in the West to frame their

---

2. I made this decision after a conversation with my colleague at Colombo Theological Seminary, Prabo Mihindukulasuriya.

understanding of guilt and the need for forgiveness. That also helped the sense of accountability that fueled the trust that characterized Western societies. Today the religion of many is one of self-effort. People are asked to have confidence in themselves and achieve their fullest potential through their own initiative. The vague spiritualities popular in the West envision an impersonal life source behind everything, and their understanding of reality is pantheistic (believing that everything is god). In this environment it is not surprising that, even in the West, shame over sin serves as a deterrent to wrongdoing more than guilt over having transgressed God's law.

When society determines what is right and wrong, shaming (rather than punishment by God) is a key deterrent to wrong. Sex outside marriage, whether heterosexual or homosexual, is not a big deal. Many even believe that giving expression to one's sexual desires (homosexual or heterosexual) is a human right. Yet, society has determined that making sexist statements at work, abusing authority to take sexual advantage of others, and especially sexual abuse of children are shameful and wrong. I certainly agree, but the omission of extramarital sex (which God hates) from the list of wrong deeds is significant.

Roland Muller says, "During the period of 1960 to 2000 western civilization has begun a slow but steady shift towards the shame/honor paradigm. Today young people are very reluctant to label anything as right or wrong. Instead, things are assigned the label as 'cool' or 'not cool.'" Muller concludes, "In the eyes of many high school students, being cool is equivalent to being honorable. Being not cool is the equivalent of shame."[3] I believe this trend has continued to intensify in the West since 2000.

In such an environment, people find ways to avoid the shame of admitting wrongdoing. I have already mentioned how people pretend they don't know who is responsible for an action. Everyone may know that an honored member of their group is guilty—one's father or mother, or one's pastor, or the director of an organization. But they act as if they do not know. That way they preserve the honor of the group, which is considered the right thing to do.

A friend of mine in Sri Lanka told me how one day his boss severely scolded him for something that had happened in the office for which

---

3. Roland Muller, *Honor and Shame: Unlocking the Door* (n.p.: Xlibris Corporation, 2000), 52.

my friend was not responsible. The boss used brutal and insulting language, and others heard it. Later another employee privately told the boss that someone else was to blame. The next day, the boss began to compliment my friend in front of the rest of the office for the good way in which he did his work. It was his way of avoiding having to say, "I'm sorry."

Two women in a local church were involved in a bitter conflict. Both were hurt by things the other said and did. A leader in the church, realizing that the hostility between these two members was beginning to hurt the whole church, organized a meeting with the two women to resolve the problem. At the meeting, it emerged that both had contributed to the problem by doing inappropriate things. One woman accepted her wrongdoing and apologized to the other. The other woman did not admit to having done anything wrong. Instead she went up to the first woman and hugged her, saying, "Let's forget about this and move forward." She avoided the shame of confession. I must say that in our culture the hugging itself was a brave act and should be acknowledged as such. In honor-and-shame-oriented cultures, where community solidarity is strong, sin is very much of a relational thing. And the problem was tackled relationally. But was it sufficient? We will discuss that later.

Table 1 summarizes how these values operate.[4]

Table 1

Shame-Based Orientation	Guilt-Based Orientation
External sanctions for good behavior	Internal conviction of sin
Shame and honor	Guilt and forgiveness
Offense reduces one's standing in the group	Offense transgresses a moral law
Loss of face	Loss of innocence
Communal	Individualistic

Thankfully, the Bible acknowledges the importance of honor and shame. It was written to a culture where honor and shame were very

---

4. I am indebted to the writings of Pilch and Malina in the next footnote for the information in this chart.

important and due attention was given to these values.[5] Duane Elmer says that the occurrences of shame in the Bible are "considerably more than those of guilt."[6] So the Bible gives us adequate food for thought on how Christians should deal with sin in honor-and-shame-oriented cultures. Excellent books have been written on how to minister in such settings.[7]

Honor and shame are more effective as motivations for holiness in community-oriented (or collectivist) cultures than in individualistic cultures. Honor and shame are community values. What others think of our life and behavior is important in a biblical community. Therefore, it should be important in Western cultures also because community solidarity is a biblical idea and is not confined to the non-Western world. Interesting studies have been done on the frequent appearance of the phrase "one another" in the Bible. There are about fifty places in the Epistles where the Greek word translated "one another" (*allēlōn*) refers to relationships between Christians. We saw in chapter 3 that biblical discipling takes place not in an individualistic setting but in a group setting where the community is a major encouragement along the path to godliness.

The Death of Christ and Shame

Tennent has highlighted the theological significance of the shame aspect of the death of Christ. Understanding the full implications of the death of Christ is important in the life of a disciple of Christ. And the shame Christ bore is a key aspect of his death.

Right from the story of the fall, the Bible presents shame as a key consequence of sin. When Jesus died, he took on that shame.

---

5. This has been documented extensively by the writings of John J. Pilch and Bruce J. Malina. See especially, Malina, *The New Testament World: Insights from Cultural Anthropology*, 3rd ed. (Louisville: Westminster John Knox, 2001); Pilch and Malina, eds., *Biblical Social Values and Their Meaning: A Handbook* (Peabody MA: Hendrickson, 1993). A new edition of this book has been published by Cascade in 2016. See also David A. de Silva, *Honor, Patronage, Kinship, and Purity: Unlocking New Testament Culture* (Downers Grove, IL: InterVarsity Press, 2000).

6. Duane Elmer, *Cross-Cultural Connections: Stepping Out and Fitting In around the World* (Downers Grove, IL: InterVarsity Press, 2002), 174. Hannes Wiher includes words relating to justice also in his listing. He reports that major terms for honor and shame appear 968 times in the Bible, and major terms for guilt and justice appear 1350 times. Wiher, *Shame and Guilt: A Key to Cross-Cultural Ministry* (Bonn, Germany: Verlag für Kultur und Wissenschaft, 2003), 215.

7. E.g., Werner Mischke, *The Global Gospel: Achieving Missional Impact in Our Multicultural World* (Scottsdale, AZ: Mission One, 2015); and Jayson Georges and Mark D. Baker, *Ministering in Honor-Shame Cultures* (Downers Grove, IL: InterVarsity Press, 2016).

The shame of the death of Christ may be at first a stumbling block, as people see being shamed as a defeat. Therefore, we must remind people that right through his arrest, trial, and crucifixion Jesus was in control of the situation, even proclaiming that he could have avoided the death but took it on as part of his work (Matt. 26:53–56; John 10:18; 18:11, 36). It was not a defeat but a victory (Col. 2:13–15), as is evidenced by his declaration "It is finished" (John 19:30). Hebrews says that "he endured the cross, despising the shame." The result is that he is now "seated at the right hand of the throne of God" (Heb. 12:2). The latter statement points to his glorious resurrection and ascension, which attested to the victory won on the cross.

So the death of Christ was not a defeat. The Gospels and Acts are eager to show that it was planned all along. As Peter said: "This Jesus, delivered up according to the definite plan and foreknowledge of God, you crucified and killed by the hands of lawless men. God raised him up, loosing the pangs of death, because it was not possible for him to be held by it" (Acts 2:23–24).[8]

The shame of the arrest, trial, and death was real, as a cursory reading of the passion narratives would bear out. But when one understands that Jesus was our substitute, this becomes good news. People know the shame of sin and wrongdoing even better than the guilt of it. It can be a liberating thought for them to realize that Jesus has borne this shame. After describing the shame connected with the passion, Tennent says, "A mere execution would have atoned for guilt, but not for the shame. . . . Jesus bore our shame as well as our guilt."[9] A person who had served in Yemen, which is a 99.9 percent Muslim nation, told me of a Yemenese statement: "Nothing removes shame except blood." Once the idea that Jesus was our substitute is understood, the thought that he bore our shame would be good news.

We must not downplay the importance of the death of Christ as removing the guilt of our sin and God's wrath over it. As I said in the last chapter, we must find ways to share this so that our people will understand. Yet, because the shame of the death of Christ deals with

---

8. For a fuller discussion on this theme, see Ajith Fernando, "The Cross Challenges Humanistic Self-Sufficiency," chap. 10 in *The Supremacy of Christ* (Wheaton, IL: Crossway, 1995).

9. Tennent, *Theology in the Context of World Christianity*, 91.

familiar sentiments, it may be an entry point in the presentation of the cross. Once the attention and agreement are won, we can go on to explain the more difficult but vitally important message about guilt.

All this is also relevant in the West, where, as we saw above, the sense of guilt is rapidly vanishing and being replaced by shame. Some say that, therefore, the message of Christ as removing our guilt should be replaced by a message of liberation from shame through Christ.[10] A more biblical approach is that of Christopher J. H. Wright, who advocates taking both guilt and shame as key factors addressed in the death of Christ.[11] Wright quotes a familiar hymn in which both these emphases appear:

> Bearing shame and scoffing rude
> In my place condemned he stood;
> Sealed my pardon with his blood;
> Hallelujah! What a Saviour![12]

Conversion Can Result in Loss of Honor

One of the dreaded consequences of becoming a Christian is the loss of honor in the community to which the convert has belonged. This is a critical issue, and if Christians do not learn to face this, they could stumble along the way. I have dealt with this in chapter 5, which is on facing suffering, persecution, and loss of honor.

The Biblical Community Is a Covenant Community

I have said that in honor-and-shame-oriented cultures the concept of community solidarity is very important. It is so in biblical cultures also. Old Testament Israel was a community where the people were bound together by a covenant. (In chap. 3 I have dealt with how important this is in discipling Christians.) The lifestyle of covenant living with its corporate acts of commitment, festivals, and pilgrimages

---

10. See Alan Mann, *Atonement in a "Sinless" Society: Engaging with an Emerging Culture* (Milton Keynes, UK: Paternoster, 2005), 31–59. Mann, however, says that shame in the post-industrialized West is different from that in shame-honor societies, being "an intensely private affair" (37).

11. Christopher J. H. Wright, *The God I Don't Understand: Reflections on Tough Questions of Faith* (Grand Rapids, MI: Zondervan, 2008), 127–42.

12. Philip P. Bliss, "'Man of Sorrows,' What a Name" (1875); from *The Worshiping Church: A Hymnal* (Carol Stream, IL: Hope, 1990), no. 226.

featured shared values that were key to Israel's behavior. Many Christian groups are defective in practicing the biblical idea of a covenant community. This is needed not only in community-oriented (collectivist) societies but also in individualistic societies, where it would stand out as one of the countercultural features of Christianity.

Biblical Motivations Using Honor and Shame

The Bible often presents honor and shame as motivations to holy living. In fact, it has a lot to say about the shamefulness of sin and the shame people will experience at the judgment. Teaching these truths can encourage receptivity to the call to repentance.

Sin Is Shameful

Recently, I went through the whole Bible and made topical listings of all I could find about honor and shame. I found sixty-four passages that talk about the shamefulness of sin, including some long passages. For example:

- Matthew devotes a whole chapter to Jesus talking about the shamefulness of hypocrisy (Matt. 23:1–39).
- Paul says, "But sexual immorality and all impurity or covetousness must not even be named among you, as is proper among saints. Let there be no filthiness nor foolish talk nor crude joking, which are out of place. . . . Take no part in the unfruitful works of darkness, but instead expose them. For it is shameful even to speak of the things that they do in secret" (Eph. 5:3–4, 11–12).
- In a section about family life Paul says, "If anyone does not provide for his relatives, and especially for members of his household, he has denied the faith and is worse than an unbeliever" (1 Tim. 5:8).
- Paul even uses shame as a strategy to win back disobedient Christians: "If anyone does not obey what we say in this letter, take note of that person, and have nothing to do with him, that he may be ashamed. Do not regard him as an enemy, but warn him as a brother" (2 Thess. 3:14–15). In a relational culture, it is a bitter pill to suffer when others "have nothing to do with"

you. Sometimes I feel that the relationship that many have with the church is so shallow that they may not feel this shame. They may just move on to another church, an option not available in the first century.

The above listing is only a sampling of the biblical use of shame to help people to live holy lives. Sometimes when I talk about this, people react quite negatively, suggesting that I am presenting an unworthy motive for holiness. But that motivation is clearly found in the Bible. Today our society regards as shameful some actions once considered acceptable, like beating one's spouse, sexually abusing a child or a junior in the workplace, or acting out of extreme prejudice. Christians too need to find appropriate ways to nurture communities that consider sin shameful. Teaching and conversation about the shamefulness of sin are vitally important.

It Is Shameful to Deny Sin

I said above that confessing sin is a shameful thing in honor-and-shame-oriented cultures. And we saw examples of how people try to avoid this step. But in the biblical culture, *denying* sin is presented as a shameful thing. John says, "If we say we have no sin, we deceive ourselves, and the truth is not in us. . . . If we say we have not sinned, we make him a liar, and his word is not in us" (1 John 1:8, 10). Here John is saying that people who don't admit to their sinfulness are fake Christians. Christians confess because it is shameful not to do so. We must conscientiously seek to inculcate this new value system among Christians. A lot of biblical passages proclaim this attitude—passages many Christians overlook in their teaching!

The honor that is preserved by the failure to repent is shallow. Often others know a Christian has sinned. They protect his name by not confronting him about it. If he is a leader, he is honored for his position. But he wins no spiritual respect. He can wield earthly authority but not the spiritual authority that is a key to Christian leadership. We should seek to stop that kind of sham from being perpetuated in our churches. It is a major hindrance to the revival we so much need today.

Proper motivation through shame works in communities that practice the oneness of mind that is characteristic of true biblical community life as described in Acts 2 and 4 (see below, p. 212). If community members don't feel one with their leaders, then when a leader decrees that something is shameful, that may trigger resentment more than life change. Nurturing alternate communities that follow biblical principles is a key to transforming the worldviews of honor-and-shame-oriented cultures. The discipleship group can be one such community.

The Judgment for Sin Is Shameful

In my study of honor and shame mentioned above, the most frequently occurring category of shame I found was the shame that comes when God judges people. Sometimes the judgment is on earth, especially in the Old Testament passages. Other times it is at the final judgment. I found 190 passages that talk about the shame that comes with judgment. This is not only an Old Testament idea. Twenty-four of the passages are in the New Testament. The rich farmer is called a "fool" when his death is announced, because "he is not rich toward God" (Luke 12:20–21). Another rich man, now in hell, is seen begging for relief from a pauper, now in heaven, whom he once ignored (Luke 16:24). Talking about the shortsightedness of hypocrisy, Jesus said, "Nothing is covered up that will not be revealed, or hidden that will not be known. Therefore whatever you have said in the dark shall be heard in the light, and what you have whispered in private rooms shall be proclaimed on the housetops" (Luke 12:2–3). As Howard Marshall put it: "Hypocrites will be unmasked."[13]

All these texts talk of the shame of judgment for people who die without seeking God's grace to deal with their sin. The prospect of eternal shame or honor gives Christians the strength to bear temporary shame on earth. Jesus says, "Whoever is ashamed of me and of my words in this adulterous and sinful generation, of him will the Son of Man also be ashamed when he comes in the glory of his Father with the holy angels" (Mark 8:38).

---

13. I. Howard Marshall, *The Gospel of Luke*, The New International Greek Testament Commentary (Grand Rapids, MI: Eerdmans, 1987), 512.

We must encourage Christians to take the prospect of judgment seriously. It is a reality vital to a Christian understanding of life. Teaching about it is a challenging task in a generation that is not familiar with the concept of being accountable to God. Certainly, a sermon or two would help. Alas, in some churches we almost never hear sermons on judgment! But one or two sermons a year would be insufficient to affect such a major shift in thinking.

As I said in chapter 8, not only should we teach unfamiliar doctrines; we also need to be talking about judgment in ordinary conversations.[14] While we may not preach many full sermons on judgment, that crucial doctrine could be mentioned in passing in the middle of a sermon as a reality that affects our life now. I often say in my preaching that I think about heaven every day because that influences how I value all things. I mention how I have already planned my funeral and listed the songs I want sung at it. People are shocked when I say things like this. But I do it to nudge them to look at life from an eternal perspective. Judgment must be part of the day-to-day thinking and talking of Christians.

Honor for Those Who Repent

Jesus also vividly describes the honor that comes to those who confess their sin. The tax collector who "beat his breast, saying, 'God, be merciful to me, a sinner!' . . . went down to his house justified," unlike the Pharisee who gloried in his claims to righteousness (Luke 18:13–14).

The father runs to meet his son who had wasted his life with shameful behavior, culminating in a pigpen. Mark Strauss comments, "The scene is striking since even today, a distinguished Middle Eastern patriarch in robes does not run, but always walks in a slow and dignified manner. Running was viewed as humiliating and degrading."

The son's prepared confession is cut short as the father lavishes honor on him. The "best robe" and "a ring" are given to him. The servants are to put "shoes on his feet," which distinguished a son from servants. These are all symbols of honor. So is the feast, prepared with a fattened calf rather than a goat or a sheep, which possibly "indicates that the whole village is to be invited, confirming the father's desire to

---

14. On this, see Ajith Fernando, *Crucial Questions about Hell* (Wheaton, IL: Crossway, 1994), 125–64.

reconcile his son to the community."[15] "Music and dancing" follow (see Luke 15:11–32). This son is invested with great honor within the community, and his return to the community is welcomed with great celebration.

Notice the two key features of this response of the father: honor and joyous acceptance into the community. These are two of the key values in honor-and-shame-oriented societies. How important it is for our Christian communities to be welcoming of repentant sinners. Sadly, though people come to salvation by grace, after that, many live the Christian life through law. The important thing is their performance, not Christ's gracious and loving gift. People who focus on their performance will not welcome those who return after sin. Like the elder brother in the parable, they think that after all they have done, they are ignored, and the returning sinner is given far too much honor. They say things like "Just wait and see. He will fall again very soon." Those who focus on grace refuse to speak that way. They focus on the possibilities of grace to help the repentant sinner live a transformed life.

Acceptance and hope offered by the discipler help erring disciplees to believe that they can indeed make it. And that will help quench the darts of Satan, who tries to discourage them into believing that they are too weak to live righteous lives. Disciplers and all Christian communities need to communicate this grace-inspired sense of values. In such communities, confession of sin is viewed as something honorable. And people are motivated to follow the path of repentance.

The Bible, then, gives an alternate system of honor and shame to the one found in society. It is aware of the importance of these values and seeks to meet the deep needs and aspirations of the people in relation to honor and shame. As is typical of honor-and-shame-oriented societies, there is a heavy emphasis on the communal and relational aspects, which are used to enhance restoration after sin.

Sin and Our Relationship with God

The relational emphasis in honor-and-shame cultures harmonizes beautifully with the Christian way of life, where our relationships with

---

15. Mark Strauss, in *Zondervan Illustrated Bible Backgrounds Commentary*, vol. 1, *Matthew, Mark, Luke* (Grand Rapids, MI: Zondervan, 2002), 448.

God and each other are primary factors in life. We must help disciplees to cherish and nurture their relationship with God right from the start of their Christian lives. They may come to Christianity primarily with a magical view of God as one who meets felt needs rather than as a loving Father. The joy of the Lord, which is such an important aspect of life, is the joy of a love relationship with a God who deeply loves and cares for us. Living the Christian life is not essentially following a bunch of rules. As Jesus said, "This is eternal life, that they know you, the only true God, and Jesus Christ whom you have sent" (John 17:3). After describing the different ways the word "know" is used in the Bible, William Barclay concludes, "To *know* God is therefore not merely to have intellectual knowledge of him; it is to have an intimate personal relationship with him, which is like the nearest and dearest relationship in life."[16] John and Betty Stam were missionaries in China who were killed by the Communists in 1934 when they were twenty-seven and twenty-eight years old. John once said, "Take away everything I have, but do not take away the sweetness of walking and talking with the king of glory."[17] That is the beauty of our love relationship with God.

I have found that generally the most prominent sentiment among Christians when they think of the death of Christ is amazement over the love that made him die for us. While this falls short of the full understanding of the cross, it is a good start to one's relationship with God in Christ. It is a love relationship, and it is initiated by a lavish display of sacrificial love by Christ. Yet, while people believe in their minds that God loves them, it may take a long time for them to realize that they are loved by God personally. Helping disciplees to believe that God really loves them is one of the great challenges a discipler faces. We will look at this issue in chapter 13.

Our relationship with God has a vital bearing on our pursuit of holiness. People in honor-and-shame-oriented cultures (and other cultures too) may not take rules very seriously. In fact, they are used to breaking rules and don't think of doing so as very serious (unless they

---

16. William Barclay, *The New Daily Study Bible, The Gospel of John*, vol. 2 (Edinburgh: Saint Andrew, 2001), 244.

17. Quoted in Sherwood Elliot Wirt and Kersten Beckstrom, *Living Quotations for Christians* (New York: Harper & Row, 1974), 266.

are caught). They must learn the value of God's rules as they grow in Christ. In the meantime, their first understanding of holiness can build on the thought that sin violates the love relationship they have with God. To think that we have grieved the God who did so much for us and whom we love is a repulsive idea. In fact, Paul uses this idea within a passage that gives us rules for the life of holiness when he says, "Do not grieve the Holy Spirit of God" (Eph. 4:30).[18] We avoid breaking rules because doing so grieves God.

Sin and Our Relationships with Each Other

This idea of Christianity being essentially relational is also significant when a Christian community confronts sin among its members. When problems appear in a person's life, it is wise to first deal with it relationally. Long before formal disciplinary inquiries and warning letters are sent, a leader needs to talk with the wrongdoer the way a father or mother would. There may need to be anger and sternness, but the whole encounter is colored by love. In my forty-one years of ministry, there have been very few times when I have wept in front of others. Among those few times were occasions when I was praying with a person after he had confessed a serious sin. That is our first reaction—deep sorrow. Then, without giving up our role as loving parents, we exercise discipline.

I have seen many discipline-related situations ruined by official letters sent too early in the process. Everything in the letter was accurate and true. But it would have been better to talk to the person before sending the letter. Impersonal responses can result in painful splits as the person leaves the group angry with its leaders. Our relationship with God is relational. Specific sins can ruin that relationship. When dealing with those specific sins, we do so relationally. It is not a situation of relationally overlooking guilt but one of relationally confronting sin. I have seen ministries ruined in Sri Lanka owing to unnecessary conflicts arising from Westernized leaders reacting in an impersonal and legalistic way to problems with non-Westernized members.

---

18. Dennis Kinlaw describes how, as a child, he learned this truth about the Christian life, which he later understood and explained using philosophical categories, in *Malchus' Ear and Other Sermons* (Wilmore, KY: Francis Asbury, 2017), 14–16.

It may be easier to shoot off a letter than to talk personally to an angry or backslidden person. You will be deeply hurt when you hear that this sinning child in the faith is blaming you. You will think, "After all I have done for him, see the way he is talking to me." But just as Jesus died to save us from our sins "while we were still sinners" (Rom. 5:8), we endure the pain and do all we can to help sinners recover from their sin. We cannot be emotionally lazy as we strive to bring back lost sheep. Always when someone sins, our key response should be to ask how we can help this person and the church to recover. And we will do all we can to facilitate that recovery.

Respecting Protocol

It is necessary that when we confront sin, we respect cultural protocol, which is very important in honor-and-shame-oriented cultures. Paul spoke harshly to an official without knowing who he was, and when he was told that it was the high priest to whom he was speaking, he immediately apologized, saying, "It is written, 'You shall not speak evil of a ruler of your people'" (Acts 23:5). Paul tells the relatively young Timothy, "Do not rebuke an older man harshly, but exhort[19] him as if he were your father" (1 Tim. 5:1 NIV). In unpleasant situations involving a young leader and an older man, cultural etiquette requires that the young leader speak in a respectful tone when rebuking an elder.

Again, this may seem unwise to people with a very rational, efficient, fact-oriented approach to people and projects. But we need to find a balance between respecting people and prompt communication. To respect people is also to respect their cultural sensitivities. I am convinced that, even though this approach may seem to be inefficient and time consuming, the price paid is well worth it in the long run.

Applying the Principles to Lying and Taking Revenge

I want to apply what we have learned from this and the previous chapter to two aspects of the Christian life that converts find very difficult. They are the principles that Christians do not lie and do not take revenge.

---

19. The NIV rendering of *parakalei* as exhort is preferred, as it is more in keeping with the context than the ESV "encourage."

Lying

In most cultures today lying is commonplace, generally excused, and sometimes even considered necessary. Simply telling people not to lie does not seem to help. The Bible was written to an honor-and-shame-oriented culture, and it records many instances of lying. But it strongly condemns lying and exhorts the faithful to avoid lying.[20] Twice Proverbs says that lying lips are an abomination to the Lord (Prov. 6:16–17; 12:22). I have found that one of the greatest cures for lying is community solidarity informed by biblical values concerning what is honorable and shameful. Included in this solidarity is the value that lying is shameful.

Our ministry has been primarily with people from backgrounds that tolerate lying. We have found that the kind of oneness described in Acts 2 and 4 has helped many who were accustomed to lying to give it up. In the Jerusalem church, the believers "were of one heart and soul," and that solidarity extended to their possessions: "and no one said that any of the things that belonged to him was his own, but they had everything in common" (Acts 4:32).

We have tried to be open about our financial lives. For example, we have an open-salary-book policy, along with a salary policy heavily based on the needs of staff workers. So a staff worker can find out what another receives. This can be awkward at times, with people asking unpleasant questions about why some are getting a certain allowance or privilege while he or she is not getting that. But the reward is ownership by all within the community. Ownership brings with it the right to protest about what one doesn't like. It also encourages honesty. We have tried to moderate our lifestyle, keeping it relatively simple, so that the poor will not be distant from us. Those of us who travel abroad are open and accountable about financial dealings relating to our travel. This way others do not feel distant from those with access to foreigners. And we have insisted on being truthful to each other.

In such an environment, the honor-shame motivation can work powerfully. The members develop an attitude that makes it shameful

---

20. E.g., Lev. 19:11–12; Deut. 25:13–16; Pss. 4:2; 15:3; 31:18; 52:3; 58:3; 119:163; 120:2; 144:7–8, 11; Prov. 10:18; 13:5; 14:25; 17:4, 7; 19:22; 21:6; 30:8; Isa. 59:1–3, 11–13; Hos. 4:1–2; Nah. 3:1; Eph. 4:25; Col. 3:9–10; 1 Tim. 1:10; 4:1–2; Titus 1:12–13; 1 Pet. 3:10. See also the references in footnote 22.

to lie. We have seen habitual liars gradually change to becoming truthful. We have also seen that some who do not like this level of accountability end up leaving the group. Sadly, some have stayed a considerable time and continued lying. Once this is known, they are lovingly confronted. Some change, but others don't. The key is paying the price of developing a community where there is true spiritual solidarity.

Another necessity in overcoming lying is for Christians to understand and accept that they are accountable for their actions to a holy God. As I said in the last chapter, people do not think of God in this way all over the world. Western society was fashioned on the idea that there is a God to whom people are accountable and whom people will meet at the judgment. In this environment lying was not tolerated, and trust was a major value driving the societies as people were taught to be honest. Now with a pantheistic deity replacing the God of the Bible, gradually the idea of accountability to God is disappearing. As a result, the importance of truthfulness can decline. A look at TV news suggests that this trend is significant. And the millions spent on security cameras shows that the trust that once drove the supermarket culture is no longer there.

A marked change in thinking is needed if accountability to God is to influence the day-to-day lives of those who come to Christ from another faith. A key to this is proper teaching about God and his ways.[21] I wonder whether this is why God chose to highlight the seriousness of sin with the judgment on Ananias and Sapphira (Acts 5:1–11). It is the first sin recorded in the early church; so it is obviously of great importance. The gift they brought was part of the proceeds from the sale of a land, and it must have been a large gift. Their lie was that they gave all the proceeds of the sale to the church. Today most leaders would ignore that "small lie." But it was severely judged, and the church learned that lying is simply not acceptable among Christians because it provokes God's wrath. Twice we are told that "great fear came upon" the people (Acts 5:5, 11). When I preach on this text, I usually have a dramatic reading of the passage. It presents the amazing story in an

---

21. I mentioned the effectiveness of the chronological approach to teaching the truth of the Bible in the previous chapter (see also appendix 3).

unforgettable way. There are many other passages in the Bible which talk of the fearful prospect of judgment for lying.[22] Clearly, then, in the Bible, the fear of judgment is a deterrent to lying.

One of the major reasons why people lie is fear of the consequences of telling the truth.[23] The way Christians overcome this fear is by showing that God is the one we must fear most because he is greater than all humans. We believe in God's sovereignty and trust him to help us through the consequences of being truthful. We will see this truth more clearly in the next chapter (see Matt. 10:28).

Another key is that the leaders should demonstrate how important truthfulness is by the way they speak and act. I often tell our Youth for Christ staff and volunteers that, in youth work, we work with young leaders who may make mistakes that bring shame to the organization. That goes with youth work, and we are willing to take on that shame out of our commitment to our people. But there is one thing we cannot tolerate, and that is lying. When people lie, we can't help them improve or overcome their weaknesses, and we can't have true fellowship with each other. Jesus showed how careful we must be about our words when he said that our words should be reliable, and therefore people should not need to ask us to take oaths (Matt. 5:33–37). Instead, "Let your 'yes' mean 'yes,' and your 'no' mean 'no.' Anything more than this is from the evil one" (Matt. 5:37 CSB).[24]

An important aspect of this culture of truthfulness we nurture is the practice of admitting our error when we say something untruthful. Sometimes an exaggeration slips out of my mouth when I am speaking. When describing something that happened in a group of twenty people I may say something like, "There was a large group there." The moment I realize what I have said, I correct myself, even though it is humiliating to do so. Sometimes after my discipleship group meeting at church I will send a text messaging apologizing for something I said there. Usually it is something bad I said about someone, even though I was sure it was true. Even if true, it was not necessary to say it. In the first few months since we started meeting, the members would respond

---

22. Pss. 59:12–13; 63:11; 101:7–8; Prov. 6:12–15; 12:19; 19:5, 9; 21:6; Mic. 6:12–13; Rev. 21:8.

23. I am grateful to Sam Kim of Asbury Theological Seminary for alerting me to this.

24. This is a more literal translation than the ESV for this verse.

with surprise at the apology, as if to say that it was not necessary. But with time, hopefully they learned that truthfulness is necessary for a Christian. This way we help create a culture where accountability and truthfulness are valued. Shared values are very important in honor-and-shame-oriented cultures.

Taking Revenge

It is very difficult for new believers in most cultures to accept that Christians must not take revenge. When I tell them this after someone has hurt them, some respond that I can follow that principle as a mature Christian, but it is impossible for them. In many cultures, when someone has dishonored you, it is wrong not to restore your honor or that of your family or friend through revenge. Dishonoring the wrongdoer is seen as the way to restore honor. However much we teach about this, the natural reaction to being hit by another is to hit back. Jesus's statement "But if anyone slaps you on the right cheek, turn to him the other also" (Matt. 5:39) is considered impossible to practice in today's world.

Here too the dual emphasis on community and the doctrine of God helps. The community changes its value system by turning the refusal to take revenge into an honorable practice—a high value. We expound this principle often in our teaching and preaching. We show how true healing takes place when there is forgiveness. When teaching what it means to obey God, we will use as illustrations vivid stories of Christians who forgave and refused to retaliate. We present the heroism of honorable forgiveness and the healing it brings. As I have said often in this book, values are changed through constant exposure to the truth.

The doctrine of God gives the logic of why revenge is not necessary. Paul says, "Beloved, never avenge yourselves, but leave it to the wrath of God, for it is written, 'Vengeance is mine, I will repay, says the Lord'" (Rom. 12:19). The logic of this is that dishonor will indeed come at the final judgment to those who hurt us (unless they repent). God will repay. We show how the doctrine of judgment is an antidote to bitterness. People who have been hurt are angry that wrongdoers have gotten away with it. They haven't. God will repay.[25] Later in

---

25. I owe this insight about the connection between judgment and bitterness to John Piper, *The Purifying Power of Living by Faith in . . . Future Grace* (Sisters, OR: Multnomah, 1995), 262–66.

Romans Paul will say that this repayment of evil is sometimes done by government authorities, to whom God has entrusted the task of rewarding good and punishing evil (Romans 13). If we tried to take revenge, we would make a mess of it. Instead, we do something we *can* do, something that will help heal us: we activate love in the place of hatred. So Paul goes on to say, "To the contrary, 'if your enemy is hungry, feed him; if he is thirsty, give him something to drink; for by so doing you will heap burning coals on his head'" (Rom. 12:20). The result of this process, says Paul, is honor for us, for we have won a victory: "Do not be overcome by evil, but overcome evil with good" (Rom. 12:21). The logic is based on the doctrine of God, but the language uses honor-shame criteria.

The motivation for not lying and not taking revenge is not only that avoiding those responses is the right thing to do. Doing the right thing may not be an attractive motive to someone enraged by wrong or in a vulnerable situation. We remind people that abstaining from lying and taking revenge is also the best thing for us. We are not making some great sacrifice by being obedient to God's way. At the beginning of Romans 12, Paul teaches that we are to be different from others; we are to offer our bodies as living sacrifices and not be conformed to the world. One aspect of this difference is not taking revenge (12:17). The result of this sacrificial nonconformity is that transformation takes place by the renewal of our minds (12:1–2a). And, in turn, we "will be able to test and approve what God's will is," that it is "good, pleasing [probably pleasing to God] and perfect" (12:2b NIV). Try it, says Paul, and you will see that it's the best thing to do!

We must labor to help our people to have this transformed mind—with its new sense of values that looks at truthfulness and the refusal to take revenge as honorable things.

From Community Solidarity to Spiritual Accountability

I have described the power of community solidarity. Communities make decisions collectively and consider right and wrong to be community values. But I have found that community solidarity does not automatically lead to spiritual accountability. People who have a strong sense of community solidarity may not be open with others in the group about their personal spiritual lives and struggles. For example, in Sri Lanka, Buddhist communities practice strong social solidarity. But when it comes to personal salvation, people are on a personal journey. "*I* go to the Buddha for refuge" is a basic affirmation in Buddhism. In Christianity we say, "*Our* father in heaven."[26] The learned Sri Lankan Buddhist monk Narada Maha Thera says, "There are no petitionary or intercessory prayers in Buddhism. . . . The Buddha does not and cannot grant earthly favours to those who pray to him. A Buddhist should not pray to be saved, but should rely on himself and strive with diligence to win freedom and gain purity."[27] Community life may be strong; but salvation is through individual effort.

The Christian life is all of grace; and one of God's appointed means for us to receive grace is other members of the body. Our experience of grace makes us open to the vulnerability that spiritual accountability brings. A trust grows based on the experience of God's grace and love, which are often mediated through others in the group. That is the theory! But the change in attitude toward accepting spiritual accountability usually takes time to develop.

We need to respect honor-shame sensitivities and protocols as we seek to nurture these attitudes. Then God uses the experience of his grace that people have together to foster trust and openness. This is especially mediated through the care, nurture, fellowship, and openness of the leader of the group. This dual method of being culturally sensitive and of showing loving concern can open a person's heart. A person I was mentoring was hesitant to trust me enough to open up about his personal life for several months. But after an unusually long time he changed and became a dear brother in the Lord. Much later he told me that the final catalyst in the process of changing his attitude was something I had done for him at considerable cost during a crisis. That convinced him that he could trust me enough to be open with me.

The members of a group must grow in nurturing an atmosphere of trustworthiness and commitment to each other. There should be zero tolerance for betraying confidence. It is sad to see how many Christians today are hurt by others misusing information shared with

---

26. I am grateful to my friend Suren Raghavan for this insight.
27. Narada Maha Thera, *The Buddha and His Teachings* (Colombo: ANCL, 1980), 287–88.

them in confidence. With this fear in the background, they are cautious about opening up to others, especially about their sins and weaknesses. This is an acute problem in honor-and-shame-oriented cultures, where making derogatory comparisons is sadly very common. People are hurt when their weaknesses are contrasted with other more "successful" people.

Again, we return to the importance of the discipleship group being grace oriented. The grace of God strengthens us to look at others with a burning desire to see grace having its full impact on their lives. People with that desire will not talk about secrets that will hurt those who have been open about their own weaknesses. That attitude of trustworthiness will sooner or later result in trust and a willingness to be vulnerable enough to share about problems, weaknesses, and sins. Leaders must patiently and lovingly serve their communities until this atmosphere develops. As I said above, with some people it takes a very long time for such trust to develop. Don't give up! Once that level of trust is achieved, then when people fall, the community will do all it can to help "restore [them] in a spirit of gentleness" (Gal. 6:1). That's what Paul means when he says, "Bear one another's burdens, and so fulfill the law of Christ" (Gal. 6:2).

———

You can see that, like the guilt-and-forgiveness paradigm, the honor-and-shame paradigm is fueled by grace and the doctrine of God. Grace and a knowledge of who God is and what he will do are what liberate a community to use shame and honor as means of growth in the lives of believers.

12

Experiencing Liberation and Power

But if it is by the Spirit of God that I cast out demons, then the kingdom of God has come upon you.

Matthew 12:28

The above words of Jesus look at his coming to earth as an assault over the powers of Satan through the work of the Spirit. I read Matthew 12:28 during my devotions while writing this book, and I asked myself, "How much does my ministry reflect this reality?" My answer was, "Not enough." This verse presents the third orientation for looking at right and wrong in our experience and in the Bible. We discussed the other two—guilt and forgiveness and honor and shame—in the last two chapters. Now let us look at how the power of God at work within people liberates them from fears that bind them and opens the door to an experience of God's power.[1]

Fear/Bondage and Power/Liberation in Society

I said in chapter 10 that before many believers come to Christ, their understanding of divine beings is somewhat magical rather than moral. The gods can be persuaded to give what people request if the requests

---

1. I am grateful to the late New Testament scholar William J. Larkin Jr. of Columbia International University, who introduced me to the need to think theologically about this issue.

follow the right formulas. There are different gods to whom one could appeal to meet different needs. But there isn't a sense of accountability to these gods for personal actions. So sometimes the main contributors to the shrines of some gods are people who do a lot of illegal things, like unscrupulous business people and underworld godfathers. People perform various rituals to avoid bad luck or angering the gods and to open the door to good fortune.

These cultural factors make Christian practices of confession and spiritual accountability seem unnecessary and undesirable. Why go through that humiliation if you can offset consequences of actions through rituals? It is with such a ritualistic approach to personal morality and religion that many people come to Christ. More than being a set of truths to believe and a way of life to follow, religion has to do with tapping the power that will help them overcome fear and live secure lives.

The religious life of most people shows vestiges of the so-called tribal or primal[2] religions that have been in existence for thousands of years. Basic to these religions is "a belief in a spiritual world of powers or beings that are stronger than man himself."[3] People act and decide about right and wrong based on fear of what might happen to them. They follow formulas that bring them protection or fortune. They want a way out of fear, and in Sri Lanka they resort to shamans, exorcists, astrologers, and superstitious practices to help appease or overcome whatever forces they feel control their security and progress in life. They give gifts to shrines devoted to various gods who are believed to have certain powers. They go to different gods for revenge, for success in business, for protection in travel, and for a host of other needs.

Buddhism claims to be a way of life and not a religion. It is said to be an ethical discipline that does not require the help of gods (nontheistic). But in practice most Buddhists are essentially theistic in their

---

2. I am using the term "primal" in the sense of basic rather than original or first. The Bible's record of the origin of religion is that the first humans worshiped the one true God and that, after their rebellion, religion deteriorated to other forms, including the tribal animistic religions. Contrary to what many liberal thinkers claim, this is a story of *retrogression* of religion rather than *evolution* of religion, which starts with tribal religions and climaxes with the worship of one supreme God.

3. Harold Turner, "World of the Spirits," in *Eerdmans' Handbook to the World Religions* (Grand Rapids, MI: Eerdmans, 1994), 130.

outlook. Buddhists in Sri Lanka often use the greeting "May the gods bless you." They usually have auspicious times for all key events. When they start the construction of a building, they bury expensive items within the foundation so that evil will be warded off. The building often has a hideous figure, like a devil's face or a scarecrow, on display to distract the observer and thus avoid the problem of "evil eye"—looking at a thing and wishing evil upon it. Sometimes "evil eye" refers to the misfortunes that come simply from looking at something with envy. Little babies usually have a big round black mark painted on their foreheads, again to avoid evil eye.[4]

This approach to religion has become popular in the West too. Most newspapers and magazines have space for horoscopes, psychic counselors, and the like. Many Westerners go to witches, wizards, spiritual healers, and practitioners of necromancy (communicating with the dead) and participate in séances to tap supernatural powers for their own good.

These things are all expressions of fear, which is one of the most important emotions motivating people's actions: fear of demons and spirits, bad luck, ill health, enemies, economic reversals, and a host of other things. Some resort to the security of gangs to overcome their perceived enemies. Right and wrong are determined by how well an action measures up according to fear and liberation values. So a daughter marrying a very good man whose horoscope does not fit is accused by her parents of doing something very wrong. If a man violates a ritual and thus brings bad luck to his family, that is considered a more serious sin than getting drunk and beating his wife.

This is the approach to life that many bring when they come to Christ. Everyone has some vestiges of this approach. In this chapter I will show how the gospel speaks to it.

Fear and Liberation in the Gospel

One of the key features of the ministry of Jesus was his assault on the kingdom of Satan. John says, "The reason the Son of God appeared

---

4. This description of popular Buddhism is taken almost verbatim from Ajith Fernando, *Sharing the Truth in Love: How to Relate to People of Other Faiths* (Grand Rapids, MI: Discovery House, 2001), 145.

was to destroy the works of the devil" (1 John 3:8). The first miracle recorded in Mark and Luke is the healing of a demon-possessed man (Mark 1:21–26; Luke 4:33–37). Of the thirteen miracles recorded by Mark, "exorcism is the most frequently occurring type of healing" (four times).[5] Jesus saw his death as a decisive blow against Satan. At the end of his ministry, as he was approaching his death, he said, "Now is the judgment of this world; now will the ruler of this world be cast out" (John 12:31). About Jesus's death, Paul said, "He disarmed the [demonic] rulers and authorities and put them to open shame, by triumphing over them in him" (Col. 2:15).

This is a powerful message to people living in fear of demons and bad luck! One of the reasons for the central event of Christianity, the death of Christ, was to overcome the evil forces that they fear. If the decisive blow against Satan was given at the cross, his final defeat is certain. Paul says, "The God of peace will soon crush Satan under your feet" (Rom. 16:20). The resurrection of Christ was the proof that his death was a victory (Acts 2:23–24, 36). These are basic truths that we must teach Christians who have lived under the fear of demons and evil forces.

The Bible also says that Satan still has power and attacks believers. Paul says he was afflicted by "a messenger of Satan to harass" him (2 Cor. 12:7). Peter warns, "Your adversary the devil prowls around like a roaring lion, seeking someone to devour" (1 Pet. 5:8). In anticipation of the attacks of Satan, Paul says, "Put on the whole armor of God, that you may be able to stand against the schemes of the devil" (Eph. 6:11). Teaching people these truths is also an important part of the discipling process.

Those who have had no previous overt connections with demonic rituals and oppression may primarily experience Satan's attacks in less overt forms, like subtle temptations or depression. But those who have opened their lives to overt demonic activity prior to conversion, or who live in environments where such activity abounds, may find themselves attacked in more direct ways. Some disciples of Christ, like Mary Magdalene (Mark 16:9) and the Gerasene demoniac (Mark 5:18–20),

---

5. Darrell Bock, *Jesus according to Scripture* (Grand Rapids, MI: Baker; Leicester, UK: Inter-Varsity Press, 2002), 100–101.

came to follow him through an experience of deliverance from demons. People from such a background sometimes are vulnerable to Satan's attacks, even after they have become Christians, especially when they face a crisis and see no positive answer to earnest prayer. Their relatives and friends keep hounding them about the need to seek guidance from an astrologer or an exorcist. It is sad but true that some succumb to the pressure. Such people could also be severely oppressed through charms planted by enemies or through direct demonic attacks.

When people renounce their faith to follow Christ, they are often warned about being attacked by the gods they have forsaken. Having lived under the fear of these gods, they are vulnerable to fear and sometimes even to the temptation to forsake Christ. Therefore, it is important to teach, as basic to Christianity, that Christ is more powerful than all the forces they fear. To ignore the reality of such forces would be both foolish and unbiblical. Paul is clear that we battle such powers. He says, "For we do not wrestle against flesh and blood, but against the rulers, against the authorities, against the cosmic powers over this present darkness, against the spiritual forces of evil in the heavenly places" (Eph. 6:12).

Paul also emphasizes that Jesus has defeated these forces. He speaks of

> the immeasurable greatness of [God's] power toward us who believe, according to the working of his great might that he worked in Christ when he raised him from the dead and seated him at his right hand in the heavenly places, far above all rule and authority and power and dominion, and above every name that is named, not only in this age but also in the one to come. (Eph. 1:19–21)

Christ is way above any other force or power. It is significant that these two statements by Paul are made to the Ephesians, whose pre-Christian life was highly influenced by occult practices (Acts 19:11–20). Paul combines the liberation aspect of salvation with the forgiveness aspect when he says, "He has delivered us from the domain of darkness and transferred us to the kingdom of his beloved Son, in whom we have redemption, the forgiveness of sins" (Col. 1:13–14). Both these truths need to be taught to God's people.

So the answer to fear of demons and occult power is not to deny their reality but to present the deeper reality of God Almighty, who is greater than all these forces and will finally defeat them completely. This is why it is important for us to proclaim the truth that when Jesus died, he was victorious over demonic forces, and that his resurrection gave proof of his victory.

As I said before, if we deny the reality of demonic forces, not only are we unbiblical; we are also unwise, because we fail to equip people for some of the major challenges they will face in life. People must be warned of Satan and his devices and be equipped to battle him.

Victory over Temptation

Satan Tempts

When most Christians think of Satan, they think of how he tempts them to sin. Still, disciplers need to warn disciplees about that reality. Jesus told Peter, "Simon, Simon, behold, Satan demanded to have you, that he might sift you like wheat" (Luke 22:31). Paul wrote of his "fear that somehow the tempter [Satan] had tempted" the Thessalonians (1 Thess. 3:5). While Judas had to bear responsibility for betraying Jesus, the Bible says that a key step in his decision was when "Satan entered into" him (Luke 22:3; see John 13:27). Even Jesus was tempted by Satan (Matt. 4:1). We need to warn disciplees: "Be soberminded; be watchful. Your adversary the devil prowls around like a roaring lion, seeking someone to devour" (1 Pet. 5:8).

God Enables

Yet, as with all challenges, God promises victory. The Bible says that one reason for Christ coming to the world was to destroy the works of the Devil, whose activity is connected with our sinning: "Whoever makes a practice of sinning is of the devil, for the devil has been sinning from the beginning. The reason the Son of God appeared was to destroy the works of the devil" (1 John 3:8).

God uses various means to give Christians victory over sin. The Bible promises that he will help us at the time of temptation. A verse that new believers often memorize (and should) puts this well: "No temptation has overtaken you that is not common to man. God is faithful, and he will not let you be tempted beyond your ability, but with the temptation he will also provide the way of escape, that you may be able to endure it" (1 Cor. 10:13). That is a key verse to drill into the hearts of new believers. Peter assures us that "the Lord knows how to rescue the godly from temptation" (2 Pet. 2:9 NASB). God will help us be victorious over temptation.

In my personal battle with sin, few things have helped me as much as the truth that God has promised us victory over temptation. If I did not have this assurance, I may have given up fighting temptation and simply given in to sin. I cannot give up, as I know God's power is greater than the power of temptation. As John wrote, "Little children, you are from God and have overcome [false spirits], for he who is in you is greater than he who is in the world" (1 John 4:4). Paul explains that this help comes through the Holy Spirit when he says, "By the Spirit you put to death the deeds of the body" (Rom. 8:13).

When it comes to sin and temptation, the primary focus should always be on God's ability and grace rather than on our inability. In fact, one of the incentives to stay holy and to return to God the moment we sin is that we are homesick for God. We long to restore our relationship with him. And he has done all that is needed for that. As John assured us, "My little children, I am writing these things to you so that you may not sin. But if anyone does sin, we have an advocate with the Father, Jesus Christ the righteous. He is the propitiation for our sins" (1 John 2:1–2). Disciplers must always place before their people this dual perspective: there is no excuse for sin, but there is always provision made for our restoration after sinning.

We Participate

Of course, we need to participate in the battle too. We are to "give no opportunity to the devil" (Eph. 4:27). Negatively, that means we are to "flee youthful passions" (2 Tim. 2:22a). As John Stott explains:

> We are not to come to terms with it, or even negotiate with it. We are not to linger in its presence like Lot in Sodom (Gn. 19:15–16). On the contrary we are to get as far away

from it as possible as quickly as possible. Like Joseph, when Potiphar's wife attempted to seduce him, we are to take to our heels and run (Gn. 39:12)."[6]

Positively, we are to "pursue righteousness, faith, love, and peace" (2 Tim. 2:22b). This would include our decisions to do right. It includes our giving time to prayer. Jesus said, "Watch and pray that you may not enter into temptation" (Matt. 26:41). Someone has said, "Seven prayerless days make one weak." We must feed on God's truth personally and in corporate settings. The value of this is shown in two more verses that new Christians need to memorize:

> How can a young man keep his way pure?
> By guarding it according to your word. (Ps. 119:9)

> I have stored up your word in my heart,
> that I might not sin against you. (Ps. 119:11)

We should hammer into the minds of our disciplees a thought variously attributed to John Bunyan, Susanna Wesley, and D. L. Moody: "This book will keep you from sin; or sin will keep you from this book."

Friends Encourage

After asking Timothy to flee wrong and pursue right, Paul adds, "along with those who call on the Lord from a pure heart" (2 Tim. 2:22c). God uses sincere Christians to help us in this battle with sin. That could represent the discipleship group and especially the discipler. We are sometimes more afraid to sin in the presence of our friends than in the presence of God! Knowing this sad anomaly, God made provision for it by encouraging us to get the help of friends. Accountability with them—that is, having to report to them about our lives—and encouragement and rebuke from them are used by God to help us along the path to holiness. With the ease of falling into temptation on the Internet, it would be wise to install accountability software in which the discipler or another friend could act as the guardian who gets reports of one's internet activity. This influence of friends is described

---

6. John Stott, *Guard the Gospel: The Message of 2 Timothy* (Downers Grove, IL: InterVarsity Press, 1973), 74.

in Hebrews 10:24: "And let us consider how to stir up one another to love and good works."

Friends also help when Christians fail by yielding to temptation or in some other way. When Christians stumble, they risk going deeper into sin, or discouragement, or self-loathing. By listening to them, friends take a huge burden off them. Friends can counteract the negative thoughts swirling in their minds by feeding them with God's healing truth. Caring friends can help them snap out of the destructive trajectory they are on and avail themselves of God's grace. We need to keep reminding believers that "where sin increased, grace abounded all the more" (Rom. 5:20). As the preacher put it, "Two are better than one. . . . For if they fall, one will lift up his fellow. But woe to him who is alone when he falls and has not another to lift him up!" (Eccles. 4:9–10).

Friends are vital for Christians seeking to overcome habitual sins and addictions. In chapter 10 I described a worship leader who was in the habit of speaking to his wife in a hurtful way. In a case like that, by regularly checking with a disciplee about his behavior at home, the discipler can help him overcome such a habit. Otherwise, disciplinary action may be necessary for him to be healed of the weakness behind this sin. The help of others is particularly important with overcoming addictions. Prayer alone may not suffice to help someone addicted to drugs or pornography to overcome the habit. God uses accountability with another or with others to help heal them. Group therapy is also commonly used in secular methods for treating addiction. Again, accountability software helps with addiction to pornography. Addiction to mobile devices and social media is another challenging area that disciplers need to talk about.

Unwise spending on credit or by taking loans is a temptation that plagues many Christians today. This is an area that needs careful monitoring as it can ruin the economic and spiritual life of an individual or family and rob peace and joy. Disciplers, then, must conscientiously bring up known weaknesses and areas of vulnerability when meeting their disciplees.

Here, then, are some keys to overcoming temptation: the power of God, available to us through the Holy Spirit; believing in the possibility of victory with the Holy Spirit's help; our availing ourselves of God's grace by fleeing from youthful passions and instead pursuing God's thoughts; and the help of fellow Christians, including disciplers.

The Fear of Judgment

I said above that the primary motivation driving many people is fear of superior forces. The Bible also presents fear as a motivation for action. It uses the prospect of judgment to warn people of the folly of disobedience. The Bible teaches that people ought to fear God, the most awesomely great force one can encounter. And it teaches that there is no doubt that all people will encounter God one day.

The first sin recorded in the first church in Acts was lying, a sin that is commonplace and often overlooked in most cultures today. Ananias and Sapphira lied about a gift they gave to the church. The gift was part of the proceeds from the sale of a property, and it must have been very large. But they lied by claiming to have given the total proceeds. Peter confronted them, and both of them died. As a result, "great fear came upon the whole church and upon all who heard of these things" (Acts 5:11; see also 5:5). Yet this fear does not seem to have harmed the church. Three verses later we are told that "more than ever believers were added to the Lord, multitudes of both men and women" (Acts 5:14). The Bible presents some kinds of fear as good. Fear can be a friend that alerts us to danger and sends us along the path to freedom.

Jesus said: "Do not fear those who kill the body but cannot kill the soul. Rather fear him who can destroy both soul and body in hell" (Matt. 10:28). People today are afraid of demons and misfortune, and they build a whole system of values and practices based on that fear. Jesus was telling us that we do not need to fear even the chief of demons, Satan, because the One who is with us is more powerful than he. This is the One "who can destroy both body and soul in hell." The liberating reality of the gospel is that this One can be our loving heavenly Father, who will protect us from all harm and danger.

This statement of Jesus introduces a key biblical theme: the fear of judgment helps us to live holy lives. Jesus said:

If your right eye causes you to sin, tear it out and throw it away. For it is better that you lose one of your members than that your whole body be thrown into hell. And if your right hand causes you to sin, cut it off and throw it away. For it is better that you lose one of your members than that your whole body go into hell. (Matt. 5:29–30)

Jesus is saying that the fear of judgment is a motivation to shun sin and follow the path of holiness. Paul likewise says, "We must all appear before the judgment seat of Christ, so that each one may receive what is due for what he has done in the body, whether good or evil." Then he continues, "Therefore, knowing the fear of the Lord, we persuade others" (2 Cor. 5:10–11). The prospect of judgment gave him a fear that helped him live an obedient life.

One implication of all this is that we need to warn people severely about the dangers of going back to practices and rituals they followed in their previous lives. The Old Testament contains many examples of people being judged for adopting the practices of neighboring nations. After describing the judgment that befell disobedient people in the Old Testament, Paul says, "Now these things happened to them as an example, but they were written down for our instruction, on whom the end of the ages has come" (1 Cor. 10:11). Then he adds, "Therefore let anyone who thinks that he stands take heed lest he fall" (1 Cor. 10:12). Disciplers must warn disciplees about the terrible consequences of disobedience.

There is also a positive side to motivating people to obedience through fear of divine judgment. Those who conquer by being faithful to the end will have a great reward. Jesus tells the lukewarm church of Laodicea, "The one who conquers, I will grant him to sit with me on my throne, as I also conquered and sat down with my Father on his throne" (Rev. 3:21). The prospect of such eternal honor gives one the courage to confess sin and to pay the price needed to live the life of holiness.

These are but a small sampling of texts that present the fear of judgment as a motivation to living a holy life. The right kind of fear is an important topic when discipling people for whom fear has been a driving emotion.

Ministering God's Freedom

Our Ministry to Others

Sometimes repair work is needed to clear vestiges of an occult past in the lives of new believers. I have found it necessary to go to homes of new believers who fear that there have been occult influences in their lives or their houses (such as a charm hanging from the ceiling). When I and others go, we do not deny these influences but, acknowledging them, proclaim Christ's victory over them and claim deliverance from them through prayer. There have been times when I have removed the charms and thrown them away. This kind of ministry should be taken very seriously today in a pluralistic environment where many people come to Christ thinking that dabbling with charms, séances, and the like is harmless. They must be told that we should have no dealings with those forces. Some come to Christ so influenced by such forces that total deliverance may not come immediately after their conversion.

While the church will debate the issue of whether or not a Christian can be demon possessed, we know that Christians can be oppressed by Satan in different ways and with varying intensity. When evidences of demonic influence appear, we must immediately deal with them. Of course, we need to bear in mind that often people mimic possession while hardly realizing what they are doing. But at other times there are clear evidences of possession, which require prayer for deliverance.

Sometimes we may need to say a prayer of deliverance rebuking Satan, who is harassing a Christian through fear or through occult actions or curses by an enemy. Sometimes Satan needs to be rebuked for trying to break the harmony among a group of believers. This is one of Satan's favorite methods to neutralize Christians. Some come to Christ carrying what we may call a family curse because of anger, enmity, abuse, dabbling in the Satanic, and other such activities. These can hold a believer in bondage, and we may need to pray specifically for that person's deliverance. While in some circles there may be an overemphasis on generational curses passed down in a family's history, we must not ignore the warning in the Ten Commandments that God "is a jealous God, visiting the iniquity of the fathers on the children to the third and the fourth generation of those who hate [him]" (Ex.

20:5). The evil family atmosphere people grow up in can affect their behavior and make them susceptible to God's judgment.

Those who have been addicted to things like drugs and sex are also under Satan's control. An important step in their deliverance might be an unmistakable experience of the power of God in their lives.[7] In Jackie Pullinger's remarkable ministry with hundreds of drug addicts in Hong Kong, a key aspect of deliverance has been an experience of the Holy Spirit, usually with speaking in tongues.[8] Such an experience may help people who have lost all hope of victory to awaken to the possibility of coming out of their rut as they see God intervening dramatically in their lives. It can bolster the faith that opens them to receiving God's grace to heal and restore their lives.

Sometimes Satan attacks Christians through moods like depression and rage. Leaders must be alert to this, and if they sense there is a demonic element at work, they need to address it. Timothy M. Warner tells the story of a missionary teacher who had become so debilitated that she had to be sent home by her mission because she could not carry on ministering. After two years of struggle, she was ready to give up—even to stop trying to be a Christian. One day she felt God telling her, "Why don't you fast and pray and cast them out?" "She wrote out the commands for the evil spirits troubling her to leave 'in the name of Jesus who shed his blood for me,' and she read them every thirty minutes during that day." That day she was completely delivered.[9]

Disciplers Become Vulnerable to Attack

Warner points out that when he and his wife became more involved in ministering to people with problems caused by demons, they also came under attack in various ways. This is something anyone involved in this kind of ministry should be aware of. Satan will pay special attention to those who invade his territory. I know of servants of God

---

7. I am grateful to my friend Amarajith de Silva for alerting me to this point.

8. See Jackie Pullinger, with Andrew Quicke, *Chasing the Dragon: One Woman's Struggle against the Darkness of Hong Kong's Drug Dens*, rev. ed. (London: Hodder and Stoughton, 2006).

9. Timothy M. Warner, "Power Encounter with the Demonic," in *Evangelism on the Cutting Edge*, ed. Robert E. Coleman (Old Tappan, NJ: Revell, 1986), 93. Warner has written a more comprehensive book on the topic, *Spiritual Warfare: Victory over the Powers of This Dark World* (Wheaton, IL: Crossway, 1991).

who, after ministering in this realm, succumbed to his attacks and fell into serious sin. A friend of mine who knew I was writing this book, urged me to mention that Satan will attack people who seek to disciple others.[10] All ministry makes us vulnerable to Satan's attacks. Neutralizing God's servants is one of his favorite strategies.

I recommend three things for people taking on such a ministry. First, they should not go into it alone. Warfare is usually done not by lone soldiers but in a group. Sometimes an issue comes up suddenly and there may be no one to give support. Then we need to trust the sufficiency of grace and launch into the battle. Cell phones, however, help us alert others to pray for us. Second, those going to help people troubled by demons need to go after much prayer. When the disciples asked Jesus why they were not able to cast a demon from a boy, he said, "This kind cannot be driven out by anything but prayer" (Mark 9:29). Spiritual ministry requires spiritual power. If we become spiritually weak through prayerlessness, we become prime candidates for failure.

Third, they should have people praying for them. Using vivid language, Paul tells the Romans, "I appeal to you, brothers, by our Lord Jesus Christ and by the love of the Spirit, to strive together with me in your prayers to God on my behalf" (Rom. 15:30). Paul uses warfare language, "strive together" (*sunagōnizomai*), here. After his great passage about armor for spiritual warfare, he asks the Ephesians to persevere in prayer for him (Eph. 6:18–20). As he goes out to battle, he wishes others to join him in the battle by praying. Paul requests prayer for himself a total of eight times in his epistles.[11] I urge you to recruit people who will pray for you; and once you have found them, cultivate them by giving them frequent specific requests for prayer.

The Importance of Experience to Belief and Growth
The Order Reversed

In 1982 the esteemed missionary anthropologist Paul Hiebert wrote a groundbreaking article about the need for missions to consider

---

10. I am grateful to my friend Douglas Ponniah for alerting me in this way.
11. Rom. 15:30–31; 2 Cor. 1:11; Eph. 6:18–20; Phil. 1:19; Col. 4:3–4; 1 Thess. 5:25; 2 Thess. 3:1; Philem. 22.

people's interactions with spiritual forces.[12] The article, "The Flaw of the Excluded Middle," begins with the question the disciples of John the Baptist asked Jesus: "Are you the one who is to come, or shall we look for another?" (Luke 7:20). Hiebert says, "Jesus answered, not with logical proofs, but by a demonstration of power in curing the sick and casting out evil spirits."[13] This accords with the verse quoted at the start of this chapter: "But if it is by the Spirit of God that I cast out demons, then the kingdom of God has come upon you" (Matt. 12:28). Experiencing God has an important part to play in the growth of a disciple of Christ, and disciplers need to be alert to this. It gives a knowledge of how God works, which is an important aspect of Christian growth (Eph. 1:17–20). A lot of counterfeit experiences and extreme expressions of legitimate experiences are being advocated today. Therefore, it is necessary for disciplers to help disciplees grow into a healthy experience of the presence and power of God in their lives.

Most of us were taught a growth paradigm that goes like this:

Facts → Faith → Feeling (Experience)

That is the way we usually grow. We learn the facts given in the Bible, we believe those facts, and that results in our experiencing the reality of what we believe (feelings). But that is not the only way God works in the Bible. Sometimes the order is reversed, like this:

Feeling (Experience) → Faith → Facts

People experience something of the work of God, and that makes them open to believing that God works in this way, and they believe the biblical truth on which this experience is founded. The facts are always basic. Experience is evaluated by its conformity to Scripture. But sometimes people closed to a scriptural truth can become open to it through an experience.

A biblical community should always be a place where members see God at work. This includes discipleship groups. They should

---

12. Paul G. Hiebert, "The Flaw of the Excluded Middle," *Anthropological Reflections on Missiological Issues* (Grand Rapids, MI: Baker, 1994), 189–201. This chapter first appeared in *Missiology: An International Review* 10, no. 1 (January 1982): 35–47.

13. Hiebert, "Flaw of the Excluded Middle," 189.

be a people experiencing God together. Disciplers need to help disciplees to master the art of learning from experience and of approaching experience in a biblical way. For example, what is normative—that is, necessary for everyone—and what is unique to some individuals but not necessary for all? And what is clearly not in keeping with Scripture?

Triggering Basic Belief

The governor of Cyprus, Sergius Paulus, was interested in the message of Barnabas and Saul, and he summoned them, seeking to hear the word of God. But a Jewish sorcerer, Elymas, tried to stop them and turn the governor away from the faith. Saul responded by rebuking Elymas and stating that he would be blind for a time. This happened, and the man had to be led by his hand (Acts 13:6–11). "Then the proconsul believed, when he saw what had occurred, for he was astonished at the teaching of the Lord" (Acts 13:12). He saw what had occurred, but he was not what we might call a "power convert." The display of power helped him to be open to listening to the *Word*, and he believed because "he was astonished at the teaching of the Lord." It was the teaching that he believed. We too must help people to focus on the Word. The display of God's power arrests people so that they are open to hearing the Word.

A woman from a Buddhist background suffering from demon possession was invited to our church by one of our members. Earlier she had spent a lot of money going to exorcists for deliverance. She would be all right for a few days and then relapse to her former condition. She attended a Bible study conducted by my wife before Sunday worship. One day, when the Bible was opened, she began to shiver and show signs of possession. Our members took her to our pastor's home next to the sanctuary and prayed for her. She got well and this time remained well for a longer period, but she began to show symptoms of possession a few weeks later. Yet she kept coming to church. And the people in church prayed for her each time the symptoms reappeared. After a few months she was delivered completely in answer to prayer. Today, over twenty years later, she is a vibrant Christian. She often responds when we call for testimonies in church. Interestingly her testimony is always about how she was a sinner who was forgiven and saved by Jesus, not about the healing she received. The healing opened her to the gospel. She is a Christian not because of the healing but because of the gospel.

Healing is not the only experience that attracts people to the gospel. Hiebert relates a story about how, when smallpox hit a town in India, the people had a diviner come to appease the goddess of smallpox. They wanted everyone in the village to contribute, but the Christians refused, much to the anger of the villagers. Then a Christian child caught the dreaded infection. An elder came to Hiebert and asked him to pray. They had a prayer meeting for her healing, but a week later the child died. "I felt thoroughly defeated," Hiebert says. But the elder told him, "The village would have acknowledged the power of God had he healed the child, but they knew in the end she would have to die"; yet he added, "When they saw in the funeral our hope of the resurrection and reunion in heaven, they saw an even greater victory—over death itself—and they have begun to ask about the Christian way."[14]

These two stories help us understand the place that experience has in Christianity. God can use it to lead people to the truth. But God is not bound to act always in the same way. He always acts in ways that bring glory to his name. But the glory may come through miracles or through sufferings.

Learning New Truths

Peter was already a follower of Jesus when Jesus told him to let down nets for a catch. He responded: "Master, we toiled all night and took nothing! But at your word I will let down the nets" (Luke 5:5). He obeyed his Master, even though under normal circumstances a seasoned fisherman like Peter would have seen this as a foolish thing to do. The result was a huge catch of fish that resulted in a new understanding of who Jesus was. Peter said, "Depart from me, for I am a sinful man, O Lord" (Luke 5:8). Jesus told them,

---

14. Hiebert, "Flaw of the Excluded Middle," 189–90, 200–201.

"Do not be afraid; from now on you will be catching men. . . . [and] they left everything and followed him" (Luke 5:10–11). The surprising catch of fish, resulting in new understanding about Jesus, ushered in a new level of devotion to Christ.

Peter subsequently became the leader of the first Christian church. He was in Joppa when a voice in a vision telling him to eat unclean food revolutionized his life. He was led to the home of a Roman centurion and preached the gospel to non-Jews there. And, as he explained later to the church, "the Holy Spirit fell on them just as on us at the beginning" (Acts 11:15). Declaring, "Can anyone withhold water for baptizing these people, who have received the Holy Spirit just as we have?" (Acts 10:47), he ended up baptizing them (Acts 10:48). The truth that Gentiles must also receive the gospel had been enshrined in the Great Commission that Jesus gave. But it took a vision and the sight of Gentiles speaking in tongues to make Peter understand how that worked out in practice. Here was a mature Christian who learned new truths through his experience.

Today also Christians can understand new scriptural truths through experiences. Eta Linnemann was a young woman in Germany preparing for theological studies when she went to a retreat. The scheduled preacher did not come, and instead they had an unknown "gospel preaching" pastor speak. She says that one day "this pastor dared to tell us that we were sinners and needed a Savior." That day "she agreed with him and accepted Christ."[15] She came home a changed woman, and a year later she left home to study under the world's most famous New Testament scholar, Rudolf Bultmann. Bultmann did not believe that the Gospels were actual historical accounts. The miracles and resurrection probably did not take place, he said. The so-called prophecies were based on events that had happened and were read back into the narrative and put into the mouth of Jesus as predictive prophecies. Under Bultmann's influence and that of other professors, she gave up her simple trust in the Word of God.

---

15. "Eta Linnemann Testimony," Grace Valley Christian Center (website), Wednesday, November 28, 2001, http://www.gracevalley.org/teaching/eta-linnemann-testimony/. I am grateful to Robert Yarbrough, who translated Linnemann's books into English, for directing me to this website. I depend on this resource and the work cited in the following footnote for details concerning Dr. Linnemann.

Linnemann eventually became a highly esteemed professor in New Testament in a German university. She wrote books and scholarly articles using the historical-critical method, which denied the historical reliability of the Bible. But she had no joy or peace in her heart. She began to question what she was doing and the authenticity of it. That led her "into profound disillusionment." She says, "I reacted by drifting toward addictions which might dull my memory. I became enslaved to watching television and fell into an increasing state of alcohol dependence."[16]

Then she read a doctoral dissertation that talked about miracles in Africa that were just like the miracles in the Gospels. They really seemed to have happened. This was a major trigger for change in her life. One day a student in one of her classes said that similar miracles had happened in the town where they were. She also heard the testimony by a Wycliffe Bible translator from Nepal about the eloquent and bold way in which a newly converted Nepali Christian who was imprisoned spoke to the judge. She realized that with his limited experience, this man could not have spoken like that on his own. It had to be a fulfillment of the prophecy of Mark 13:9–11, where Jesus promised that words would be given in such situations by the Holy Spirit. Once her mind was open to the possibility of God acting in miraculous ways, her heart was opened to surrendering afresh to the claims of Christ as found in the Bible.

She says she was born again. But she had already "accepted Christ" as a youth, resulting in genuine life change. God knows when she was really born again. What *we* know is that after seeing God at work, her belief about the impossibility of miracles and prophecy had to be discarded and her mind was willing to accept the truths of the Bible. And she became a new person. Interestingly, she then enrolled in a Bible school where she experienced what we would call discipling. God does change Christians through experience. And disciplers need to be alert to this and guide them to understand what God is doing in their lives.

Assurance of Salvation

A third way that experience can help us grow in the faith is by God's action in assuring us of our salvation. In the early church,

---

16. Eta Linnemann, *Historical Criticism of the Bible: Methodology or Ideology*, trans. Robert W. Yarbrough (Grand Rapids, MI: Baker, 1990), 18.

speaking in tongues was a sign that people had truly been converted (see Acts 10:44–48; 11:15). Twelve Ephesian believers had a
similar experience of confirmation of salvation under the influence
of Paul's teaching (Acts 19:1–7). The church will debate whether
speaking in tongues is a necessary sign for all Christians. But the
point here is that an experience gave assurance of salvation.

To be sure, the most reliable means of having the assurance of
salvation is believing what the Bible says about salvation. John
says, "But to all who did receive him, who believed in his name, he
gave the right to become children of God" (John 1:12). Jesus said,
"Truly, truly, I say to you, whoever hears my word and believes
him who sent me has eternal life. He does not come into judgment,
but has passed from death to life" (John 5:24). Both these texts
present salvation as a present reality for those who believe. We
must show Christians the importance of believing what the Bible
says.

However, God assures us through personal experiences also.
Paul says, "The Spirit himself bears witness with our spirit that we
are children of God" (Rom. 8:16). The Bible presents God as one
who communicates with the individual believer. Most often this
communication takes place when we are reading the Bible. But
sometimes an experience may give us that keen sense that God has
assured us that we belong to him. He may do it through a text we
read that speaks exactly to a situation we are facing at the time.
Or it may be an unexpected check that comes in the mail at a time
of great need. Or it could be an audible message, or a distinct impression in the heart that we recognize as the voice of God. Many
today are skeptical about the validity of objective truth but open to
subjective experiences. God can use subjective experiences to lead
them to accept fully the objective truths in the Bible.

Chrishantha is the leader of our drug rehab ministry and is like
a son to me. He came to Christ from a very rough background,
having spent time in prison for taking and selling drugs. He had
once followed the values of a gang leader. But he was wonderfully
transformed by Christ. Yet some changes in his rough character
came slowly.

Several years ago, when I was abroad, I got the news that he had been severely assaulted by some of the young people in the village where we have our rehab center. I was very upset by this news and called him the moment I returned home. One of the first things he told me was, "Now I know I am a Christian." He explained that when he was assaulted, several of the students at our center wanted to hit back, and they could have gained the upper hand. But Chrishantha stopped them.

As he was walking back to the center, he suddenly felt immense joy. He realized that his not wanting to hit back was completely uncharacteristic of his old self. As we saw in the last chapter, the principle of not taking revenge is one of the things about Christianity that most converts in Sri Lanka find very difficult to accept. Chrishantha realized that he did not even have a desire to do so. That was not the way the old Chrishantha acted. This was God's work in him: he was indeed a Christian!

Our communities need to recognize and celebrate such experiences. We need a culture of openness to hearing testimonies. The greatest experience to celebrate, of course, is salvation. The Old Testament has many exhortations for God's people to recall and thank God for his actions in recent and ancient history. This has always been a regular feature of the life of faith. Sadly, some Christian groups become so sophisticated that they don't get excited over the wonderful things God does in the lives of believers. The Psalms show us the prominent place of testifying to God's acts in the life of faith.

Most Christians go through periods that could be described as "the dark night of the soul," when God seems to be silent and their spiritual life feels cold and lifeless. We must not be critical of people going through such times. The Psalms and books like Jeremiah show that many of God's great servants also had such experiences. At such times we cling to our belief in God and in what the Word says. But the memories of wonderful experiences we had with God in the past can also tide us over during the tough times. In the middle of a passage of bitter lament and complaint, Jeremiah recalls one of his happy experiences:

Your words were found, and I ate them,
   and your words became to me a joy
   and the delight of my heart,
for I am called by your name,
   O LORD, God of hosts. (Jer. 15:16)

We know those experiences are real; we once experienced God in our lives. So we don't abandon God when we feel spiritually dead.

One of the best ways for Christians to express their experience of the assurance of salvation is through hymns. In the English-speaking world, the revival under the Wesleys in the eighteenth century produced beautiful hymns celebrating salvation, such as the following by Charles Wesley (1707–1788):

My God, I am thine,
What a comfort divine,
What a blessing to know that my Jesus is mine!
In the heavenly Lamb
Thrice happy I am;
My heart it doth dance to the sound of thy name.

True pleasures abound
In the rapturous sound;
And whoever hath found it hath paradise found.
My Jesus to know,
And feel his blood flow,
'Tis life everlasting, 'tis heaven below.[17]

In the next century, hymns that became known as gospel songs, associated with evangelists like D. L. Moody and hymnwriters like Fanny Crosby, Ira D. Sankey, and Philip Bliss, carried this tradition of celebrating the joy of salvation. One of the greatest hymnwriters of the nineteenth century was the blind Fanny Crosby. She wrote:

Blessed assurance, Jesus is mine
O what a foretaste of glory divine
Heir of salvation, purchase of God
Born of His Spirit, washed in His blood

---

17. Charles Wesley, "My God, I Am Thine"; from *The Methodist Hymn-Book* (London: Methodist Publishing House, 1933), no. 406.

Perfect submission, all is at rest
I in my Savior am happy and blessed
Watching and waiting, looking above
Filled with His goodness, lost in His love.[18]

Can you see the combination of belief and experience in these songs? They capture the atmosphere that should pervade our discipleship groups. After asking the Ephesian Christians to "be filled with the Spirit," Paul says, "addressing one another in psalms and hymns and spiritual songs, singing and making melody to the Lord with your heart, giving thanks always and for everything to God" (Eph. 5:18–20). This is part of Christian conversation: singing to each other about the marvels of grace. We need more songs celebrating the beauty and joy of salvation.

The Fullness of the Holy Spirit

A loaded expression, "the fullness of the Holy Spirit" describes the desire we have for our disciplees. How one enters into and experiences this has been debated in the church. But Paul's imperative to the Ephesians "be filled with the Spirit" (Eph. 5:18) leaves us with no doubt that this is an essential experience for all Christians. The requirement that those doing administrative work in the church should be people "full of the Spirit" (Acts 6:3) is still relevant. We desire for our people to experience all that God wishes for them. We want to see every hindrance to this fullness, anything causing them to "grieve the Holy Spirit of God" (Eph. 4:30), to be taken away.

For this we yearn, for this we pray, and for this we work. Just as Jesus said, speaking of his own death, "For their sake I consecrate myself, that they also may be sanctified in truth" (John 17:19), we make every effort to pray for them to become godly people. Our hearts' cry is, "O God, fill them with your Spirit and make them holy! And may we do whatever is necessary for that to happen."

---

18. Fanny J. Crosby, "Blessed Assurance," (1873); from *The Worshiping Church: A Hymnal* (Carol Stream, IL: Hope, 1990), no. 514.

Some may think that this chapter does not have a place in a book on discipling. But if experiencing God is basic to Christianity, then we must talk about it with our disciplees and yearn for it to be seen in their lives. There are many reasons for the relatively slow growth of the Protestant church in Asia till the last century, despite many significant missionary efforts. One reason is surely that the religion that was preached was not sufficiently spiritual to Asia's highly spiritually oriented people. Many saw Christianity as a dry, cerebral religion and were not attracted by it. It looks like the entire world has recently become alert to the reality of and need for spiritual power. This, then, is an opportune time to return to emphasizing the experience of the power of God found in the gospel.

13

Healing for Wounds

Love . . . keeps no record of wrongs.

1 Corinthians 13:4–5 (NIV)

The Christian life is portrayed in the Bible as a joyous walk with God. We are asked to "rejoice in the Lord always" (Phil. 4:4). At the heart of this joy is the thrill of being God's children. This was a source of amazement to John, who said, "See what kind of love the Father has given to us, that we should be called children of God; and so we are" (1 John 3:1). Using passionate language, Zephaniah shows how being the object of God's affection is a source of great joy to God himself:

> The LORD your God is in your midst . . . ;
> he will rejoice over you with gladness . . . ;
> he will exult over you with loud singing. (Zeph. 3:17)

God is rejoicing over his children in an exuberant way! This thought can ignite immense joy in us.

Not All Christians Experience Joy

Most disciplers will find that some of those they disciple (and maybe they themselves) do not have the joyous experience of reveling in

God's love in this way. They show an earnest desire to be fully committed to Christ. But they seem to find it difficult to accept that God really loves them. This shows in their behavior. When certain areas of their lives are touched, they overreact with deep hurt or depression or anger. Some struggle with abnormally strong temptations. Often there is a history of pain and rejection that makes it difficult for them to think of themselves as objects of God's love and joy. The wounds created by bad experiences trigger these abnormal reactions.

What kinds of wounds hamper Christian joy? There could be a deep disappointment, such as a father or mother abandoning the family, which feels to a child like rejection. It could be deep resentment resulting from abuse at the hands of unkind parents. It could be a sense of hurtful rejection from other children poking fun in elementary school. It could be the feeling of worthlessness brought on by parents' insensitive comparisons with other children. It could be rejection, humiliation, discrimination, or insult based on racial, class, caste, or some other prejudice. It could be injustice experienced in one's workplace or church. When we see an unusually intense reaction to an issue, it could be a sign that a deep hurt has been touched.[1]

Sexual abuse often has deep and long-lasting effects. Abused people often live with shame mixed with unwarranted guilt. This can cause deep-seated anger over being exploited, especially if a victim has reported the abuse, and parents or authorities have not responded with necessary concern. Sometimes when a child is abused by an older relative, parents blame the child, saying that he or she may have left room for the accused person to act in this way, or scolding the child for trying to bring shame on the family through such an accusation. Sometimes there is a quick call to forgive the wrongdoer without really facing up to the wickedness of what he or she has done.

Sexual abuse of a minor may result in sexual confusion or excessive sexual desire because he or she was not mature enough to understand what happened. This could result in promiscuity or a hidden battle with sexual lust that suddenly erupts in a public sin. I know of

---

1. I reached this conviction after studying David A. Seamands, *Healing for Damaged Emotions* (Colorado Springs: David C. Cooke, 2015). The original edition was published by Victor Books in 1981.

situations where everyone was shocked when respected Christian leaders committed completely unacceptable sexual indiscretions; but when inquiries were made, it became known that childhood experiences with an adult had warped their thinking about sex. They had secretly struggled with sexual feelings that culminated in the prominent sin. Sometimes the result of sexual abuse is a distaste for sex, which also can severely affect a person's life.

These issues must be dealt with adequately, otherwise they can hinder receiving God's joy-producing grace. But they are very painful to bring up. Often they are secrets buried deep within a person, fueling self-pity or anger. My pastor friend Adrian de Visser, who has written a very helpful book on emotional healing,[2] says that it would be good to bring up these issues with new Christians. Once they become mature Christians and have an image to protect, they may be reluctant to talk about such embarrassing experiences.

My own journey with this issue began with reading and then teaching our staff workers from the book *Healing for Damaged Emotions* by David Seamands. Soon after we completed our study, our nation was engulfed in a violent riot, which gave major impetus to a three-decade-long war, leaving tens of thousands dead and physically and emotionally wounded. We felt that studying that book prepared us for what followed.

Before we go deeper into this chapter, I need to say that we are all bruised people. Often when our bruises are touched, we can react in unwise and uncontrolled ways. Hopefully, we keep these weaknesses at a manageable level so that we, as wounded healers, are able to minister God's healing to others. Our own experiences help us approach this subject with humility, compassion, and patience as we work for the maturing of the people we disciple. Emotional healing is rarely instantaneous. We must persevere knowing that the Holy Spirit is willing to work in the difficult areas of people's lives to bring them wholeness.

I am approaching this chapter from the perspective of a discipler and not a skilled counselor. Sometimes when we encounter serious

---

2. Adrian de Visser, *Journey of Grace: Finding Emotional Healing in a Broken World* (Orlando, FL: Kudu, 2014).

issues, we may need to refer people to someone more specialized in difficult cases.[3] Christians are often reluctant to take this step. But sometimes things like depression and rage are caused by physical or mental factors that could best be treated professionally. We should do this with caution, because many today look for quick answers to their pain through pharmaceuticals, which can be dangerous and avoid dealing with root causes. But we must remember that medicines taken responsibly can bring needed relief and may help prevent behaviors that are harmful to distressed persons and others around them.

Our Aim in Looking for Healing

The paths of healing that God uses with hurting people can differ, but our desire for all is the same. We aim for them to believe and experience what the Bible says about the things that have hurt them: that God can heal them and turn the situation into something good. Then it can be said of them that they have a love inside that "keeps no record of wrongs" (1 Cor. 13:5 NIV). The verb translated "keeps . . . record" (*logizomai*) means here that love does not consider or reckon wrongs to be significant. This term is used, in accounting, for a bookkeeper filing an entry for later reference. Paul uses the same verb when he says of God that he was "not counting [our] trespasses against [us]" (2 Cor. 5:19). Just as God no longer considers our sin to be the bottom line, we no longer consider the sins committed against us to be the last word. We can say, as Joseph said, "You meant evil against me, but God meant it for good" (Gen. 50:20). Now there is no need to think about it as something that has ruined our lives.

Our aim as disciplers should be to help our disciplees to understand these implications of being God's children. Layers of hurtful experiences may hold them back from understanding and experiencing these implications. We want to see their minds cleared so that they can be freed to see that the sovereign God will turn their painful experience into something good. I have dealt with many of the issues discussed

---

3. There is a helpful appendix, "When to Refer to Professional Counseling," in the excellent book by Dennis McCallum and Jessica Lowery, *Organic Discipleship: Mentoring Others into Spiritual Maturity and Leadership* (Columbus, OH: New Paradigm, 2012), 301–13. The contents of this appendix are from a lecture given by psychiatrist Amy Merker, MD.

in this chapter in a fuller way in my book *Reclaiming Love*.[4] Here I will briefly discuss some ways in which God can use disciplers to bring healing to the lives of disciplees.[5]

Being with God and Realizing What the Scriptures Say about Us

The Bible is loaded with amazingly heartwarming statements about who we are as Christians. Disciplers need to remind new Christians about that. Earlier I mentioned that young Youth for Christ staff often exhort youth about their Christian responsibilities. Exhortation is important, as we showed in chapter 6. But I caution these staff about an overemphasis on exhortation and insufficient emphasis on the riches of grace that a Christian inherits by being God's child. We will fully understand the meaning of the amazing truth that we are loved by our heavenly Father only when we get to heaven. Disciplers need to do all we can to help our people understand this more and more. Neil T. Anderson has helpfully popularized the idea that we should take time to affirm these statements about who we are. He recommends lists of passages that Christians can memorize as God's therapy for the bondages that cause us to miss out on God's best for our lives.[6]

We need to direct our people to these truths. Because the wounds run deep, it may take some time before these truths go deep enough to minister healing. We must patiently remain with people, trying to help them to accept these truths. An illustration of this is the healing experienced by one of God's choice servants in Cambodia, Sokreaksa (Reaksa) S. Himm. Reaksa lived during the time of the "Killing Fields" in Cambodia under the rule of the Khmer Rouge led by Pol Pot. Reaksa was scheduled, along with his family, for elimination by this oppressive and evil regime. He saw his father and most of his family

---

4. Ajith Fernando, *Reclaiming Love: Radical Relationships in a Complex World* (Grand Rapids, MI: Zondervan, 2013), 91–101. See especially chap. 5, "Patience Encountering Justice"; chap. 9, "Accepting Who We Are: The Antidote to Envy"; and chap. 15, "The Discipline of Not Reckoning."

5. For Christian books that give more detailed guidance on helping people experience emotional healing, see de Visser, *Journey of Grace*; Brad Long and Cindy Strickler, *Let Jesus Heal Your Hidden Wounds: Cooperating with the Holy Spirit in Healing Ministry* (Grand Rapids, MI: Chosen, 2001); Peter Scazzero, with Warren Bird, *The Emotionally Healthy Church: A Strategy for Discipleship That Actually Changes Lives* (Grand Rapids, MI: Zondervan, 2010); David A. Seamands, *Healing for Damaged Emotions*; and Stephen Seamands, *Wounds That Heal: Bringing Our Hurts to the Cross* (Downers Grove, IL: InterVarsity Press, 2003).

6. Neil T. Anderson, *Victory over the Darkness: Realizing the Power of Our Identity in Christ* (Ventura, CA: Regal, 1990). See especially 45–47 and 57–59.

killed, and he himself was brutally clubbed and left for dead. In all, eleven members of his family, as well as a sister-in-law and nephew, were killed. Reaksa was thirteen years old when all this happened.

Somehow he managed to recover from the beating and escape. Before leaving the mass grave in which he had lain with his dead family members for several hours, he made three promises to them: "Mother, father, brothers and sisters, as long as I live, I will try to avenge your deaths. If I fail in this, then I promise that I'll become a monk. If I can't fulfill these promises, then I won't live in Cambodia anymore."[7]

After some years, Reaksa went to a refugee camp in Thailand, where he met Jesus Christ. Subsequently, he traveled to Canada, and the long painful process of healing began. Therapists told him that he had an extreme case of post-traumatic stress disorder (PTSD). Helped by others, Reaksa began to make determined progress along the road to healing.

One of the first signs of his progress was learning to cry. Reaksa continued to struggle with recurring nightmares that haunted him for many years, and during this time, he found the book of Psalms to be a wonderful source of support and comfort. He writes, "Here [in the Psalms] was someone like me who had known despair, and who was not afraid to cry out to God in pain and anguish." He began to read a psalm every day, and, he says, "as I read, my trust in God's goodness and power was strengthened. I felt more secure."

Psalm 23 became his favorite psalm. "Whenever I read it, I felt safe in the presence of God."[8] Reaksa began to use this psalm as a daily evening meditation, and soon the nightmares stopped. Not once did he dream "about being hunted by the Khmer Rouge and the Thai soldiers," he wrote. "It seems as though my need for security and comfort while I sleep is met by this psalm, because I know I can trust God."[9] Eventually, Reaksa broke his third promise to his family by traveling back to Cambodia. Today, he is involved in bringing healing to those who, like him, suffered during that terrible period in Cambodia's history.

---

7. Sokreaksa S. Himm, with Jan Greenough, *The Tears of My Soul* (London: Monarch, 2003), 76. This illustration is taken almost verbatim from my book *Reclaiming Love*, 95.

8. Himm, *Tears of My Soul*, 115–16.

9. Himm, *Tears of My Soul*, 117.

This is the kind of healing we hope for our disciplees. It was a slow process, and many factors were involved in his healing, including the help of qualified counselors. But a key was the truth found in the Bible. We must gently lead our disciplees to look at their time with God in prayer and Bible reading not only as a duty to perform but also as a time for being affirmed in the presence of a loving Father. Moses said,

> The eternal God is your dwelling place,
>> and underneath are the everlasting arms. (Deut. 33:27)

There is a security that comes to our life when we realize that we have been in the presence of such an awesome God. This has a way of healing our shame and opening us to accept who we really are: beloved children of a heavenly Father. As David said,

> Those who look to [God] are radiant,
>> and their faces shall never be ashamed. (Ps. 34:5)

Recognizing Experiences Which Show That God Loves Us

A second means to healing wounds and the problems that accompany them is experiencing God doing things specifically for the believer. I talked about this in the discussion on the assurance of salvation in the last chapter. I have heard people who have experienced deep disappointment in life say things like "Nothing works for me" and "Even God has not looked after me." Sadly, that attitude can prevent them from receiving God's healing. As they focus on their misfortune, it can make them blind to recognizing the things God is doing for them.

As we pray for our disciplees, we need to plead with God to show them how much he cares for them. Our hope is that many experiences of God's provision and care will change their attitude toward God and impress upon them that they are indeed God's precious children. We can gently point them to recognizing God's care for them. Though they may resist change in their attitude, we must persevere in showing them the goodness of God. As the song says, "God is so good," and he is actually "so good *to me*" also.[10]

---

10. "God Is So Good" (1933), attributed to Velna A. Ledin (italics mine). In public domain.

Healing Mediated by the Community of Believers

Acceptance from the Community and the Discipler

In chapter 3 I talked about the importance of community life to the growth of a Christian. Many people who have come to Christ in our ministry experienced painful rejection for much of their lives. In some cases, poverty left them marginalized and deprived; in others, a dysfunctional home left them with deep wounds, especially when parents worked abroad or consumed alcohol or drugs. When these hurting people came to us, they experienced a warm welcome, and soon they felt that the community of believers was like a home to them. This played a significant role in their salvation. After their conversion, the intimate fellowship within the community played a role in healing their wounds. Often people understand the glory of their identity in Christ and the fact that God accepts them as his beloved children through the acceptance they receive from members of the body of Christ.

This discovery of what it means to be accepted by God happens even more effectively through a discipling ministry. What people have missed at home they receive through a spiritual mother or father who unreservedly cares for them and reserves extended time just to be with them. It is a great boost to those whose spirits have been crushed by rejection and hurt to know that another person is truly committed to their welfare. Because of the many disappointments some have faced, they may not believe at first that the discipler unreservedly cares for them. But after some time, it becomes evident to them that it is true. They realize, "This person truly cares about me and is committed to my welfare."

Onesimus was a runaway slave who had defrauded his Christian master. You can imagine his emotions after he came to Rome and met Paul, who led him to Christ. How beautiful it must have been to hear the words of Paul to his former master, Philemon: "I appeal to you for my child, Onesimus, whose father I became in my imprisonment. (Formerly he was useless to you, but now he is indeed useful to you and to me.) I am sending him back to you, sending my very heart" (Philem. 10–12). It must have done his heart good to know that the legendary apostle and friend of his aggrieved master was writing those words about him to the one he had defrauded.

This is not all. Paul sent a letter to the Colossians, carried by Tychicus and Onesimus, in which he says that he has sent Tychicus, "and with him Onesimus, our faithful and beloved brother, who is one of you." He continues, "They will tell you of everything that has taken place here" (Col. 4:9). The dishonest runaway slave of a Christian master is sent back to the master's home church as Paul's ambassador! That is the kind of life-transforming commitment and trust of disciplers that helps heal the wounds of once-despised people!

Of course, the highly program-oriented kind of discipling that is common today will not produce this result. Our disciplees must know that we are willing to pay the price of caring for them. They must know that we represent what Jesus taught when he told us to love each other as he loved us (John 15:12). Jesus expanded that statement, saying, "Greater love has no one than this, that someone lay down his life for his friends" (John 15:13). Of course, it is not humanly possible for us to die for everyone; but we can die for those for whom we have a special responsibility, like our physical and spiritual children.

Often, however, believers get too much of their identity from the Christian group they belong so. Sooner or later, they will experience hurt and conflict in the body. They might overreact to it, feeling devastated and becoming disillusioned. The disillusionment will be even worse if the discipler and the disciplee take opposite sides in a conflict. Sometimes believers are devastated when their requests to the community of believers are rejected. They can forget all the kindness shown to them over a significant period of time and view the rejection of one request as the rejection of them personally. Disciplers must always encourage disciplees to get their primary significance from God and not from any discipler or group to which they belong. Usually there is a process of transition from seeking too much security from the group to finding more security from God. Disappointments can expedite that transition. We should guide our disciplees to use their experiences of disappointment as means of learning to look primarily to God for their security.

Kindness by Those Representing the Offending Party

If the one who has caused hurt seeks forgiveness from the offended party, that is a great boost to healing. But that may not be possible.

Sometimes healing comes through the kindness shown by someone who in some way represents the offending party. Our ethnic war in Sri Lanka has resulted in hurt people from both races. When a person from one ethnic group shows humble and deep sorrow for what people of his race have done to the other ethnic group, those harmed have a greater chance of healing.

I am from the majority Sinhala race in Sri Lanka. But I have discipled many people from the minority Tamil race, the other side in our ethnic conflict. Sometimes during times of tension, when my Tamil "sons in the faith" feel afraid and angry, they have expressed their anger to me. It has not always been easy to take this. But I have felt it a privilege to hear them out, and honored that they would share with me their fears, frustrations, and anger toward my race. I believe that my sorrow and pain over what they have suffered may have helped in healing some of their wounds.

Healing is even more effective when people of one race, at risk to their own safety, take steps to rescue people of the opposing race and bring them to safety. I know many pastors and others who did that during our riots. My pastor-brother once walked right into the rioting mob and rescued vulnerable people. The mob did not harm him because he was wearing a clerical collar. We kept in our home for six months a mother and her son whose house was burned down during the riots. The son has become like a son to me since that time. He often tells me that he cannot give up hoping for blessing on our country, and he cannot hate my race because of the tie that we have forged.

Where there are wounds of conflict, promoting healing can take time and energy. Shortly after the war in Sri Lanka, I went to the north of the country that had been devastated by the assault that ended the war. I was from the rival race, and the people there generally looked at my people as those who had hurt them. I was teaching a group of Christian leaders, and I started my first talk by expressing my sorrow for the pain they had experienced. Most people were grateful for what I had said. Others were not ready to accept a simple apology. I do not blame them, considering the pain they had experienced. But, hopefully, it was a step along the path to healing. Hurt people need time to heal. Often this takes many steps, with each contributing to final healing.

A people group that has been treated badly and robbed of its significance by an oppressor will bear the scars and anger from that for many generations—even after the legal liberation of their people from bondage. This calls for humility and understanding from others. Working with the poor, I learned to accept that the anger of new Christians over class differences and treatment as inferiors may be a good thing—a righteous indignation. When people are converted, they realize that the gospel makes them significant and equal with others. When they juxtapose that with the history of being treated as inferior, those who are perceptive will rise up in anger against such treatment. This righteous anger must be channeled to constructive responses for the gospel and the uplifting of people. Leaders must be patient with those scarred by oppression and do all they can to enter their pain by becoming close to them.

I have heard people say, "Don't blame me for something done a century ago by people with whom I have no connection." That comeback is typical of people from individualistic cultures who do not understand the importance of corporate solidarity in community-oriented cultures, which view people today as linked to the actions of their community generations ago.

Similarly, if a person's sister has wronged another, and he shows deep sorrow to the hurt individual, that expression of sorrow improves the chance of healing. Apology and shared sorrow have healing value. They attack the loneliness of bitterness. The humiliation of apologizing can bring health to others. We must be willing to do all we can legitimately do to bring healing to others.

Sadly, anger is sometimes passed down through generations. Even within churches, we find animosity from family quarrels being passed from generation to generation. This hurts both the church and the individuals on both sides of the animosity. Someone must take the initiative to stop this downward spiral of woundedness through loving acts of reconciliation.

As I wrote this book on a sabbatical in the United States, I discovered that there are deep-seated animosities within all sides of the ethnic divide there. I believe that what I have said above applies to healing for Christians in all the communities in the United States too. Then, as Jesus said, the church "may become perfectly one, so that the world may know that you sent me and loved them even as you loved me" (John 17:23). This is going to be the new frontier of evangelistic effectiveness: Christian credibility demonstrated by the different groups of Christians experiencing genuine unity.

Disciplers need to be conscious of these issues and do all they can to facilitate healing in the lives of their disciplees.

Forgiving the Persons Who Caused the Hurt

Sooner or later, the person who has sustained serious wounds should forgive the offending party. Jesus is very clear: "For if you forgive others their trespasses, your heavenly Father will also forgive you, but if you do not forgive others their trespasses, neither will your Father forgive your trespasses" (Matt. 6:14–15). An unforgiving attitude blocks God's healing grace. I have dealt with this issue in some detail in my book *Reclaiming Love*.[11]

The ideal time for forgiving perpetrators is when they admit that they have done wrong and ask for forgiveness. But, as I said above, that is not always possible. If the wounded person can at least meet the wrongdoer and tell him or her about the offense, there can be some release. But that too may not be possible. And when it is not, the hurt person must forgive the offender. But we must exercise a lot of care when advising people about forgiving those who have wounded them. They have been hurt by something terrible. And God hates what was done. Sin is so serious that the spotless Son of God had to die, bearing the unfathomable load of our guilt, before the door was open for God to forgive us. That is how much God hates sin. The discipler, with genuine sympathy, needs to acknowledge the seriousness of the wrong done. The hurt person must know that the discipler shares the just outrage over what was done.

Once the wrongness of what was done is acknowledged, then the hurt person must be gently led to accept that God is greater than the

---

11. Fernando, *Reclaiming Love*, 49–65.

perpetrator of wrong and can turn the evil done into something good. That is the logic for forgiveness.

Those hurt must also be alerted to the fact that God's love is greater than the wickedness of the perpetrator, and that in that love there is healing and comfort. This gives them emotional strength for forgiveness. Corrie ten Boom, who with her sister Betsie suffered much in a Nazi concentration camp, struggled sometimes with bitterness. She writes, "Sometimes bitterness and hatred tried to enter my heart when people were so cruel to my sister and me. Then, I learned this prayer, a 'thank you' for Romans 5:5." The verse says, "God's love has been poured into our hearts through the Holy Spirit who has been given to us." So she prayed: "Thank you, Lord Jesus, that you have brought into my heart the love of God through the Holy Spirit, who is given to me. Thank you, Father, that your love in me is victorious over the bitterness in me and the cruelty around me." Corrie writes that, after praying this prayer, "I experienced the miracle that there was no room for bitterness in my heart anymore."[12]

Once the two great truths of God's sovereignty and God's love have been applied to their wounds, hurt people have the foundation for forgiving.

There are some who use their wounds as an excuse for unacceptable behavior. They don't work hard enough; they get angry too often; they harbor animosity against others; and they are too easily offended. They act like emotionally handicapped persons. While the long-term effects of wounds can be severe, we must seek to help people out of this rut. They can't go on using their hurts as a reason for living a defeated life. We must show them the need to accept the dual reality that God's sovereignty will bring good out of the wound and that God's love and comfort are greater than the pain inflicted.

Specific Acts That Enhance Healing

With the kinds of wounds we are discussing, we often need to encourage very specific acts that help people to leave behind their past. A lot has been written recently about healing prayer. Let me share what

---

12. Corrie ten Boom, *Clippings from My Notebook* (Nashville: Nelson, 1982), 83. The larger story is from Fernando, *Reclaiming Love*, 52–53.

I generally do if I find that someone I am ministering to is burdened by deep wounds. If someone has mentioned to me the things that have happened to him, I ask him to come prepared to recite to me what was done to him. He usually writes it down and reads it. With every wound described I stop him and give an appropriate scriptural word of healing. Then we pray about it and ask for God's healing. When the person is ready to forgive the wrongdoer, I ask him to do so verbally. Generally, I burn the paper listing the wounds in his presence as a declaration that its power is now ended through God's grace, love, and sovereignty.

We may need to check on whether a demonic influence on the person is causing some agitation or experiences like depression. Disciplers may need to consult someone who is skilled in ministering in such situations if we sense that a supernatural influence may be at work.

The Need for Patience

Patience is one of the keys to ministering in situations involving deep-seated wounds. Usually change does not come immediately. Even after a major victory has been won, the Devil or our own minds can resurrect old causes for bitterness, and the same cycle of anger or depression can be unleashed. This may have become so much a part of someone's personality that it may take long before the emotions are healed. Some hurts are totally healed only in heaven.

History shows how God can use people with serious psychological problems. Examples include famous servants of God with a wide influence for good. An eminent British psychiatrist, Gauis Davies, in his book *Genius, Grief and Grace*, shows that great Christians like Martin Luther, John Bunyan, William Cowper, Lord Shaftesbury, Amy Carmichael, J. B. Phillips, C. S. Lewis, and Martyn Lloyd Jones had serious personality issues. He also shows how God used them powerfully in spite of these real handicaps.[13]

As we saw earlier, while some experience healing, others refuse to be healed. They reject attempts to help them, perhaps trying to show that their pain has not been adequately acknowledged. They cling to

---

13. See Gaius Davies, *Genius, Grief and Grace: A Doctor Looks at Suffering and Success* (Ross-shire, UK: Christian Focus, 2001).

the burden of being hurt and use that as an excuse for their anger and failures in life. But we must not give up.

Early in the book of Exodus, God instructed Moses to tell the people what God was going to do for their deliverance. God said that he had heard their groaning and would act according to his covenant with them, and he would deliver them and give them a possession (6:2–8). But when Moses told this to the people, "they did not listen to Moses, because of their broken spirit and harsh slavery" (6:9). When I read this during my devotions recently, I thought: "This is so much like what I experience with some of the people I disciple. I keep asking myself why they don't reckon with the fact that God's faithfulness and sovereignty will turn their wounds into something good. Their wound-edness keeps them closed to thinking positively about their life."

Moses complained to God that if the Israelites would not listen to him, how should he expect Pharaoh to listen (6:12)? In response, "the LORD spoke to Moses and Aaron and gave them a charge about the people of Israel and about Pharaoh king of Egypt: to bring the people of Israel out of the land of Egypt" (6:13). Moses wanted to give up, but God did not give up. He urged Moses to persevere, despite the woundedness of the people. And that is what we must do, until they move along the path to healing.

Having seen the behavior of some elderly Christians, I have decided to regularly urge people to resolve issues of anger over past conflicts before they get old. The terrible consequences of harboring anger and hurt surface when people grow older. They may have been kind and polite when they were able to control their emotions and hide their feelings of hurt. With age they enter a "second childhood" where, like children, they are unable to suppress their emotions. The pain comes out with bitter anger or serious depression. They sometimes end up as unkind people making life difficult for those near and dear to them.

Few things about the gospel have challenged me as much as my belief in the ability of God to heal the pain of deeply wounded people. I come back to two great truths of Christianity that can be applied to many of the challenges Christians face. First, like the gift of salvation, God's gift of healing from wounds must be appropriated by faith. Sadly, some refuse to believe what the Bible says God can do to them.

Second, the saving work of God in our lives is completed only after we die and go to heaven. Similarly, given the fact that we live in a fallen world, we await the redemption of our bodies and our full adoption as children of God, sometimes groaning as we wait (Rom. 8:23). Total healing will come to us only after we experience our full redemption in heaven. But we can help people before then by being agents of healing. Let us persevere in that work.

———

This may seem a surprising way to end a book on discipling. But I believe it is an appropriate way. Disciplers are servants of disciplees, doing all we can to help them grow and be fruitful. The healing of hurts is one of those things. This book has talked about many such things we need to do. In this busy world, may many Christians rise to pay the price of investing in people in this comprehensive way.

Appendix 1

What We Aim for in Discipling

Good parents have a comprehensive set of aims for their children and do all they can to help their children achieve those aims. In a similar way, spiritual parents have desires for their children. I have compiled a list of actions or habits disciplers should aim to inculcate in those they disciple:[1]

1. Repenting of sin and independence from God, and trusting in Christ for salvation.
2. Daily trusting God for all that goes into making their lives what they should be.
3. Thirsting for more of God, nurturing their relationship with him, and doing all they can to bring glory to him.
4. Nurturing their life within the body of Christ, into which they enter when they are saved, and seeking to live in harmony and accountability with members of this body.
5. Daily learning more of God and his ways from the Word.
6. Spending time with God daily in prayer.
7. Ensuring that they are filled with God's Spirit.
8. Delighting in God and pursuing their joy in the Lord through belief, praise, and other Christian disciplines.
9. Pursuing the path of personal holiness and trusting God to make them holy.

---

1. I am grateful to several friends who have enriched this list by their suggestions.

10. Confessing and leaving behind every known sin in their lives.
11. Forgiving those who hurt them and, through God's love, getting rid of everything that can cause bitterness.
12. Having faith in the midst of trials and lament while looking forward in hope to how God will turn trials into good.
13. Caring for the earthly families that God has given them.
14. Sharing the good news so that lost people will come to salvation.
15. Launching into a life of service by using their gifts, wisdom, and strength to love and be a blessing to people within and without the church.
16. Becoming a disciple maker by investing in others.
17. Doing their work—at home, at school, and/or at their place of work—as best they can with all the energy that God gives them, considering it God's call to them.
18. Being responsible members of the society, nation, and world to which they belong, contributing to its welfare, and doing what they can to protect the environment.
19. Relishing their friends and getting all the help, advice, and strength they can from them.
20. Being prudent about the way they manage their time, their money, and their bodies.
21. Eagerly looking forward to and preparing for the day when they will see their blessed Lord face-to-face, and working to contribute to the victorious consummation of all things at the end of history.

Appendix 2

Other Issues to Talk about During Meetings

In this book I have not given a comprehensive treatment of all the issues a discipler should be concerned about and talk about with a disciplee. There are other books that deal with those issues. Let me list some topics here along with those I have already discussed in the book:

- Love and romance for the unmarried, and relationships with members of the opposite sex for married and unmarried.
- Sex and pornography: People who have had experiences with things like abuse in childhood will have special needs. Those experiences leave behind feelings that can emerge suddenly with devastating force.
- Principles and practices for engaging with social media.
- Vocation and issues in the workplace and/or with studies for students.
- Budgeting and handling money responsibly, especially issues relating to loans and the use of credit cards.
- Relationship with neighbors and other acquaintances.
- Weaknesses that have surfaced, such as anger, gossip, jealousy, lying, and homosexual desires.
- Responsibility for justice relating to matters like race, caste, prejudice, poverty, and nationalism.

- Looking Christianly at current issues facing the nation and the world: in politics, economics, social welfare, sports, and so forth.
- Issues encountered in relationships with other members of the discipleship group and the community of believers; especially disunity, hurt, and disappointment.

Ingredients Needed in a Follow-Up Course

Many good follow-up courses are available for use with new believers. But today we may need to start by explaining what lies behind the gospel. Many people who profess faith in Christ may not have had the gospel that Jesus is Savior and Lord as their main reason for doing so. Often what attracts people to Jesus is that he meets a personal need. They may see Jesus as the one who banishes their loneliness, or their insecurity about the future, or their unhappiness. They may be drawn by the spotless and loving life of Jesus. They may be attracted by the way Jesus treated women or the oppressed. They may be encouraged by his teaching, especially the Sermon on the Mount.

The biggest problem we have in discipling is that people find it very difficult to understand why Jesus had to die for their sins and how that could save them from destruction. Many may not have a sense of sin and its awful consequences. They may "say the sinner's prayer" when prompted to, but that does not mean they have understood the heart of what Jesus did in order to be our Savior.

What we may call a Christian worldview is the background of the gospel message. A worldview can be described as the way one looks at life and the world, the beliefs that make one think and act a certain way. A Christian worldview is informed by the biblical teachings on the following topics:

- The creation of the world and who the Creator God is
- The fall and judgment upon sin
- The institution of the sacrificial system
- The place of the Old Testament law
- The person and work of Christ
- The person and work of the Holy Spirit
- The nature of salvation
- Relating to and experiencing God personally
- Entrance into and life in the body of Christ
- The necessity of holiness
- The call to serve God and witness to others about the Savior
- The last things, including the return of Christ, the final judgment, and the eternal blessedness of the saved and punishment of the wicked

These realities help people to develop a Christian worldview in which sin, grace, forgiveness, and a loving and holy relationship with God are key elements. I realize that my worldview list is much longer than most. This is because I believe we cannot divorce faith from practice. What we believe affects the way we live. Belief, experience, and behavior are all important to understanding what Christianity is all about.

Different aids have been developed recently that help us, especially with the belief aspects of the Christian worldview. James W. Sire's *Beginning with God: A Basic Introduction to the Christian Faith*[1] is a good example. Tim Gough has applied this approach to youth ministry in his *Rebooted: Reclaiming Youth Ministry for the Long Haul. A Biblical Framework.*[2] Ethnos 360, formerly known as New Tribes Mission, has popularized the chronological approach, beginning with creation and introducing Jesus only later in the teaching process.[3] They have produced a curriculum known as "Building on Firm Foundations." How this has worked

---

1. 2nd ed. (Downers Grove, IL: InterVarsity Press, 2017).
2. London, UK: Inter-Varsity Press, 2018.
3. https://ethnos360.org/.

with tribal people is vividly portrayed in a film they have produced called *Ee-Taow*.[4]

I also recommend that in presenting the work of Christ, we do so in terms of meeting human needs comprehensively as described in chapters 10–12. We would, therefore, show how Jesus bore the guilt of our sin to bring forgiveness, how he took our shame to open the door for our honor, and how he conquered the forces of evil to give us liberation from fear and bondage.

4. *Ee-Taow: The Mouk Story*, video by Ethnos360, May 13, 2014, https://www.youtube.com/watch?v=hjRTBQcf-uc.

General Index

Scripture Index

Also Available from Ajith Fernando

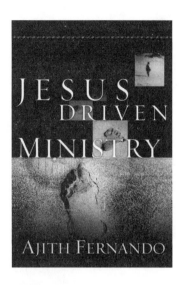

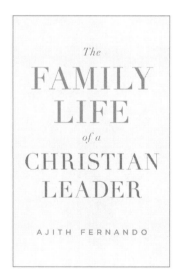

:: CROSSWAY | CROSSWAY.ORG